Mexico, From Mestizo to Multicultural

© 2007 Vanderbilt University Press
All rights reserved
First Edition 2007

11 10 09 08 07   1 2 3 4 5

This book is printed on acid-free paper
made from 50% post consumer recycled paper.
Manufactured in the United States of America.

Library of Congress Cataloging-in-Publication Data

Chorba, Carrie C.
Mexico, from mestizo to multicultural : national identity and recent
representations of the Conquest / Carrie C. Chorba.—1st ed.
p. cm.
Includes bibliographical references and index.
ISBN 978-0-8265-1538-4 (cloth : alk. paper)
ISBN 978-0-8265-1539-1 (pbk. : alk. paper)
1. National characteristics, Mexican. 2. Nationalism—Mexico.
3. Mexico—History—Conquest, 1519–1540—Historiography.
4. Mestizaje—Mexico. 5. Collective memory—Mexico.   I. Title.
F1210.C57 2006
972'.02—dc22

2006010585

A México, lindo y querido

Los hijos de Hernán Cortés siguen combatiendo
en las calles de México todos los días.

[Hernán Cortés's children are still fighting
every day in the streets of Mexico.]
—Carlos Fuentes, 1993

The challenge for mestizo Mexico after Chiapas
is to come to grips with this multicultural and
multiethnic reality.
—Carlos Fuentes, 1994

Contents

List of Illustrations

Acknowledgments

This book—from its conception to its research and writing and finally to its publication—would not have been possible without the generous help and support of many. For the all-important funding necessary to carry out this project, I thank the Department of Hispanic Studies and the Watson Institute for International Studies at Brown University for providing a U.S. Department of Education Title VI F.L.A.S. grant and a dissertation writing grant, which enabled me to carry out a full year of research in Mexico City and to begin putting that research into writing. In addition, I am indebted to the office of the Dean of Faculty—and especially to Dean William Ascher—and to the Family of Benjamin Z. Gould Center for Humanistic Studies at Claremont McKenna College, which provided me with generous financial support for summer research trips. The Gould Center also provided a special subvention that helped defray the costs of reproducing images that appear herein.

I am forever indebted to El Colegio de México, especially to Rebeca Barriga Villanueva, and to the CELL (Centro de Estudios Lingüísticos y Literarios) for generously allowing me to affiliate myself with the institution, for providing me with an office, and for allowing me access to their fine library. For always pointing me toward the people I needed to consult with, I thank Julio Ortega of Brown University, Alejandro Aura, Ignacio Solares, and Carmen Boullosa. Their ability to put me in touch with the authors, artists, and intellectuals I have had the fortune to interview has been an immeasurable gift. For all those who granted me interviews and permission to use their works, I express my heartfelt thanks and admiration.

For expert advice and help with the content of the book, I must first thank my dissertation committee at Brown, Julio Ortega and Stephanie Merrim. Their talents as teachers, scholars, editors, and mentors have had as profound an effect on my life as they have had on my work. In addition, I thank Roderic Ai Camp, whose profound knowledge of all things Mexican; tireless work as a mentor, advocate, and friend; stellar personality; and ability to inspire confidence have contributed greatly to the publication of this book. I have been truly blessed to have him as a colleague at Claremont McKenna College. For their insightful and extremely helpful comments on the manuscript, I thank Bill Beezley and Maarten Van Delden. For valuable feedback on early drafts, I thank Kimberle S. López, Susan Deeds, Henry C. Schmidt, and Stephen D. Morris.

For help in translating quotations, I am indebted to Laura Cobain. For research assistance and additional long hours near the end of the project, I thank Abbie Johnson. For help securing the permission to reproduce images, I will always be grateful to Elvia Zazueta and Daniel Derzavich Glatt. Each has provided me with invaluable assistance, and each is included among my all-time favorite students. For administrative and technological support, I thank Marie Roderick at Brown and Stacey Tomaselli at Claremont McKenna, as well as Ben Royas and all the guys and gals in Claremont McKenna's ITS Department. Never have so few scanned so much!

For their friendship and support during our days together in Providence, I thank Jamie Samons, Deborah Cohn, Patricia Sobral, and Laura Pirott-Quintero. I thank Debbie once more for introducing me to Betsy Phillips at Vanderbilt University Press, the most fabulous editor one could hope for, and for all that she has done for me and with me over the years! I send *saludos y gracias* to Jaime and Dago, Cosme, and the runners in El bosque de Tlalpan and to Leticia Cantú in Mexico. In addition, I am especially grateful to my friends and colleagues here in Claremont. Without them, this book would not have been possible. Emily (my lucky charm) and Rod, Hilary, Shana, Dan and Trina, Delia, Amy, and Stephanie have made these such wonderful years.

Last, but certainly not least, I thank my parents for taking me on my first trip to Mexico and for always offering me support. And I thank my husband, Brad, and our girls, Olivia and Audrey, who are the loves of my life.

1

Issues of Nation, Identity, and History in Mexico

Mexico's Mestizo Identity and Artistic Representations of the Sixteenth-Century Conquest in the 1980s and 1990s

In 1982, when the Mexican government placed a statue of a family that consisted of a sixteenth-century Spaniard, an indigenous woman, and a small child in the plaza of Coyoacán, one of Mexico City's upscale neighborhoods, the op-ed pages of the city's newspapers erupted in debate. According to some, the statue represented "the appearance of Mexican *mestizaje,* fruit of the union between the Spaniard and the Indian" ["el surgimiento del mestizaje mexicano, fruto de la unión del español y la india" (Arenal 1993, 4)] and possibly specifically Hernán Cortés, Malintzin (Malinche), and Martín (their mestizo son). Others balked, based on their assumption that, considering the violent nature of the conquest of Mexico, the child "had been the fruit of a violent and therefore guilty relationship that had to be hidden" ["había sido el fruto de una relación violenta, y por lo tanto culposa, que había que ocultar" (4)]. The upsurge of controversy surrounding the statue soon resulted in its removal from the plaza.

The scene depicted in the statue provoked a range of emotions among the general public. Some called the celebration of military conquest inappropriate (Riding 1989, 17). Indeed, the number of Mexicans who outrightly rejected the statue brings into sharp focus some of the most complex aspects of modern Mexican national identity, especially as it was conceived and disseminated by Mexico's postrevolutionary government in the twentieth century. First and foremost, a clear difference is evident in the way the Mexican state and the Mexican populace feel about Mexico' s reputed mestizo nature. Throughout the twentieth century, the state has traditionally promoted this national characteristic. Yet even though *mestizaje,* or miscegenation, serves as a myth of foundation in this mestizo nation, the incident in Coyoacán clearly demonstrates the public's discomfort with the notion.

Second, many Mexicans express ambivalence toward the sixteenth-century conquest—a historical period that represents painful past transgressions. And last, the statue's representation of *mestizaje* conjures up images of shameful acts, including forced racial mixing and military subjugation.

These reactions to the issue of *mestizaje* also speak eloquently to the dramatic change that was taking place in Mexico at the end of the twentieth century. Although for the better part of the 1900s, Mexican national identity was officially produced and largely based on the premise that Mexico was a mestizo nation,[1] in the 1990s the Mexican government radically changed its official position on the nation's ethnic and cultural makeup.[2]

The original constitution of 1917, written as a result of the Mexican Revolution, occupies an understandably sacred spot in the hearts of Mexicans. Yet in 1992 President Carlos Salinas de Gortari unilaterally initiated changes to the fourth article, henceforth defining the Mexican nation as having "a pluricultural composition, sustained originally in its indigenous population" ["una composición pluricultural sustentada originalmente en sus pueblos indígenas" ("Constitución" 2001, 4)]. Not only does this significant and concrete change demonstrate official governmental acknowledgment of the various ethnic groups that live on Mexican soil; in the remainder of the language it also guarantees protection and promotion of their cultures and social organizations by the Mexican state. In effect, this change opened the door to the historic negotiations over Mexico's indigenous rights and sovereignty that were internationally covered during the 1994 Zapatista uprising in Chiapas.

Both the 1992 constitutional amendment enacted by Salinas de Gortari and the 1994 Zapatista uprising in Chiapas are emblematic of the profound changes in attitude that took place in Mexico—and indeed internationally—in the 1980s and 1990s. Traditionally held notions of national unity based on the assimilation of different groups—such as *mestizaje* in Mexico and the so-called 'melting pot' of the United States—were rapidly being subverted by multiculturalism.[3]

In brief, mestizophile ideology extols not only the racial mixing of Spanish and indigenous peoples but also the creation of a new, uniform culture. Multiculturalism, in contrast, rejects assimilation "as an imposition of the dominant culture and instead prefers such metaphors as the 'salad bowl' and 'glorious mosaic' in which each ethnic and racial element in the population maintains its distinctiveness" (Glazer 1997, 10). Multiculturalism therefore advocates the maintenance of difference but also seeks symbolic and/or legal recognition of minorities in diverse and multiethnic societies.

This "politics of recognition,"[4] however, becomes a high-stakes and contentious issue as societies debate just how far they are willing to go to accommodate difference. Jacob T. Levy classifies policies that respect diversity (which, in turn, mirror demands for cultural rights worldwide) as follows: (1) exemptions from laws that penalize or burden cultural practices, (2) assistance in doing that which the majority does unassisted, (3) self-government for national minorities and indigenous communities, (4) external rules restricting the liberty of nonmembers in order to protect the culture of members, (5) internal rules for the conduct of members that are enforced by ostracism and excommunication, (6) incorporation and enforcement of traditional or religious legal codes within the dominant legal system, (7) special representation of groups or their members within government institutions, and (8) symbolic recognition of the worth, status, or existence of various groups within the larger state community (cited in Kymlicka and Norman 2000, 24).

In Mexico in the 1990s, multiculturalism began to displace the postrevolutionary nationalism that had been based on mestizophile and indigenist ideologies (Gutiérrez 1999, 206).[5] Mexico's move toward multiculturalism revolves primarily around minority rights, specifically demands for indigenous self-determination and autonomy.[6] It has been closely linked to the demands that the Zapatista movement has made on the Mexican government, for although President Salinas de Gortari's constitutional reform of 1992 provided symbolic recognition of the nation's multiethnic diversity in its indigenous peoples—or pluriculture—it lacked the teeth to turn the symbolic into real legal gains. Article 4, then, merely "conferred vague cultural rights on indigenous peoples (such as the right to 'develop' their languages, customs, and specific forms of social organization) but not political rights, other than their civil rights as individuals, which they already possessed by reason of Mexican citizenship" (Jerome Levi 2002, 33). The Zapatista uprising in Chiapas, however, has fed a national indigenous movement that is calling for both legal and legislative changes, thereby "challenging the Mexican state to support a multi-ethnic nation recognizing indigenous self-determination" (Stephen 2002, xxxvii).

The Zapatista rebellion began as an armed indigenous peasant uprising protesting the North American Free Trade Agreement (NAFTA) and other neoliberal policies of the Salinas de Gortari regime.[7] It was launched in the southernmost Mexican state of Chiapas on January 1, 1994—the same day that NAFTA went into effect. The Zapatista demands, as elaborated in the First Declaration from the Lacandón Jungle [Primera Declaración de la Selva Lacandona], include land, work, food, education, housing, health, peace, justice, freedom, and democracy (Kymlicka 1995, 196; Stephen 2002, 144). Yet in the ensuing decade of frustrating failures and intense negotiations, demonstrating the difficulties in balancing indigenous and national interests while working toward a multicultural constitution, only a handful of significant events have occurred in the standoff between insurgents and the state.[8]

The first occurred on February 16, 1996. After two years of on-and-off negotiations between the government and the Ejército Zapatista de Liberación Nacional (EZLN), the two sides signed the San Andrés Accords on Indigenous Rights and Culture [Acuerdos de San Andrés sobre Derechos y Cultura Indígenas]. In these accords, which were the only documents accepted and signed by both parties, "the government agreed to allow the Indian communities to establish local governments, to educate themselves using indigenous languages, and to mandate indigenous representation in legislative bodies" (Camp 2003, 157). The Comisión de Concordancia y Pacificación (COCOPA)—a legislative commission comprising representatives from Mexico's three political parties and charged with facilitating dialogue in San Andrés—then integrated many of these terms into a proposal for legislation to be endorsed by the president.

Throughout that year, however, Salinas de Gortari's successor, Ernesto Zedillo [1994–2000] refused to implement the accords, instead presenting COCOPA with a counterproposal of his own. Negotiations stalled. In 2002 Vicente Fox of the Partido de Acción Nacional (PAN [National Action Party]) was elected president, marking the historic ousting of the Partido Institucional Revolucionario (PRI [Institutional Revolutionary Party]) after seven decades, more democratic Mexican elections, and an alternation of power. Fox honored his campaign promise to resolve the impasse in Chiapas quickly, by complying with such Zapatista demands as closing military bases and releasing EZLN political prisoners in order to resume negotiations. In addition, in order to implement the San Andrés Accords, he returned for Senate approval the COCOPA proposal to reform the constitution with respect to indigenous rights and culture. In order to pressure the Senate and push for passage of the indigenous rights legislation, the Zapatistas assembled a highly visible caravan (popularly known as "Zapatour") that traveled from Chiapas to Mexico City in February and March 2001 (Shirk 2005, 204).

In April 2001, the House and Senate passed an indigenous rights law that was not in keeping with either the San Andrés Accords or the COCOPA proposal (Levi 2002, 36). Although the law recognized, for the first time, the rights of indigenous peoples in Mexico, as Rodolfo Stavenhagen points out,

> the text is weak on some basic issues that the Zapatistas thought they had achieved in the San Andrés negotiations, notably, autonomy, collective land rights, control of natural resources, access to the media in native languages, customary law and the legal recognition of "peoples" (rather than communities)[9] as subjects of domestic law (2003, 124).

That same month, alleging radical departure from the intent and meaning of the signed San Andrés Accords, the Zapatistas denounced the measure, cut off communication with the government, and "retreated to their positions in Chiapas without laying down their arms" (Shirk 2005, 204). Since then, the stalemate has continued, with the EZLN remaining inactive through 2004 (225). According to Jorge Volpi, a young Mexican novelist and intellectual, the EZLN "has practically vanished" ["prácticamente se ha desvanecido"] (2004, 393).[10] The situation in Mexico—both the content of the Zapatista demands for constitutional reform and indigenous rights and the government's unwillingness to pass corresponding legislation—bespeaks not only the urgent need to meet multicultural demands in multiethnic societies like Mexico's but also the existence of many deep-seated fears concerning such demands in liberal democracies.

The historical moment in which Mexico's official stance on national identity shifted from mestizophile to multicultural is of paramount importance. Mexico, along with all the Americas, had just finished years of grappling with the difficult issue of how to mark the Quincentennial of Columbus's voyages, which inevitably gave rise to a great deal of soul-searching. Within Mexico itself, nascent democratization and a decade of crises ultimately contributed to the demise of the post-revolutionary political machine of the Partido Revolucionario Institucional (PRI [Institutional Revolutionary Party]). Not only Mexico's economy but also the state and its political institutions, traditions, and defining discourse—nationalism—were experiencing inconceivable setbacks. The many levels of political and economic crisis during the late 1980s and early 1990s produced a moment of weakened nationalism in Mexico—equivalent to a Mexican identity crisis—which spurred Mexican intellectuals to rewrite themselves as a nation.[11]

At the very time that these changes were taking place, there appeared in Mexico a plethora of historical novels, plays, films, and cartoons that rewrite the events that surrounded the 1521 Spanish conquest of the great city of Tenochtitlán and its Aztec inhabitants. These works share not only a common historical basis but also the more important express intention of rewriting the conquest in a way that speaks about modern Mexican identity. The texts are significant for a number of reasons. First, by revising the past (Mexico's history) as a means of speaking about Mexico's present (politics and identity), they reflect the myriad changes that were brewing in Mexico in the 1980s and 1990s. Rewriting the same sixteenth-century events, they deliver very different messages about present-day Mexican identity. Second, they portray many of the nation's hopes and fears that resulted from the national identity crisis mentioned earlier. Because they all revisit the conquest, they inevitably delve into the thorny issue of *mestizaje* and its place in modern Mexican national identity as the nation transitions into a more open, democratic, capitalist, and multicultural society.

Overview

This book examines Mexico and Mexican national identity during the Salinas de Gortari era from the late 1980s through the 1990s, including some of the most acutely felt aftereffects of NAFTA and the Zapatista uprising in Chiapas. Its analysis includes the creative rewritings of the sixteenth-century conquest produced during that time, especially their contributions to Mexican national identity. Also examined are the ways in which (1) Mexican intellectuals represent their national identity and (2) this national identity responds to and reflects the momentous democratic and economic changes that occurred during that time in Mexico.

Analysis of the novels, the play, the film, and the cartoons selected for examination herein not only clarify their particular reinterpretations of history but also demonstrate what those reinterpretations tell us about the way Mexicans viewed themselves at the dawning of the new millennium. In an effort to recreate the debates and issues of the era, the text cites from a reference list that contains a vast number of works from the 1980s and 1990s.

Theorizing that profound challenges plagued Mexican nationalism at the end of the twentieth century, this book shows that a single moment in the nation's history—the conquest—served as a lightning rod for many of the most important issues of Mexican national identity. Spurred by the international commemoration and debates that surrounded the Quincentennial of Columbus's voyages, many Mexican artists and intellectuals took the opportunity to return to the history of the conquest, delving into such topics as mestizo origins, the state of the indigenous population in modern-day Mexico, and the gritty tale of the evangelization of the New World. Posing difficult questions about Mexico's national character, they opened up debate about assimilation, plurality, and the effects of modernization on Mexican national identity.

The treatment of Mexican nationalism found herein is important to both Mexicanists and scholars of nationalism: It explores the ways in which the reinterpretation and manipulation of national identity, produced and reinforced by state institutions for the specific purpose of national unity, can foster national pride, explain away failings, or sharply criticize official policies.

Examined in these pages are six creative reinterpretations of the sixteenth-century conquest produced during the late 1980s and the 1990s that also explored the mestizophile character of twentieth-century Mexican national identity.[12] Although Mexico as a nation has long struggled to define itself, the close reading of these recent creative works—during a time of particularly acute political and economic crisis and historical reflection—demonstrates the conflicted relationship of this ostensibly mestizo nation with its historical origins. More important, this book establishes a connection between the particular historical moment in time (the 1980s and 1990s) and the artists' attempts to resolve internal conflict, construct a positive self-image, accept and valorize cultural differences, or cope with the myriad changes brought on by modernization.

Significantly, these works represent the end of an era favorable to mestizo national identity, as the Mexican government, intellectuals, and the populace have begun to (1) conceive of their nation as pluricultural or multiethnic and (2) take steps toward meaningful recognition of that diversity. As such, the works analyzed in this book mirror the political, economic, and social unfolding of Mexico in the last decades of the twentieth century. Although Mexican demography may have remained unchanged in the past few decades, there exists a true need for a new common ground on which Mexicans can construct their national identity and unity in the twenty-first century.

In order to provide a better understanding of the Mexico of the 1980s and 1990s, the remaining sections of this chapter trace (throughout history and up to the Salinas de Gortari years) various key factors of Mexican national identity: the concept of mestizophile thought, the creation and dissemination of a national(istic) history, and the long-standing political pillar of *PRIísta* rule. They demonstrate how postrevolutionary ideals, mandatory textbooks, various crises, and the Quincentennial debates of 1992 molded Mexico's sense of itself.

Chapter 2 follows with an in-depth look at the difficult issue of Mexican *mestizaje*—both biological and spiritual—to illuminate the ways in which Mexico's mestizo origins have been traumatized or idealized. In his 1994 novel, *Nen, la inútil,* Ignacio Solares attempts to detraumatize biological origins by rewriting a rape scene between Mexico's Adam and Eve (a conquistador and an indigenous woman) within the context of a love story. In the 1998 film *La otra conquista,* Salvador Carrasco seeks to nuance Mexicans' understanding of the syncretic origins of the Virgen de Guadalupe through the tale of an indigenous scribe's religious conversion, in which violence replaces epiphanies and transculturation replaces assimilation. As such, Solares's work attempts to revitalize Mexico's mestizo identity, whereas Carrasco's revises it.

Chapter 3 discusses two texts that demonstrate Mexico's move away from a mestizophile national identity and toward a national identity that embraces its plurality. Carmen Boullosa's 1989 novel, *Llanto: Novelas imposibles* (see Boullosa 1992), and Carlos Fuentes's 1993 story "Las dos orillas" (see Fuentes 1993a) both discard the limiting notion of the mestizo to explore the ethnic makeup of Mexico and advocate two pillars of (if only symbolic) multicultural recognition of diversity: cultural tolerance and understanding. The two texts question the composition of Mexico's mestizo identity and deem its modern culture to be primarily Hispanic. As a result, Boullosa's text is able to admit the many Mexicos that the assimilationist policy of *mestizaje* obscures, whereas this affirmation in Fuentes's story ultimately undoes the text's multicultural utopia.

Chapter 4 explores the effects on Mexico's mestizo identity that may follow from rampant globalization, neoliberal economics, and the battle for indigenous rights in the 1990s. *La Jornada*'s cartoon series *El Ahuizotl* lampoons the 1992 Quincentennial commemorations by conflating the sixteenth and twentieth centuries. The cartoons equate (1) the Spanish military invasion with the North American political and cultural invasion and (2) the Spanish religious crusade with the North American crusade for free trade. Similarly, Víctor Hugo Rascón Banda's 1998 play, *La Malinche,* fuses Spanish conquistadors with North American tourists, bringing Malinche's story up to date. Central to the pieces analyzed in Chapter 4 is a nationalistic backlash fueled by the fear that Mexicans' unique characteristics were being lost to globalization. Interestingly, when faced with multiple currents of change, the artists return to a more indigenist rendering of Mexican national identity.

All of the works selected for analysis in this book (with the exception of one)[13] were produced during the Salinas de Gortari presidency (1988–1994); more important, however, all make specific contributions to the national identity discourse in Mexico. They respond to the crisis in Mexican mestizophile national identity by returning to its sixteenth-century origins, thus revealing important information about the declining pertinence of mestizophile ideology and the process of transition to multiculturalism in Mexico. The works discussed in Chapter 2 demonstrate one of the reasons for this decline: traumatized origins. The works analyzed in Chapter 3 reflect the process through which such a transition is made: acceptance of plurality and tolerance of difference. The works examined in Chapter 4 reveal the fears inherent in such profound shifts in national identity, especially as they were also accompanied by dramatic political and economic changes. Finally, the Concluding Remarks discuss Mexico's national identity and prospects for national unity in the face of post–Salinas de Gortari events, such as those involving the EZLN, the alternation of power in the 2000 presidential elections, and the Fox presidency (particularly the administration's educational reforms).

Nationalist Discourse and Identity Discourse in Mexico

Before embarking on historical or textual analyses, it is necessary to define and clarify a number of terms: *Nationalist discourses* consist of discursive strategies that attempt to define the elements that constitute a nation. Delineation of the nation's unique cultural, economic, political, or demographic characteristics fosters national unity through its portrayal of the traits of a community to which citizens believe they belong. Many states produce nationalist discourses as a means of inducing patriotism and defining a nation over and against its aggressors, but for the eight decades that the PRI ruled in Mexico, nationalist discourse was also fundamental in justifying the single-party government of *PRIísta* administrations.[14] Because Mexico's de facto single-party system was synonymous with the state, the government's proclamations concerning such elements as national unity, national identity, and national culture carry more overt authority in Mexico than in other nations.[15] Although nationalist discourse is common throughout the Americas, both North and South, some scholars argue that Mexico holds the distinction among all other Latin American nations of being one of the most tenacious producers of this brand of narrative.[16]

Of special interest in the studies of Mexico is the amplitude of thought dedicated to national identity, a specific element of nationalist discourse[17] that speaks to questions concerning the population's national being and origins. Within Mexico's nationalist discourse, intellectuals have long studied their culture and debated national identity in a specific way. In the past century, Mexicans and Mexicanists have constructed an *identity discourse* that attempts to define who Mexicans are—as individuals and as citizens. Whereas nationalist discourse treats the "what" of the nation, identity discourse speaks to the "how," or the character, of its people. Much has been written on the subjects of *lo mexicano, mexicanidad,* and *mexicanismo*—all forms of identity discourses—and many theories of Mexican essence, personality, and psychology have attempted to define (determine, circumscribe, and explain) what it is to be Mexican.[18] Mexican national identity, at one time or another, has stressed the racial, cultural, or psychological aspects of being. Three primary branches of thought—indigenist, Hispanist, and mestizophile—alternately place Mexico's social, political, and cultural virtues as originating in pre-Cortesian, Spanish, or mestizo roots.

Following the Mexican Revolution of 1910, the impulse to assign certain qualities to the concepts of *lo mexicano* or *mexicanidad*—for the good of the country—flourished in a philosophical and ideological movement that would dominate intellectual and nationalist production for decades.[19] At the time, national unification constituted one of the most urgent goals of postrevolutionary governments. After a century of independence (1810–1910) that was largely unsuccessful in appeasing tensions between liberals and conservatives, Mexico desperately needed a new, coherent, and cohesive discourse that would effectively cement its populace as citizens of a modern nation. After the Revolution, the state and its supporting intellectuals proudly declared Mexico a mestizo nation in their attempts to unify a heterogeneous population.[20] The state's controversial reliance on cultural and racial identity based on mestizo origins, however, conflicts with the assertion that the Mexican *nation* begins with such historical events as independence or the Revolution. This fact illustrates the marginalized position of the conquest and colony in Mexican institutional historiography—a point to which we return later.

So, as a result of the postrevolutionary need to unify a diverse Mexican populace in the early twentieth century, the state-generated discourse evolved from nationalist discourse into full-fledged identity discourse. Through their proclamations and policies of national unification, the postrevolutionary government and intellectuals sought to assimilate and integrate various racial, ethnic, political, and economic sectors of society into a single pueblo, or people. Throughout the twentieth century, then, Mexico's intellectuals produced a voluminous discourse concerning the Mexican national character to further the goal of national unification.

The definition of the postrevolutionary Mexican favored neither Hispanism nor indigenism. Nationalist discourse, in its search for a particular essential representation of Mexico, consecrated a new being: the mestizo. Thinkers such as José Vasconcelos, Andrés Molina Enríquez, Alfonso Caso, and Manuel Gamio founded theories of racial, cultural, and psychological nationhood in their mestizophile writings, which served to bridge the gap between a liberal postrevolutionary *patria* and the majority of the population (Brading 1981, 142).[21] This construction of a new collective image involved the valorization of the mestizo figure, elevating it from the status of pariah—a position it had held since colonial times—to that of the emblematic Mexican.

Many intellectuals believed that Mexico would become the nation it sought to be—unified—only when it had become a mestizo nation.[22] The postrevolutionary government began to commission and heavily subsidize cultural production by novelists, painters, and sculptors that lauded the figure of the mestizo as the future of the Mexican citizenry and nation. Thus, the push for real and symbolic national unity permeated society from the 1920s to the 1940s by combining education, the arts, and politics in order to homogenize Mexicans in culture and in consciousness. Literacy campaigns (in Spanish) took to the provinces to integrate the populace linguistically, and monuments to the Mexican people—and to their history and myths—were commissioned.

By the midpoint of the twentieth century, Mexico already possessed a long tradition of self-searching and state-generated identity discourses. The state not only touted the figure of the mestizo as the emblematic Mexican but also celebrated mestizo identity as a way of assimilating different sectors of society into a mainstream national culture. Yet, as a totalizing vision, this mestizophile identity discourse reduced society to a single racial and ethnic essence, thus subordinating—if not denying—the heterogeneous reality of the country. Mexico's national consciousness was fertile ground for the planting of a singular defining work, one that defined the national character and sidestepped the thorny issue of race.

It was at this moment, in 1950, that Octavio Paz first published *El laberinto de la soledad* (see Paz 1993), which enjoyed instant popularity and remained a canonical text of *lo mexicano* until the 1980s. Paz's work, a kind of identity discourse, describes the Mexican essence as solitary, melancholy, orphaned, insecure, and violent. He characterizes Mexicans as wearing masks that, while showing the world a smiling face, protect and hide a lonely, fearful interior. Paz describes Mexican life, customs, and history as a series of contradictions: life versus death, masks versus authenticity, solitude versus fiestas, conqueror versus conquered.

Although the book appeared decades after the end of the Revolution, Paz's project dovetails with that of the postrevolutionary consecration of the mestizo as the emblematic Mexican in that it searches for the specifics of *mexicanidad* and of Mexican reality. Since then, however, many scholars have criticized Paz's ideas as essentialist, if not incorrect. In *The Cage of Melancholy,* Roger Bartra (1992) dismantles Paz's portrayal of Mexico's inferiority complex as a needless continuation of Samuel Ramos's psychoanalysis of Mexican nationality in his 1934 *El perfil del hombre y la cultura en México*. Ramos's work argues that Mexico suffers from an inferiority complex that originated with the conquest and colony and has continued because of Mexico's inability to become more European (see Ramos 1976). Bartra demonstrates how this argument is essentially a reworking of negative stereotypes of Native Americans and peasants (1992, 81). As such, Paz's work may essentialize the Mexican mestizo and generalize that character onto the entire nation, but it also lays bare many of the negative aspects of the state-generated mestizo identity.

In the late 1980s, as Bartra was deconstructing Paz's popular yet essentialist identity discourse, two other currents—one political, one ideological—were beginning to take hold and would ultimately overshadow *mestizofilia* by the end of the century. First, beginning with the 1988 presidential elections and the appearance of a viable political opposition to the PRI, democratization began to emerge in Mexico. This opening of the political playing field coincided with a shift toward multiculturalism and therefore a loosening of the decades-long stranglehold that mestizophile ideology had on Mexican national identity. Carlos Fuentes, Mexico's most renowned writer, noted this confluence in 1995 when he saw a transition to "an admission of an identity more vast than what we ourselves see, an identification with democracy and a conviction that civil society and its culture have to be the protagonists of the future" ["una admisión de una identidad más ámplia de la que nosotros mismos vimos, una identificación con la democracia y una convicción de que la sociedad civil y su cultura tienen que ser los protagonistas del futuro"] (1996). As the *PRIísta* political system crumbled, so did the viability of its mestizophile discourse as the singular unifying factor in postrevolutionary national identity.

Manipulations of the Past and Legitimations of the Present in Mexican National Cultural Production: Murals, Museums, Monuments, and Textbooks

Despite the many attempts to pinpoint Mexican identity, it remains a continuously changing entity within identity discourse. The interpretation and revision of history and myth in Mexico play an important role in Mexico's sense of self, and the power of these mutations cannot be underemphasized. Although history and myth are not always necessarily components of either identity discourse or a people's character, they can be manipulated to prescribe certain components of national character.

The Niños Héroes de Chapultepec represent these manipulations and prescriptions well. The Niños Héroes were military cadets who, when faced with capture by North American troops at Chapultepec castle in 1847, allegedly wrapped themselves in Mexican flags and jumped from the ramparts to their deaths rather than surrender (Riding 1989, 38). Although they are still important national heroes to the Mexican people, during the Salinas de Gortari presidency of 1988–1994, when Mexico was trying to seal NAFTA negotiations with the United States, they were not a viable icon. Their images were subsequently quietly dropped from the paper money and reference to the group was omitted as part of the 1992 revisions to Mexico's official and mandatory public school history texts, the *Libros de texto gratuitos* (Robles 1992, 22). The efforts to downplay the Niños Héroes reflects the dramatic change in Mexico's official stance toward its northern neighbor from resistance to greater accommodation. With their elimination from currency and texts, the Niños Héroes increasingly vanish from Mexico's popular consciousness. In time, the revisions with respect to this historical icon encourage Mexicans—as a people—to be less recalcitrant and more conciliatory toward the United States.[23] Although clear cause and effect may not be established, analysis of the discourse that rewrites a historical event reveals possible ramifications for national identity.

Because history plays a central role in Mexico's collective mind, Mexicans have long used the past as a basis for their self-searching and cultural identification. Among Latin American nations, Mexico has been called the most *memorioso*— having the best historical memory (Villegas 1992, 34). Many Mexican intellectuals even deem Mexico "a country with a living past" ["un país de pasado vivo"] (Aguilar Camín 1993c, 14), an understandable statement in a country where the past is literally right under foot.

Perhaps no other events demonstrate this as well as those that took place in February 1978 in Mexico City. Workers from the Electric Light Company were digging in the Centro Histórico, under the streets that run through the colonial architecture downtown, when they discovered a large carved stone. Further examination and excavation brought the ruins of the Aztec Great Temple or Templo Mayor into the light of day for the first time in centuries (Fig. 1.1.). Today the monumental archaeological site contains both the ruins and a museum filled with artifacts from the temple. While the excavations were being carried out, public demand for access to the site became so great that Eduardo Matos Moctezuma, the coordinator of the Great Temple Project, was forced to open the ruins for two hours each Saturday. Despite the fact that only a few artifacts were visible to the public, the lines of people waiting to get in were endless (Matos Moctezuma 1996). Mexicans' interest in their past is evident on a daily basis, as they take advantage of ample access to the country's many monuments. Each Sunday, when national museums are free, they are flooded with schoolchildren doing research for reports and homework assignments.

The power of this "common" history to unite Mexico's people is evidenced by the nation's coat of arms and foundational symbol: the eagle eating a serpent atop a nopal cactus (Fig. 1.2). Originally conceived as the divine sign of abundance that showed the wandering Aztec tribe where to settle and build Tenochtitlán, the seat of their empire, this image is today put forth by the nation as one of pride, aggression, and a centralized identity. *Mexicanidad,* however, cannot be reduced to mere Aztec roots—as in the national emblem—since dozens of other indigenous groups have shared and continue to share Mexican territory.[24] The symbol succeeds in uniting, then, not for its ethnic origins but for its geographic significance. By adopting this mythical symbol as the nation's coat of arms, the government—and implicitly the populace—affirms the spatial center of Mexico, Mexico City, as its spiritual (founded in ritual) and governmental (representing the nation's origin)

Figure 1.1. In 1978 the ruins of the Aztec Great Temple [Templo Mayor] were discovered by electrical workers digging under the streets of Mexico City. Photograph courtesy of INAH.

Figure 1.2. The Mexican national coat of arms is based on the Aztec legend about the founding of the imperial center, Tenochtitlán. The Aztec people wandered for years until they encountered this sign (where Mexico City stands today). Although an important part of Aztec history, the coat of arms as a national symbol does not reflect Mexico's rich ethnic diversity.

center as well. Thus, from an ancient myth comes a collective symbol that not only situates the national center within its geographic center but also essentially legitimizes the federal government through a defining nationalist discourse.

Societies frequently frame their history in terms of legends and myths, and governments commonly stir patriotic passions through the use of such inventions, but the Mexican state is unique in its continual and ever-present representation of history to its citizens. Since the Revolution, Mexican governments of the PRI have patronized cultural and intellectual production as a means of forwarding their goals of not only national unification but also continued legitimization of the Revolution and its resultant institutions.[25] These manipulations of antiquity—be they renovations, excavations, or stylized mural depictions—all strive for the post-revolutionary ideal of unity through nationalism.

In the 1920s, the state established the Escuela Mexicana de Pintura. While Vasconcelos was the minister of public education, he actively employed many of the school's muralists—Diego Rivera, José Clemente Orozco, and David Alfaro Siqueiros—to paint the visual billboards of cultural nationalism in Mexico.[26]

Viewed as an opportunity to teach the populace its history and reaffirm the state's revolutionary origins, the murals laud the indigenous past as the source of Mexico's cultural wealth; condemn the imperialism of both Spain and the United States; and sing the praises of liberty, revolution, and independence in Mexico. Carlos Monsiváis, the Mexican intellectual and cultural critic, deems Mexican muralism "one of the most moving phenomena of a society in need of external and internal affirmations, on the hunt for pride and vindication" ["uno de los fenómenos más conmovedores de una sociedad necesitada de afirmaciones externas e internas, a la caza de orgullos y revindicaciones"] (1994, 1425). Postrevolutionary mural painting also provides the state with the opportunity to once again tout Mexico's pre-Hispanic cultures, as second-grade text books teach that "the muralists rescued from the ancient Mexicans the tradition of painting on the walls of temples and buildings" ["los muralistas rescataron de los antiguos mexicanos la tradición de pintar en las paredes de los templos y los edificios"] (*Mi libro de segundo* 1982, 625). The murals are replete with images of indigenous figures represented as seminal to and integrated into the mainstream of national culture. They now exist in and on government buildings (implicitly equated with Aztec temples in the previous quotation) as monuments to the country's heroes and revolutionary ideals.

The Mexican state also puts forth a proud, reaffirming version of its ancient past in the exhibits of its many museums and archaeological sites. By presenting and preserving its past in this way, the state creates a historical unity for the nation that seeks to join the many diverse aspects of the populace and the past in one intercultural synthesis. Néstor García Canclini contends that Mexico's museum system is an exemplary official staging of the nation's past. Exhibitions are based on strategies that seek to spiritualize the indigenous aesthetic, ritualize indigenous history and archaeology, and monumentalize the nation's historical patrimony (1990, 158–177).

Perhaps the best-known example of monumentalization is the Museo Nacional de Antropología de México in Mexico City, which houses artifacts from the Aztec, Olmec, Toltec, Maya, Mixtec, Zapotec, and Teotihuacán cultures. This museum, despite its immense popularity with both Mexicans and foreign tourists, has been criticized as an outright idealization of the nation's indigenous past. Soon after the museum's 1964 inauguration, Octavio Paz, Mexico's Nobel Prize–winning poet laureate, decried its revisionist consecration of the pre-Columbian past and its nationalist slant. In his 1969 "Crítica de la pirámide," he writes:

> To enter the Museum of Anthropology is to penetrate an architecture built of the solemn material of myth. . . . The cult propagated within its walls is the same one that inspires our schoolbooks on Mexican national history and our leaders' speeches: the stepped pyramid and the sacrificial platform. Why have we looked among pre-Hispanic ruins for Mexico's archetype?

[Entrar en el Museo de Antropología es penetrar en una arquitectura hecha de la materia solemne del mito. . . . El culto que se propaga entre sus muros es el mismo que inspira a los libros escolares de historia nacional y a los discursos de nuestros dirigentes: la pirámide escalonada y la plataforma del sacrificio. ¿Por qué hemos buscado entre las ruinas prehispánicas el arquetipo de México?] (1993, 315)

The museum appears to achieve the goals of the continuous current of thought, which touts the pre-Hispanic past as the root of Mexican cultural identity. Again, there exists a disjunction between the defining discourses of the state. Whereas the mestizo is regarded as the future of Mexico in the postrevolutionary essays of Gamio, Vasconcelos, and Molina Enríquez, in terms of monuments, lost indigenous cultures are being consecrated as Mexico's cultural basis.

In the patriotic and anti-imperialist images of the murals and in the daunting ruins of ancient civilizations, Mexicans are shown the greatness of their cultural roots and inculcated with the sense of a common past. Yet the most effective means for the state to disseminate national culture and to make citizens of the populace has been its public education program, which not only equalizes the knowledge imparted to generations of schoolchildren but also serves to legitimize the ruling party.[27]

In 1960 the state consolidated its role in the instruction of Mexican children, when it declared as mandatory the use of its *Libros de texto gratuitos*.[28] The texts, which are free, mandatory, and widely distributed, promote social integration and national identity by providing a singular version of the nation's history.[29] Under President Adolfo López Mateos, the 1964 texts openly declared that they would accentuate in students "the feeling of duty toward the motherland, of which they will one day become citizens" ["el sentimiento de sus deberes hacia la Patria, de la que algún día serán ciudadanos"] (*Mi cuaderno* 1964, n.p.). The state can therefore foment social consensus in order to maintain its hegemony (Villa Lever 1988, 20) while also presenting Mexicans with a largely mestizo national identity.

However, it is worth noting here that in the Salinas de Gortari administration's 1992 texts, the first hints of official language valorizing diversity begin to emerge. In the reading on the colony—traditionally a point at which Mexico's *mestizaje* is discussed, sixth-grade students are told that "the vast extension of the territory favored social diversity" ["la gran extensión del territorio favoreció la diversidad social"] (*Mi libro de historia de México* 1992, 64). Furthermore, all texts, no matter the year or the level, seek to have students identify key components of the Mexican nation. The texts for first- and second-graders throughout the 1980s stress the Tenochtitlán–Mexico City palimpsest,[30] again aligning the nation with the centrality of the capital and its foundation on the ruins of the Aztec culture. In 1994, however, we see a section entitled "Diversity Enriches Us" ["La diversidad nos enriquece"], in which students read, "We people are different. We have diverse customs, stature, and skin color" ["Las personas somos distintas. Tenemos diversas costumbres, estatura y color de piel"] (*Libro integrado* 1994, 167).

Yet let us take a close look at the wording in the 1992 texts. In terms of the diverse roots of Mexican identity, for example, the 1992 *Mi libro de historia de México* for sixth graders says:

> In the novo-Hispanic society, Indians, Spaniards, Africans, and castes coexisted. These groups mixed and created the mestizo society that distinguishes us. Most Mexicans have Indian, European, or African ancestors. The Mexicans' way of life and customs are the product of this mixture.

> [En la sociedad novohispana convivieron indios, españoles, africanos y castas. Estos grupos se mezclaron y crearon la sociedad mestiza que nos distingue. La mayoría de los mexicanos tienen antepasados indios, europeos o africanos. Las formas de vida y costumbres de los mexicanos son producto de esta mezcla.] (1992, 67)

With this statement, despite its acknowledgment of a diversity of roots, the books very clearly relegate difference to the distant past, or the realm of "ancestors."[31] The books go on to mark modern Mexican society and culture as mestizo or mixed. In this way, they stress unification by emphasizing mixture or assimilation.

Thus, the *Libros de texto gratuitos,* which have now accompanied three generations of Mexicans throughout primary school, are a powerful state tool that conveys everything from historical anecdotes to national identity. Whereas through the 1980s the state's texts mostly affirm Mexican society as mestizo, beginning in the 1990s, they show the dramatic effects that one president's agenda can have on how Mexico's children perceive their nation and its citizenry.

National identity is disseminated not only in the content of the *Libros de texto gratuitos* but also in the all-important iconography on the front cover of the series. From 1960 to 1972, the first twelve years—or two presidencies—of the existence of the mandatory texts, a portrait by Jorge González Camarena graced the front cover of each book. The painting depicts an indigenous woman, Victoria Dorenlas, who ostensibly embodies *la madre patria* (Fig. 1.3). The image was also co-opted by the presidents during that time, Adolfo López Mateos (1958–1964) and Gustavo Díaz Ordaz (1964–1970), as part of government propaganda and official mural production (Herrera 1962, 11). Despite allegations that the image was not and is not an accurate representation of *mexicanidad,* the portrait was reinstated on the history texts when president Carlos Salinas de Gortari revised the *Libros de texto gratuitos* in 1992. One reporter described the image as follows:

> The homeland of 1992 ... is a young dark woman who is well nourished, possibly a model for a men's magazine, unsuccessfully attempting to identify her-

self as indigenous. She wears a Roman tunic and she is pushed toward her destiny by an eagle with open wings and an abundance of fruits and symbols of a cornucopia that has not been used as a metaphor for Mexico for decades.

[La Patria de 1992 . . . es una joven morena y bien alimentada, modelo posible para alguna revista masculina, con frustrada intención de que se identifique como indígena. Viste una túnica romana y es empujada hacia su destino por una águila con alas abiertas y la abundancia de frutos y símbolos de un cuerno que hace décadas no se usaba como metáfora de México.] (Cazés 1992a, 9)

The use of this confusing, ambiguous image aptly symbolizes the state's ambivalence toward its own messages of racial identity. Although the 1992 texts equate *mestizaje* with *mexicanidad* and even begin to recognize Mexico's ethnic diversity, the patria is envisioned as indigenous and draped in Western garb of classical provenance.[32]

The controversy that surrounded the inclusion of this image on the 1992 covers was, in fact, the least of Salinas de Gortari's worries. It seemed that each president, limited to one term in power, was trying to leave his own personal and indelible mark on Mexican national identity by consecrating his administration's version of the past, thereby influencing national identity. Since their debut as mandatory in 1960, the texts have been revised in 1972, 1989, and 1992.[33] In 1992, despite a large-scale competition for authorship of the history texts and a huge expenditure of money, the quality and ideology of the books was thoroughly attacked.[34] Among the most common complaints disseminated by newspapers and magazines at the time were that the history was overly abridged; anecdotal; superficial; and full of errors, omissions, and deficiencies. One article summed up the criticisms as follows: "poor in content, deficient, deformed, erratic, contradictory, repetitive, inexact, imprecise, partial, schematic, enunciative, simplistic, incoherent, manipulated, idealized, reactionary, conservative, and tendentious" ["pobres de contenido, deficientes, deformados, erráticos, contradictorios, repetivos, inexactos, imprecisos, parciales, esquemáticos, enunciativos, simplistas, incoherentes, manipulados, ideologizados, reaccionarios, conservadores y tendenciosos"] (Ramírez 1992, 6).

Many articles discussed which heroes had been eliminated from history—among them El Pípila, a favorite miner who is said to have played a decisive role in the ouster of Spaniards from the town of Guanajuato during the fight for independence. Others criticized the fact that national "traitors" and "despots," such as Iturbide, Santa Anna, and Porfirio Díaz, were vindicated, whereas popular heroes such as Emiliano Zapata and José María Morelos were minimized (Garrido 1992, 10).

Those who defended the revisions included the historian Luis González y González, who opined, "Now there are neither demonizations nor canonizations. Nothing. For the first time, men of flesh and bone appeared, in their complexity,

Figure 1.3. For decades, *La Patria* (1962), by Jorge González Camarena, has graced the covers of Mexico's *Libros de texto gratuitos*, or free textbooks. These texts, which are free to all students and mandatory in public schools, are powerful governmental tools for instilling national identity in future citizens. Courtesy of SEP (Secretaría de Educación Pública).

not as heroes or villains, but simultaneously as both" ["Ahora no hay ni sataniza-ciones ni canonizaciones. Nada. Por primera vez surgieron hombres de carne y hueso, en su complejidad, no como galanes o villanos, sino simultáneamente como las dos cosas"] (quoted in Vera 1992, 13). Despite González y González's praise of the texts, popular outcry reached fever pitch, necessitating public hearings with representatives from the SEP (Secretaría de Educación Pública) in attendance. Before the conflict was resolved, Paco Ignacio Taibo II, an activist and leading author of detective novels, was calling for a popular revision of the revisions. He demanded the creation of "a national commission for revising the history books, composed of all the teachers, parents, and their children, who, in their homes, must make the necessary corrections by hand. In each chapter, they will have to write down with pencil how things actually occurred" ["una comisión nacional revisora del libro de historia, conformada por todos los maestros, los padres de familia y sus hijos, quienes, en su casa, deben hacer a mano las correcciones necesarias. En cada capítulo, tendrán que apuntar con lápiz cómo ocurrieron realmente las cosas"] (Vargas 1992, 6). Despite this call for a large-scale, popular penciling-in of the peoples' version of history, the actual solution to the problem came at a huge cost to the Mexican people. The government warehoused the six million textbooks and commissioned new ones, costing the public roughly thirty billion pesos (almost 10 million dollars) (Aguirre 1992b, 12).

The intensity of the debate over what type of history should be taught in schools prompted one reporter to write, "There is nothing more alive than History. Nothing ignites more passion than what happened centuries ago, since the interpretation of memory moves our present" ["Nada más vivo que la Historia. Nada enciende más pasiones que lo que ocurrió hace siglos, pues la interpretación del recuerdo mueve nuestro presente"] (Romero 1992, 10). The need to debate the textbooks' revisions was attributed to everything from ideological differences between various generations of Mexican historians, reporters, and intellectuals (Becerra 1993, 375) to Mexico's need for myth: "The controversy showed that Mexicans prefer to remain faithful to a mythological truth and not to historical truth—the closer it is to mythological truth, the better it is viewed by the masses" ["La controversia mostró que los mexicanos prefieren ser fieles a una verdad mitológica y no a la verdad histórica—mientras más se acerca a la verdad mitológica, mejor visto es desde el punto de vista de la masa"] (Castañón 1996).

But it was evident that the real incendiary issues were not which hero or villain appeared or disappeared. When the Salinas de Gortari presidency set out to revise primary school textbooks, its stated goal was to make Mexican history more objective. Salinas de Gortari himself said, "It is indispensable, today, to make of national history a lesson in objectivity and self-esteem" ["Es indispensable, ahora, hacer de la historia de la nación una lección de objetividad y autoestima"] (Limón 1992, 18). Thus, the disappearances of such figures as the Niños Héroes and El Pípila can be attributed to attempts at historical demythification and accuracy. Behind this academic objective, however, there inevitably lies a political objective as well. The spark that truly ignited the debate over these texts was that, within the pages of the official history texts, Mexican intellectuals viewed the Salinas de Gortari government as trying to maintain its monolithic sovereignty and political legitimacy.

In other words, the texts came under fire not only for the "poor" quality of the history they presented but also for the propagandistic nature of that history. One critic complained about "the use that, it is affirmed, makes the present government a part of History, either by presenting its achievements self-complacently in the texts or by a more subtle revisionism of the past in search of justifications for the present" ["el uso que, se afirma, hace el actual gobierno de la Historia, ya sea al presentar autocomplacientemente en los textos sus realizaciones, ya por un más sutil revisionismo del pasado en busca de justificaciones del presente"] (Latapí 1992, 34). Lorenzo Meyer agrees, adding that "in the case of the Textbooks, what we see is an attempt to think of Mexico in terms of neoliberalism, an attempt to undo some of the myths of past governments in order to create new ones" ["en el caso de los Libros de Texto, lo que se ve allí es un intento de pensar México en función del neoliberalismo, de deshacer algunos de los mitos de los gobiernos anteriores para crear otros nuevos"] (1996). In sum, Salinas de Gortari was trying to realign Mexico's past—its heroes, villains, and events—with his present economic platform of neoliberalism,[35] radically changing the nation's traditionally postrevolutionary identity while also trying to legitimize his own departures from postrevolutionary economic practices.[36]

Yet for President Salinas de Gortari to claim any sort of official apostolic lineage (be it from foreign investment during the Porfiriato or the agrarian reform of Zapata) would mean that he himself was a legitimate ruler—which, to many, he was not. Because Salinas de Gortari had entered the presidency in a cloud of doubt and suspicion of electoral fraud (precisely when one of his campaign promises was electoral reform), his government was *not* legitimate in the eyes of many. By 1992, when his version of Mexican history was published for schoolchildren, his lack of public support contributed greatly to the scandal over the textbooks.[37] The debate over the *Libros de texto gratuitos*, then, when seen in isolation, presents a fascinating study of the high stakes for Mexico's official history. Nevertheless, when examined in the political context of the day, this polemic presents merely the tip of the iceberg.

The Decade of Crises: 1982–1992

By the time of the 1992 textbook fiasco, the full decade of crises that had plagued Mexico's economic and political institutions had the PRI struggling to stay in power.[38] Interestingly, Salinas de Gortari's presidency—combining, as it does, characteristics of both authoritarian rule and reform from within—is emblematic of the paradoxical nature of the PRI's rule in Mexico in the late twentieth century. Despite the aforementioned bold changes in the Mexican constitution, economic policies, and primary school textbooks that Salinas de Gortari was able to make, he was a product of the *PRIísta* political machine. "Tapped"[39] by his predecessor, Miguel de la Madrid, as the official candidate of the ruling party, Salinas de Gortari became president despite the fact that he "had no prior electoral or grassroots political experience" (Camp 2003, 191). Yet although the traditional channels through which he arrived in power—presidential succession and electoral fraud—indicate a heavy debt to the PRI, Salinas de Gortari broke with the state's revolutionary ideology in important ways. Above all, Salinas de Gortari continued de la Madrid's neoliberal economic policies and insisted that he would lead the country forward in its drive toward modernization. The very same free-market economics and insistence on modernization evident under de la Madrid and Salinas de Gortari demonstrate just how far from traditional postrevolutionary policies these *PRIísta* presidents had drifted.

With reason, then, Mexicans were not only questioning the legitimacy of Salinas de Gortari's presidency in the 1990s; they had also begun to view the entire revolutionary system—complete with the social, political, and economic institutions that it had spawned through more than sixty years of rule—as outmoded and ineffectual for their current needs as a country. Long-standing concepts of nationhood in Mexico were crumbling, and it is the goal of this text to call attention to the most deeply significant events that contributed to this disintegration of national unity. With the exception of the 1968 student protests and consequent massacre, the PRI had enjoyed—and actively cultivated—an environment that remained relatively free of opposition until the early 1980s.

The events of 1968, however, were a watershed for Mexico's traditionally authoritarian and corporatist government. Just ten days before the international Olympic Games were to begin in Mexico City, thousands of citizens had gathered in Tlatelolco's Plaza de las Tres Culturas to hear protest speeches, when the army and public security forces opened fire on the crowd. Hundreds of people, trapped in the crossfire, were killed in one of the most chilling shows of bloody repression and government violence that the Mexican state has ever carried out against its citizens. The aftereffects of that evening, known as La Noche de Tlatelolco, have had a deep and far-reaching effect.[40]

The deep current of disillusionment and distrust that took hold among the Mexican people was undoubtedly still in place in 1982 when another decisive moment of rupture shook the ruling party's foundations. That year, a catastrophic economic crisis effectively ended what had come to be known as the "Mexican miracle," or *el milagro mexicano*—decades of political stability, an average growth rate of 6 percent, rapid urbanization, and the formation of a modern middle class (Aguilar Camín 1995, 38). Just as President de la Madrid (1982–1988) tried to open the Mexican economy and readjust its traditionally internal markets toward external markets, a severe dip in global oil prices plunged Mexico into a depression that was further aggravated by a huge external debt, hyperinflation, and economic stagnation (38).

Despite this cutting economic blow to Mexican society, the government managed to maintain a level of political stability—though tenuous—largely thanks to the strength of such institutions as the presidency itself. Yet the 1980s in Mexico were anything but a decade of security. Lorenzo Meyer describes the atmosphere as "a terrible awakening for many Mexicans as future safety disappears. . . . I would describe the period as one lacking security. What was once our pride is no longer. It is now even shameful" ["un terrible despertar para muchos mexicanos de que la seguridad en el futuro les desaparece. . . . Yo caracterizaría la época como una ausencia de seguridades. Lo que fue orgullo ya no lo es. Es incluso vergüenza"] (1996). With the economic crisis, Mexicans lost hope that they would overcome underdevelopment. The drug trade was corrupting Mexican judicial and legal organizations, and the institutions that had made Mexicans so proud for so many decades during the *milagro*—political stability, agrarian reform, trade unionism, and nationalism—were rapidly deteriorating.

In addition, Mexican nationalism was also reaching new lows. Author Carlos Fuentes ties Mexican nationalism directly to the 1982 crisis:

> I think Mexican nationalism . . . suffered serious deterioration as a result of the disappointment with the oil abatement. As a result of the '82 crisis, there was a jolt, because the identity of oil and nationalism beginning with Cárdenas was very strong, and since we were not able to administer the oil wealth and we fell into a terrible crisis like the one in '82 from which we have not recovered, the idea of nationalism suffered a very, very serious deterioration.

> [Creo que el nacionalismo mexicano . . . sufrió un deterioro muy grave a partir de la decepción de la abonanza petrolera. Apartir de la crisis del '82 hubo un sacudimiento porque la identidad del petroleo y nacionalismo a partir de Cárdenas fue muy fuerte y como no supimos administrar la riqueza petrolera y acabamos en una crisis tan espantosa como lo del '82 de la cual no hemos salido, la idea de la nacionalidad sufrió un quebranto muy, muy grande.] (1996)

A vicious cycle of crisis and uncertainty gripped the country throughout the 1980s, and the populace reevaluated the conquest during the Quincentennial in this atmosphere of uncertainty. In *A la sombra de la Revolución Mexicana: Un ensayo de historia contemporánea de Mexico, 1910–1989,* Lorenzo Meyer and Héctor Aguilar Camín concur that "Mexican society in the mideighties lived with the generalized sense of a change in era, the suspicion of a great historical transition" ["la sociedad mexicana a mediados de los ochenta vivía la sensación generalizada de un cambio de época, la sospecha de una gran transición histórica"] (1994, 295).

Then, on September 19, 1985, the second of the decade's worst tragedies befell Mexico. At 7:19 A.M., an earthquake measuring 8.1 on the Richter scale rocked the porous soil of the Valley of Mexico. Thousands of buildings crumbled, one-third of Mexico City's population was left without water, and virtually all of the city was left without electricity and phone service. Fires broke out as a result of gas leaks, and the city sank into a state of chaos. It is estimated that between 15,000 and 20,000 people died as a result of the earthquake and the 6.5 aftershock that followed the next day. Concomitant with the trauma of the destruction was the realization that the government had not only failed to put in place a plan to deal with such tragedies but also lacked the ability to formulate and implement such a plan. In the face of this official paralysis, the populace took to the streets, forming volunteer brigades to pull victims from the rubble. When Ramón Aguirre, the head of the Department of the Federal District (Mexico City's appointed mayor), called for the September 21 disbanding of volunteer brigades and the "normalization" of the city two days later, the population flatly rejected his appeal. The government's credibility had all but disappeared. Much of the public believed that, in the name of progress, the government turned a blind eye toward the shabby construction of many of the collapsed structures. Resentment toward the federal government was at an all-time high in Mexico City as residents were forced to deal with the tragedy on their own. A placard displayed during one of the many protests demanding government aid read, "This is the generation of the earthquake, and we no longer believe in the 'normalcy' of authoritarianism" ["Ésta es la generación del terremoto, y ya no creemos en la 'normalidad' del autoritarismo"] (see Monsiváis 1988, photos 14–15).

It was within this context of instability that Carlos Salinas de Gortari emerged as the PRI's choice for the 1988–1994 presidency (Fig. 1.4). During his campaign, therefore, Salinas de Gortari held a series of meetings on culture and national identity during which he and many renowned intellectuals discussed the political platform with the populace. In these *Diálogos para el consenso,* Salinas de Gortari artfully conveyed his sensitivity toward the hopes and fears that Mexicans held for the future. He managed to combine a message of modernization and reform with the tried-and-true issues of Mexican identity and national unity—now called consensus.

Salinas de Gortari's emphasis on unity and consensus was critical, since, for the first time in decades, a viable political opposition[41] emerged in the 1988 presidential campaign. As a result, Salinas de Gortari tapped into extant popular hopes for democracy and created a renewed sense of Mexican nationalism. He declared that "the role that belongs to a government convinced of democracy and with democracy, lies in the search for that link between nationalism and culture, between the defense of identity and sovereignty and the will of the people" ["el papel que corresponde a un gobierno convencido en la democracia y con la democracia, estriba en la búsqueda del punto de enlace entre nacionalismo y cultura, entre la defensa de la identidad y de la soberanía y la voluntad del pueblo"] (1988, 19).[42] Fears of the unknown—progress toward modernization or democracy—were tempered with comforting messages of unity and new *mexicanidad.*

Many of the intellectuals who campaigned for Salinas de Gortari echoed the comfort, the hope, and the nationalism that their candidate proposed. Aguilar Camín confirmed the continued paternalism that Salinas de Gortari's presidency would offer: "We are living in a time of uncertainty . . . when the country has the feeling that it needs to be defended because it feels vulnerable. I think it is the job of government to defend it" ["Vivimos un momento de incertidumbre . . . que el país tiene la sensación de que necesita ser defendido porque se siente vulnerado. Creo que una tarea del gobierno sería defenderlo"] (1988, 14). Still, the question of how a government that was working feverishly toward an open-market economy and free trade planned to defend its citizens, who had traditionally been protected by government controls, was not posed. Javier Barros Valero introduced candidate Salinas de Gortari to a crowd, stating:

Figure 1.4. Presidential candidate Carlos Salinas de Gortari shakes hands with supporters during his 1988 election campaign. Salinas de Gortari's emphasis on Mexico's cultural plurality, or *pluricultura*, reflected international currents of multiculturalism and the Mexican people's growing demand for democratization. Courtesy of arteHistoria.com.

Carlos Salinas de Gortari proposes that citizens agree about how to transmit the values and practices of our own tradition to stimulate creativity and renovation: He proposes that we modernize our social practices. He calls upon us to strengthen the roots of our unique identity, because he knows that it, along with economic self-sufficiency and political unity, is a requirement for a greater task: the guarantee of national sovereignty and independence.

[Carlos Salinas de Gortari nos propone a la ciudadanía acordar sobre cómo transmitir los valores y los usos de nuestra propia tradición para estimular la creatividad y renovación: nos propone modernizar nuestras prácticas sociales. Nos llama así para fortalecer las raíces de nuestra singular identidad, porque sabe que ésta, junto con la autosuficiencia económica y unidad política, es requisito de una tarea mayor: garantizar la soberanía y la independencia nacionales.] (1988, 21)

Lo mexicano—the Mexican essence—was again being touted as a source of strength and wealth, this time as the basis on which a developed and unquestionably independent nation would emerge.[43]

A more pluralistic, open-ended *mexicanidad* was the key to Salinas de Gortari's messages of consensus, or national unity, as well. In his campaign discourse, Salinas de Gortari focused on the wealth of Mexico's indigenous cultural legacies and the contributions of today's indigenous peoples, mentioning only in passing the "colonial heritage" ["herencia colonial"] (1988, 17) of the nation. He then confirmed, "Our culture is all of that and more, and its importance lies in the creative conjugation of its plurality. We have been able, over time, to formulate a Mexican way of life, a deeply rooted way of being Mexican unlike that of any other people" ["Nuestra cultura es todo eso y más, y su importancia radica en la conjugación creadora de su pluralidad. Hemos podido, con el paso del tiempo, formar un modo de vida mexicano, una forma muy arraigada de ser mexicanos que no es idéntica a la de ningún otro pueblo"] (17). Salinas de Gortari goes on to laud Mexico's national culture as the key to future development and progress, adding that the state (synonymous with his *PRIísta* platform) will play a decisive role in caring for Mexico's culture and channeling Mexico's ideas and dreams (17). He is thus able to insist on diversity within cultural unity and political consensus, claiming that the PRI will both guard the past and modernize the future.

The historian Enrique Krauze also ensured that all were welcome in Salinas de Gortari's consensus: "I think that consensual does not mean totalizing, it does not mean globalizing, it does not mean to make all people and opinions into one. I think there is a pluralistic essence in the text" ["Creo que consensual no quiere decir totalizante, no quiere decir globalizar, no quiere decir hacer de cada persona y de cada opinión una. Yo creo que hay una esencia plural en su texto"] ("Diálogo" 1988, 12).[44] Within the long-standing state discourses on national unity, *mestizaje,* and cultural nationalism, which traditionally reduced *mexicanidad* to its essence, Mexico's heterogeneity—or plurality—was now being recognized and championed by both politicians and intellectuals. Instead of including reductionist, character-based models of *mexicanidad*—such as those espoused by Paz and Ramos—official discourse changed, admitting that the nation, constituted by a multifaceted *pueblo,* was unified by lifestyle and (it was hoped) its support of the *PRIísta* government.

Citing García Canclini's idea of hybrid cultures[45]—wherein many cultures may intermix and coexist without necessarily fusing or losing their individual trait—in the mid-1990s, the author Juan Villoro stated, "The subject of national identity has now taken on new importance, and I think that most Mexicans actually are interested in a multiple identity, in a multicultural identity" ["El tema de la identidad nacional ahora ha cobrado nuevos visos y creo que la mayoría de los mexicanos se interesan más bien por una identidad múltiple, por una identidad multicultural"] (1996). The official turnaround toward viewing Mexico as a pluricultural society coincided with both international currents of multiculturalism and, within Mexico, public demand for democratization and a concerted effort on the part of the PRI and candidate Salinas de Gortari to project their willingness to democratize during the 1988 campaign. Termed *salinastroika*[46] by many, the party platform combined widespread plans to modernize the country and open it to the free market while working to reform election laws to ensure honest elections. Change was urgently needed and candidate Salinas de Gortari promised his countrymen and -women that he would deliver it without compromising Mexican traditions.

As Salinas de Gortari discursively combined tradition and modernization, he echoed the two primary components of Mexico's nationalism: pride and optimism.[47] Salinas de Gortari proclaimed that it was "morning in Mexico," echoing the U.S. Republican rhetoric of Ronald Reagan in the 1980s. One newspaper article claimed that young Mexican yuppies "grew up and went from adolescence to adulthood during the sexennial of Carlos Salinas de Gortari, who they exalted as their personal Reagan; he promised to take them to the first world and they believed him" ["crecieron y pasaron de la adolescencia a la vida adulta durante el sexenio de Carlos Salinas de Gortari, al cual encumbraron como su Reagan personal; les prometió ingresar al primer mundo y ellos le creyeron"] (González Ayala 1995, 1).

Salinas de Gortari's most far-reaching goals for Mexico undoubtedly entailed economic growth, which he hoped would benefit all Mexicans.[48] At the outset of his presidency, he proposed a massive new antipoverty plan called Solidarity. He had also promised widespread democratic gains through political election reform. It was soon evident, however, that he was concentrating on economic changes at the expense of democratic reform. Salinas de Gortari's plans for modernization and a return to growth without inflation sought to raise the Mexican standard of living. He relied heavily on foreign investment for national development as well. Yet in the transition to free trade and free market, Salinas de Gortari privatized many government-owned corporations and eliminated many government regulations, causing massive unemployment. Rave economic performance during the first half of Salinas de Gortari's presidency led *Forbes* magazine to declare it "a revolution you could invest in" (Goldmann 1990, 48), further implying the Reaganesque dawning of the Mexican economy.

After his election, it became evident that Salinas de Gortari's bag of political tricks was not as full as he had hoped. As noted earlier, the Salinas de Gortari administration took power under a cloud of doubt about the 1988 electoral results. The official figures posted were Salinas de Gortari, 50 percent; Cárdenas, 30 percent; and PAN (the party of the center-right), 20 percent. However, a number of factors caused widespread suspicion: the length of time it took to tabulate the votes, the opposition's rapid gains, and the authorities' potential manipulation of the whole process (Meyer and Aguilar Camín 1994, 284). Bartra concludes, "It is necessary to add that there is no evidence to indicate that the 1988 elections were without fraud; on the contrary, a close examination of the results assures that fraud continued to play an important role: without it, the PRI candidate would not have obtained the votes that were assigned to him and that consequently won him the election" ["Es preciso agregar que no hay ningún indicio que en las elecciones de 1988 no hubo fraude; por el contrario, un examen de los resultados permite asegurar que la franja del fraude continuó jugando un papel importante: sin ella, el candidato del PRI no hubiera alcanzado la votación que se le asignó y que le permitió ganar las elecciones"] (1989, 24). In 1988 the Mexican state was experiencing the worst crisis of legitimacy in its history, and any gains that candidate Salinas de Gortari had made in reviving nationalism were lost by the end of his *sexenio*, or six-year presidency.

By the beginning of the 1990s, the crisis of nationalism had deepened. Adolfo Gilly, a Mexican historian and essayist, had written, "Mexican nationalism is in crisis because its state is in crisis. . . . This crisis could be described, too, as a rupture between the cultural identities of Mexicans and the Mexican State as it subsists today" ["El nacionalismo mexicano está en crisis porque está en crisis su Estado. . . . Esta crisis podría describirse, también, como una ruptura entre las identidades culturales de los mexicanos y el Estado mexicano tal como éste todavía subsiste"] (1995, 63). Salinas de Gortari's discourses on plurality as a candidate did not materialize into popular democratic gains during his presidency. Bartra simply deems the entire system a failure, stating, "The PRI is becoming more evidently the party of rural backwardness and marginalized factions, the party of nonmodern Mexico and—of course—predemocratic Mexico" ["EL PRI es cada vez más obviamente el partido del atraso rural y de las franjas marginales; el partido del México no moderno y—desde luego—del México predemocrático"] (1989, 24). In 1988, as he toured the country, candidate Salinas de Gortari attempted to sell to potential voters a Mexico of proud cultural traditions framed by a more modern economy and more democratic political institutions. Nevertheless, as these claims were exposed as empty and fallacious and the state system as decreasingly viable, Mexico's sense of its national identity crumbled even further.

Without traditionally strong state discourses to reinvent Mexican nationalism, national identity suffered fragmentation. Although a real source of uncertainty, this weakened sense of identity and nationalism can be, and currently *is being,* replaced in Mexico with one that is more pluralistic, more multicultural. The 1994 uprising in Chiapas brought indigenous diversity and sovereignty to the forefront of national debates, while confidence and pride surround recent democratization, which Mexicans have pushed for since the crises of the 1980s. Although Mexican society and its government continue to negotiate the terms by which they approach multiculturalism—whether through indigenous autonomy or not—the fundamental changes that this realignment in Mexico's sense of nation and identity entails cannot be underestimated.

Mexican nationalist discourse and national identity had been constructed and disseminated by the same political party for decades, but in the late 1980s and early 1990s, a new plural national identity was forming around the fragmentation and failures of that party. Mexicans had witnessed the government's authoritarian repression of its own citizens in 1968, widespread economic mismanagement in 1982, and complete official inefficiency in the aftermath of the 1985 earthquake. It is not surprising, then, that the government was losing its traditional corporatism and its consensus with its constituency. Civil society had begun to organize on its own, and the expectation was that open democracy would be the next government model, but those same hopes for a competitive party system had just been dashed in 1988. The sense of uncertainty that pervaded the 1980s implicated and called into question every facet of the Mexican nation: its political institutions and their revolutionary foundations, its economic promise, and its very nationhood—the people's national identity.

Serendipitously, during the 1980s, Mexico began to participate in the commemoration of the Quincentennial of Columbus's voyages to the New World. As nations and their specific interest groups debated international plans and the many polemics that surrounded them, Mexico found itself engaged in a deep inquiry into the most painful issues of its history and its identity. The opportunity to revise the historical record and renew its identity discourse would prove both challenging and gainful. Instead of being fed a historical discourse wholly generated by the state, Mexicans had access to a variety of divergent views of the sixteenth century during the Quincentennial, mirroring disagreements not only among intellectuals but also within the larger society. Just as the issues of historiographic manipulation, crisis, and nationalism are invaluable to the analyses that follow, the polemics and debates of the Quincentennial, to which we now turn, demonstrate the currents of thought that influenced and informed the artists discussed herein.

Reevaluating Mexican Origins and Identity:
The Quincentennial Debates

In 1982 the Spanish government began long-term and large-scale preparations for the five hundredth anniversary of the discovery of America. During the ten years leading up to the October 12, 1992, celebration, the entire enterprise sparked heated debate. Soon after it ended, the events were thoroughly analyzed. Nearly every nation and every group of people involved in or affected by European expansion to the West opined about, organized, and contributed to the international fervor evoked by that date. In Mexico the debates that ensued dredged up many painful historical issues. Nevertheless, the very questioning of the distant past and its relationship to the present also served to clarify a host of national identity issues. As we have seen, in the 1980s, Mexican nationalism and identity were experiencing numerous setbacks. The Quincentennial debates added generously to the process of Mexico's self-searching.

As we saw in the discussion of national identity, the Mexican state, which declares the Mexican nation to be mestizo, has a difficult and complex view of the conquest and colony as foundational moments in the country's past. Although this view acknowledges that racial mixing began at the time of the conquest and colony, rather than present the conquest or colony as national cornerstones, it opts to laud the events of the Revolution and independence. Public opinion and institutional historiography treat the circumstances of the sixteenth century with no less ambivalence.

The responses of Mexicans and Mexicanists to the question of the location of the birth of the Mexican nation, an absolute necessity for identity discourses, run the gamut. Justo Sierra, a powerful nineteenth-century intellectual, believed that during the conquest Cortés founded the Mexican nationhood [*nacionalidad*], whereas with independence, Father Hidalgo gave rise to the *Patria* (Vázquez 1970, 106).[49] For Sierra, Mexico's nationhood is exemplified in its mestizo beginnings, but Mexico's nation begins as it throws off the yoke of colonialism. Although it is true that Mexican official history articulates the 1821 independence as the beginning of nationhood (Schmidt 1978, 21), some scholars (e.g., Aguilar Camín) point to nineteenth-century Creole patriotism, and a few others (e.g., Fuentes) indicate the conquest as the nation's origin.

Here again, we see the marginal place of the conquest and colony in Mexico's national consciousness—especially given the widespread rhetoric on Mexico's mestizo condition. Because these moments in history embody painful and shameful issues, such as massacre, rape, trauma, exploitation, and submission to dominance, they are largely overlooked and underanalyzed. The conquest is commonly referred to as a nightmare, a symbolic wound to Mexicans (Martínez 1992, 10). To overcome the trauma, nationalist discourse has traditionally posited the sixteenth-century arrival of Spaniards to the Mexican coast as the beginning of all of

Mexico's ills (Meyer 1993, 43; 1996). Corruption, exploitation, and misery seem to have disembarked from Spanish *carabelas* along with Cortés's troops. By denigrating the conquest, however, nationalism discredits Mexico's Hispanic inheritance and the role it played in the nation's formation.[50]

Despite the general suppression and ignorance of these historical events, the conquest continues to be a very visceral presence for many Mexicans. Fuentes deems it "the principal, mental headline on every Mexican's mental newspaper.... It continues to occupy a central place in our historical memory, in our memory of identity" ["el principal encabezado mental del periódico mental de cada mexicano.... Sigue ocupando un lugar central en la memoria histórica, en la memoria de la identidad"] (1996). But he adds that Mexicans wrongly identify largely with the conquered indigenous nations, as they demonize Cortés and the Spaniards for having obliterated the Aztec paradise. That Cortés's conquest of Mexico still stirs so many ambivalent feelings is not surprising. In fact, these feelings reflect the multitude of attitudes about the European expansion, conquest, Christianization, and colonization of the New World.

The debate over what to call the Quincentennial provides us with a telling example of the complexity of its meanings. Spain's official proposal that the Quincentennial be called Celebration of the Discovery of America sparked immediate reaction. Many people throughout the Americas were scandalized that Europeans still thought they had "discovered" the continent—as if beforehand it had not existed. One Latin American angrily observed, "It would not be pointless to ask the Spaniards, 'Why, to this date, have you not built a monument to remind you of the eight centuries of Muslim domination? How much longer are you going to wait? When will you begin festivities for eight hundred years of subjugation?'" ["No es ocioso preguntarle a los españoles '¿Por qué, hasta la fecha, no han construido un monumento que les recuerde los ocho siglos de dominación musulmana? ¿Cuánto más van a esperar? ¿Cuándo van a iniciar los festejos por los ochocientos años de sojuzgamiento?'"] (Abud 1992, 2). Then, at a 1984 meeting of Latin American Quincentennial commissions, the Mexican delegation—headed by Miguel León-Portilla, a renowned historian specializing in Nahuatl history and culture—proposed that the 1992 activities be called the Commemoration of the Encounter of Two Worlds. The next day, headlines read, "Mexico denies that Spain discovered America!" ["¡México niega que España descubrió a América!"] (León-Portilla 1996).

It was not at all the Mexican delegation's intention, however, to deny the past. Rather, *encounter* was chosen for its wealth of meanings. As León-Portilla points out, the word *encounter* can mean "meeting," "nearing," and even "the violent clash of troops or fighters" (1996).[51] By referring to an encounter and labeling its remembrance a commemoration instead of a celebration, the Mexican delegation diplomatically bridged the most polar attitudes about the Quincentennial.

But not everyone was persuaded of the wisdom of diplomacy in dealing with such charged issues as massacre, slavery, and cultural imperialism. Some proposed that the activities be called the Invasion of America; the Destruction of the Indies (Iniciarte 1992, 61); or liquidation, genesis, and apocalypse (Hinojosa 1992, 39). Mexican historian Silvio Zavala debated even the listing of only two worlds, and Guillermo Bonfil Batalla, a leading indigenist, commented, "I prefer the term 'collision,' because it seems more descriptive" ["Prefiero el término encontronazo, porque me parece más descriptivo"] (Bonfil Batalla 1996, 45). The Quincentennial project, which began as the proud marking of Columbus's crossing of the Atlantic, took on a wide variety of meanings. European expansion was blamed for the stifling of indigenous cultures, and all the excesses of the conquest and impositions of the colony were scrutinized as well.

Deciding on suitable nomenclature was challenging enough, but what about the issue of what the commemoration should mean to today's Americans—both North and South? Many believed that the Quincentennial should be a learning experience, one of analysis that would prevent us from committing the same historical errors in the future (Abud 1992, 18), whereas others asked poignantly, "What are we to celebrate or commemorate? . . . Are we to celebrate the bloody brutality of the Conquest? The three centuries of colonization whose inequality we resent today and is our most serious problem?" ["¿Qué debemos celebrar o conmemorar? . . . ¿Debemos festejar la brutalidad sanguinaria de las conquistas? ¿Los tres siglos de Colonia cuya desigualdad resentimos hoy y es nuestro mayor problema?"] (Benítez 1992, 11). Some longed for this event to revive pan-Americanism by demonstrating the commonalties among Latin American countries (Bonfil Batalla et al. 1991, 43). Paraguayan writer Augusto Roa Bastos believed that pan-Americanism and the consolidation of Latin American identity could be coupled with alliance and union with Spain and Portugal (1987, 8), but others flatly refused to participate, sarcastically calling the Quincentennial a Eurocentric marketing ploy and an attempt by Spain to secure a prominent role in the European Union (Ortega 1992, 18).

All the same, most people focused on the events of five hundred years before and proposed new analyses of our epistemology of and attitudes toward that historical era. Yet there were many who could not abide a conciliatory stance toward the past. Members of the Seminario de Estudios Prehispánicos para la Descolonización de México of the Universidad Nacional Autónoma de México (UNAM) noted perceptible changes in terminology that reflected a new, decolonizing reading of the conquest: "The epic language used to describe the Conquest is being substituted by simple and plain talk of invasion; when speaking of the Indian, it is necessarily done with deference; attitudes toward the Colony are being modified to the degree that we admit our own identification with those originally colonized" ["El lenguaje épico usado para describir la Conquista se sustituye para hablar simple y llanamente de invasión; al tratar de lo indio, se hace necesariamente con deferencia; actitudes hacia lo colonial se modifican a medida que nos sabemos identificados con los originalmente colonizados"] (Editorial 1995, 1). This viewpoint identifies almost solely with indigenous interests, demonstrating further the ideological and discursive squaring off of sides during the Quincentennial debates.

The sheer ardor of the debates and polemics over 1492 demonstrates the Americas' urgent need to confront the past and the inextricably intertwined issues of identity elicited by this confrontation. By reevaluating the circumstances that made the Americas what they are today—culturally and linguistically Western former colonies—the Quincentennial brought to the fore difficult issues of racial and cultural identity that had to be dealt with. Even five centuries after the fact, this identity remains unresolved. To a certain extent, this is due to the resultant identity crisis provoked by the fact that Mexican nationalist discourse has vilified the conquest and colony, thus making it difficult to valorize mestizo, indigenous, and Hispanic roots. The great strides that have been made in indigenous studies in the past half century have consequently publicized the frightful effects of the so-called encounter. But the harsh condemnations of European imperialist activities that accompany this understanding have clouded the past, making objective assimilation nearly impossible.

The identity crisis referred to earlier is, as should now be quite clear, particularly deep and complex in the case of Mexico. We have seen how the postrevolutionary state constructed *mexicanidad* around glories of the indigenous past and mestizo present. The large-scale suppression of open analysis of Mexico's Hispanic and colonial legacies has skewed the Mexican sense of nationhood, but it has also been a convenient tool for some. Condemnation of the events of the sixteenth century in Mexico is a powerful unifying force for nationalist projects. This confluence of nationalism and anticolonialism also serves to legitimize the PRI by justifying the continuation of revolutionary projects, which constitute a radical break with Mexico's colonial past.

Yet despite the PRI's continuous efforts to distance itself from the colonial past, the many discussions about the Quincentennial revealed just how closely related this past is to the Mexico's present. These realizations were not always pleasant. For instance, it seemed that after nearly 150 years of independence, Mexico could not continue to explain away its shortcomings merely by blaming Spain's actions from centuries before (J. Villoro 1996). As Aguilar Camín points out, Hispanic legacy cannot be blamed for Mexico's problems today, especially given Spain's great successes in democratization and prosperity in recent decades. Therefore, the decade of the 1980s in Mexico bared the fallacious belief that its Hispanic heritage was to blame for the nation's economic underdevelopment and inability to achieve full-fledged democracy (1993c, 101). Faced with Spain's successes, Mexico could no longer blame its continued underdevelopment on this era of history.

Further aggravating this identity crisis during the years leading up to the Quincentennial was the concurrent deterioration of the PRI and its political institutions in Mexico—termed by some the great farewell to the revolutionary system [el gran adiós al sistema revolucionario].[52] As the failures of the Revolution were becoming more and more evident, many also began to see in their everyday life the political legacies of their colonial past (Aguilar Camín 1993a, 51). Fernando Benítez even writes, "The Colony continues to exist in many aspects of Latin American life: despotism, absolutism, distrust, *cortesansimo,* and ever-present inequality, which is its principal legacy. All of its countries have suffered from guerrillas, military coups, the ambition of absolute power, poor education, huge debt, and subjection to the United States" ["La Colonia sigue vigente en muchos aspectos de la vida latinoamericana: el cacicazgo, el absolutismo, el recelo, el cortesanismo y la siempre presente desigualdad, su principal legado. Todos sus países han sufrido la guerrilla, el cuartelazo, la ambición de un poder omnímodo, una educación pobre, un endeudamiento gigantesco, una sujeción a los Estados Unidos"] (1992, 313). The Mexican crises of the 1980s and 1990s, coupled with the Quincentennial's debates over the central historical and foundational events of Latin America allowed for widespread discussion of important facets of Mexico's identity. The nation's status as revolutionary was called into question, and the very colonial characteristics that Mexico so loathed and had fought so hard to erase made themselves known again.

During these same years of economic and political instability in Mexico, when nationalist feelings were at a low and even the Quincentennial activities were pointing to Mexico's unique national problems, a number of Mexican artists were poring over the historical documents of the conquest and colony. Although they searched the past for a multitude of reasons, all rewrote that past through narratives of historical fiction, and because they were treating the sixteenth century during these years of crisis, all necessarily explored issues of modern Mexican identity. The intriguing aspect of their identity discourses lies in their treatment of this national essence at a time when—in retrospect, we now know—*mestizaje* as a framework was being deeply undermined in official nationalist and identity discourses. These artists reworked and revised Mexico's mestizo identity for what will most likely be the last time, for soon after—prompted by emerging democratization, growing awareness of multiculturalism, a crumbling political system, and a vociferous indigenous rights movement—Mexico's identity discourse took a dramatic turn toward the recognition of its pluricultural and multiethnic populace.

Creative Representations of Mexican Nationalism, Identity, and History

The works in the discussion that follows combine many of the issues of nationalism, identity, and history laid out in this introductory chapter. They are novels, plays, movies, and cartoons written and/or published in the late 1980s and 1990s. In each of these works, the artists collectively interrogate and recreate Mexico's sixteenth-century history in a search for origins that resulted from the very specific crises, disillusionments, and debates of the end of the twentieth century. Each search for origins undeniably unfolds within a metaphor of *mestizaje*—be it the inception of biological *mestizaje,* the continuation of spiritual and cultural *mestizaje,* or the revelation of impossible *mestizajes.* Yet despite the common historical and metaphorical bases shared by these works, they are dramatically unique in that they highlight different historical events or employ different characters from the historical record, they alternately adhere to and mold the past in discrepant ways, and they are varied in their typifications of national identity. All of the works reveal the depth of the crisis in Mexican national sentiment as well as the urgency with which intellectuals wrote either to salvage or to rework a national mestizo identity that they believed to have germinated in the events and historiography of the early sixteenth century in Mexico. We now turn to an analysis of the revisionist treatments of the conquest of Mexico and the commentary on modern Mexican national identity encountered in these works.

2

The Trauma of Mexico's Mestizo Origins

In the late 1980s and early 1990s, when many of Mexico's foremost novelists, playwrights, cinematographers, and cartoonists took part in the collective commemoration of the Quincentennial, some of them also took the opportunity to respond to the crisis of nationalism by grappling with the thorny issues presented by Mexico's mestizophile national identity discourse. At the end of the twentieth century, Mexico's national identity discourses were in turmoil, owing, as we have seen, to both economic and political failings, the Quincentennial debates, and an emerging national consciousness of multiculturalism. The notion of the mestizo as the central figure of national identity, based in the history of the conquest, became the focus of many artists, who were confronted with the problematic conceptual baggage associated with being mestizo and with the process of *mestizaje*.[1] The issues of mestizo origins and the resultant perception of mestizo dualism are central to their works. For if it can be said that mestizos constitute a "cosmic race" or a "race of bronze" that harmoniously forges indigenous and Spanish roots, it can also be said that mestizos are children of tragedy in whom an unresolved battle continues to wage. The authors and artists who rewrote the conquest at the end of the twentieth century returned to this traumatic era precisely in order to explore the origins of Mexico's *mestizaje*—the cornerstone of twentieth-century Mexican national identity—and thereby reexamine the underpinnings of official claims of national unity.

The two works analyzed here treat traumatized mestizo origins: one in terms of biology, and the other in terms of theology. The novel *Nen, la inútil,* by Ignacio Solares, and the film *La otra conquista,* by Salvador Carrasco (1998), both portray the inception of Mexican *mestizaje*—*Nen la inútil* (1994) through a romanticization of the encounter between the Spanish and the indigenous and *La otra conquista* through an exploration of the indigenous acceptance of Christianity in the form of a syncretic Spanish Virgin Mary. In order to analyze these works, however, we must first understand the negative connotations associated with Mexican *mestizaje* that form the context in which Solares and Carrasco write.

The Traumatization of Mexico's Mestizo Origins and Combative Mestizo Dualism

Because *mestizaje* began in Mexico during the very painful national historical chapters of the conquest and colony, mestizo origins have been traumatized—told as tales of violence, rape, exploitation, and submission to dominance. The 1950 publication of Octavio Paz's *El laberinto de la soledad* represents perhaps the most significant moment in the traumatization of mestizo origins. Most important to the analysis here is the author's treatment of mestizo origins and the mestizo condition. First, he equates mestizo origins with the Cortés-Malinche[2] paradigm. As elaborated by Paz, this paradigm originates from the idea that the conquistadors' cruel conquest of the land and people constituted a rape that resulted in the violent conception of the mestizo (Paz 1993, 94–96).

In her study entitled *La Malinche in Mexican Literature from History to Myth*, Sandra Messinger Cypess probes both Paz's treatment of the conquest and its key role in traumatizing mestizo origins. Cypess criticizes Paz's equation of the Cortés-Malinche paradigm with the concepts of the *chingón* and *chingada*.[3] Here, the rapist, or *chingón*, leaves the victim wounded and used, literally *chingada*. In *El laberinto de la soledad*, Paz contends that, beginning with the conquest and with Hernán Cortés taking his translator (Malintzin) as a lover, Mexicans are all *hijos de la chingada*.[4] Cypess writes that Paz victimizes Malintzin (by casting her as a voluntary participant) while simultaneously blaming the popular rejection of her for Mexico's sense of orphaned isolation and loneliness (Cypess 1991, 97). Paz further traumatizes the Mexican mestizo condition when he writes, "We condemn our origins, and we renounce our hybridity. The strange permanence of Cortés and Malinche in the imagination and sensibility of contemporary Mexicans reveals that they are something more than historical figures. They are symbols of a secret conflict that we have yet to resolve" ["Condenamos nuestro origen y renegamos nuestro hibridismo. La extraña permanencia de Cortés y de la Malinche en la sensibilidad de los mexicanos actuales revela que son algo más que figuras históricas. Son símbolos de un conflicto secreto que aún no hemos resuelto"] (Paz 1993, 95). In *La jaula de la melancolía*, Roger Bartra, also debunks Paz's portrayal of violent mestizo origins, noting that not only does Paz contradict himself about just who the *hijos de la chingada* are—foreigners or Mexicans—but he exaggerates the peculiarities of the verb *chingar* as well (Bartra 1992, 160).

Yet despite the unmistakable negativity of the Cortés-Malinche paradigm, Paz's writing on the subject demonstrates both the complexity of Mexican identity and the traditional Mexican denial of cultural roots. In a direct reference to Paz's *El laberinto de la soledad,* Carlos Fuentes asks, "From whence comes the legitimacy of a country when it denies its father, the Spanish rapist, and condemns its mother, the indigenous traitor?" ["¿De dónde surge la legitimidad de un país que niega a su padre, el español violador, y condena a su madre, la indígena traidora?"] (1992b, 127). Yet many Mexicans have internalized these origins as their own and even Cypess sees Cortés and Malinche as the "symbolic parents" of the mestizos (1991, 28). Solares, too, proposes dealing head-on with these symbolic ancestors and Mexico's cultural roots in order to better understand Mexican national identity. In *Nota* at the end of *Nen, la inútil,* he poignantly asks, "Can we Mexicans know ourselves without facing the tragic past from which we originate? . . . We are the children of tragedy and denying it only perpetuates it" ["¿Podemos conocernos los mexicanos sin mirar de frente el pasado trágico del cual surgimos? . . . Somos hijos de una tragedia y su negación no hace sino perpetuarla"] (1994, 133–34). Thus, by revisiting the conquest, Mexican intellectuals such as those whose works are analyzed in the pages that follow seek to reevaluate the tragic events of the sixteenth century in an effort to comprehend the many intricacies and contradictions of modern Mexican identity.

In addition to the traumatization of mestizo origins noted, recent depictions of an inherent combative dualism in the mestizo condition have further complicated Mexican national identity. Nearly a century ago, in the Mexican mestizophile tradition of the early twentieth century, the mixing of blood and races was hailed as the road to national unification: "the conformation of a truly Mexican national identity, unique, that puts an end to internal divisions . . . the definite end [being] the unification of a mestizo motherland" ["la conformación de una nacionalidad verdaderamente mexicana, única, que ponga fin a las divisiones internas . . . el fin definitivo (siendo) la unificación de una patria mestiza"] (Basave Benítez 1993, 84). The theoretical concept or dream of a largely mestizo nation as unified and egalitarian ran through official Mexican discourse for decades. More recently, however, Mexicans describe being mestizo in terms of an internal conflict. In his *Nota* at the end of *Nen, la inútil,* Solares describes his own personal experience of the ambiguous dualism—or "unresolved otherness" ["otredad no resuelta"] (1994, 133)—of Mexican identity by noting that one of his grandfathers was one of Pancho Villa's revolutionary Dorados,[5] while the other was of Spanish descent and an open supporter of Porfirio Díaz's totalitarian regime. He also quotes a fictional character created by Rafael F. Muñoz,[6] who quips, "I am all Mexican! I have nothing to do with Indians and Spaniards" ["¡Yo soy puro mexicano! Nada tengo que ver con indios y españoles"] (quoted in Solares 1994, 133). In the same vein, the writer and thinker Alfonso Reyes laments, "We have not found the figure, the unity of our soul. We comply with knowing that we are the children of a conflict between two races" ["No hemos encontrado la cifra, la unidad de nuestra alma. Nos conformamos con sabernos hijos del conflicto entre dos razas"] (1952, 88). In keeping with his traumatic vision of the inception of Mexican *mestizaje*, Paz believes the mestizo conflict originated with Cortés and Malinche, "symbols of a secret conflict that we still have not resolved" ["símbolos de un conflicto secreto, que aún no hemos resuelto"] (1993, 95). The prominent twentieth-century Mexican intellectual Luis Villoro describes it as "the ancestral battle: The conflict between Cuauhtémoc and Hernán Cortés lives in our blood, where neither is able to defeat the other" ["la pugna ancestral: El conflicto entre Cuauhtémoc y Hernán Cortés vive en nuestra sangre sin que alguno de los dos haya podido vencer"] (1950, 191). Thus, the distant past plays an undeniably large role in this contemporary vision of a combative national character. Had there not been a violent conquest of Mexico, the current-day conception of *mestizaje* would not be so riddled with discord.[7]

Many Mexicans see contemporary Mexico bearing out the dualistic conflictive view of national being. The Mexican author and poet Homero Aridjis describes his homeland as enigmatic:

This is always, for me, Mexico's surprise. Because when one wants to see in Mexico merely an indigenous nation, the West emerges, Western culture. And when one wants to see in Mexico a Western nation, indigenous culture appears in force.

[Para mí siempre es ésta la sorpresa de México. Porque cuando uno quiere ver en México como un país indígena, nada más, sale el occidental, la cultura occidental. Y cuando uno quiere ver en México un país occidental, sale la cultura indígena muy fuerte.] (1996)

Solares would agree, noting that the "balance" of the Mexican consciousness is often destabilized by events in contemporary history: "Curiously, when we felt most North American, during the North American Free Trade Agreement [NAFTA] period, the Chiapas issue arrived to remind us of our Central American condition and our poverty" ["Curiosamente, cuando más norteamericanos nos sentíamos, en el momento del Tratado de Libre Comercio, vino lo de Chiapas, de hecho, a recordarnos de nuestra condición de centroamericano, y de pueblo pobre"] (1996).[8] The fact that so many Mexicans speak in terms of a mutually exclusive dualism reaffirms the 1994 Universidad Nacional Autónoma de México poll of Mexicans, which shows that the majority believe that indigenous traditions are not conducive to Mexicanization or modernization (*Los mexicanos de los noventa* 1996, 86).

The Cortés-Malinche paradigm—its trauma and its combativeness—transcends the mere study of the history of the conquest and has become profoundly embedded in not only Mexican identity discourses but also the national consciousness and imaginary. Yet the inherent violence of the conquest and mestizo origins appears radically oversimplified in Paz's Cortés-Malinche paradigm, and this may have contributed to a stunted analysis of the events of the sixteenth century and their significance to modern Mexican identity. In addition, this traumatization of the Adam and Eve of Mexican *mestizaje* lends itself to one single (and singularly negative) interpretation of the founding of this mestizo nation. Although for purposes of national unity, this centralized vision of nationhood has at times been beneficial, it does not allow for multiple stories or for a variation of heritage, both of which are necessary in a pluricultural society.

Nen, la inútil, by Ignacio Solares

Nen, la inútil (1993), by Ignacio Solares,[9] responds to the crises in Mexican national identity discourse by trying to resolve the problems that mestizophile ideology presented for modern Mexican society. As we have seen, mestizophile ideology—most recently, Hispanizing—had become unpalatable in the face of growing acceptance of and support for ethnic and cultural diversity in Mexico. Over the years, the entire concept of *mestizaje* had been constructed as traumatic. Solares's text, accordingly, works to revitalize this distasteful ideology by romanticizing it—by retelling the original drama of *mestizaje* within the narrative framework of a love story (albeit a tragic love story) with a fairy-tale ending.

To a degree, the novel *Nen, la inútil* is a fictive account of events that are firmly based in history. Solares cites his use of such historical documents as the sixteenth-century testimony of the conquest by Bernal Díaz del Castillo (1992), the late nineteenth-century history of the conquest by Manuel Orozco y Berra (1880), compilations of sixteenth-century indigenous retellings of the conquest by Miguel León-Portilla (1989), and in-depth twentieth-century biographies of Cortés by José Fuentes Mares (1981) and José Luis Martínez (1992). Yet he believes that his job as a writer is to revitalize the very stories that history tells, maintaining that literature brings events to life:

> I have the impression that something remains a cold fact if it hasn't been turned into a novel. I think in this case a novelist has two advantages: that he or she can change things ... [and] the novelist can fill in history's gaps with imagination.... And I like to think that, in the end, things are not just the way they supposedly were but are also the way you shape them.

> [Y yo tengo la impresión que queda un poco como un hecho frío mientras no se lo novela. Yo creo que la ventaja del novelista en este caso serían dos: que puede ambientar las cosas ... (y) que el novelista puede llenar con la imaginación los huecos de la historia.... Y a mí me gusta pensar que finalmente las cosas ya no son como las supuestamente fueron sino también como tú se las elaboras.] (1996)

Through the descriptive and imaginative narration of events of the past, Solares believes, the past comes alive, actively constituting a new version of history.

Although two of the novel's central textual fragments narrate historically documented and well-known sixteenth-century events in Mexico—the first meeting between the Aztec emperor Moctezuma and Cortés and the adventures of shipwrecked Jerónimo de Aguilar and Gonzalo Guerrero[10] on the Yucatan peninsula—the majority of the novel is concerned with the fictional protagonists Nen and Felipe. The two characters—a young, clairvoyant Aztec woman and a typified Spanish conqueror—embody the story of encounter, shock, and appropriation that Solares sees as the beginning of modern Mexican society. Through their eyes, the encounter and conquest are rewritten and retold, thereby creating a fuller picture of the past. The unwillingness to narrate history through the eyes and acts of a single "great" or well-known man suggests that Solares privileges the margins— voices that are not normally heard outside the novel. Although the text tells of the conquest from both the Spanish and indigenous points of view, as the pages that follow demonstrate, Solares also employs marginal voices to relate a very mainstream version of history.

This narrative perspective is also very much in keeping with nascent historical and societal trends in Mexico since the 1980s. The 1980s were years filled with historical revisionism, as we have seen, and as a result of such events as the 1968 massacre and the 1985 earthquake, Mexico's population lost much faith in "great men" as societal leaders. With this breakdown of consensus and trust, arises interest in microhistories, the telling of events from a wide variety of (not always official) perspectives. The disjointed nature of the narrative in *Nen, la inútil,* which is characterized by alternating fragments, allows for simultaneous accounts of the same moments in history from two markedly distinct points of view: that of a Spanish conquistador and that of an Aztec visionary. Although these two perspectives have been studied in Mexico for decades (especially since the 1959 publication of León-Portilla's *La visión de los vencidos: Relaciones indígenas de la conquista*),[11] only since the marking of the Quincentennial has the general public been made conscious of and engaged in debate about the value of both perspectives.

In *Nen, la inútil,* the narrative's seemingly random fluctuation in time and perspective actually serves a relevant purpose with respect to both character development and the author's intent to reinsert the encounter and conquest into Mexico's consciousness as the beginning of modern Mexican society. The novel, which is divided into two parts, begins with an emblematic fragment that depicts Nen watching Spanish and Tlaxcalan soldiers march and ride into Tenochtitlán. The first part of the novel then progresses in leaps, starting toward the culminating first (historical) encounter between Cortés and Moctezuma (the emperor of the Aztec kingdom, the ninth *tlatloani*). Thus, the first half of the book is literally interlocated between parallel images of meeting the Other and the growing sense that encounter will only lead to tragedy.

The narrative progression in the first part of the novel—from the parade of soldiers that Nen views in the first pages to the two leaders standing face to face at the end of this section—probably lasted no more than a few hours in chronological time. Nonetheless, interspersed between these two narrative bookends are the fragmented journeys that Nen and Felipe make toward each other. We see Nen's development from a young girl who has horrifying dreams to a respected visionary in the emperor's palace. We follow Felipe's life: his decisions to travel to the New World and his journeys to both Cuba and Mexico. In effect, we watch him approach Nen physically through both his narration and her premonition of his journey.

The second half of the narrative moves from encounter toward its tragic consequence: the fateful night known as *Noche Triste*. It is important to note that the second part of the book begins not after the meeting between Cortés and Moctezuma but on the Yucatan peninsula months before. There Cortés sent for two shipwrecked Spaniards—Aguilar and Guerrero—to serve as interpreters. As both the novel *Nen, la inútil* and historical sources tell us, the Spaniards arrived on the Yucatan only to discover the nearly nude, savage, and bearded Other (who is, in Aguilar's case, Spanish). Although Aguilar declared his identity as a Spaniard and agreed to accompany Cortés's troops, Guerrero refused to leave the Mayan world.[12] Solares's inclusion of these vignettes allows him to set up contrasting stories of *mestizaje* in the scene that ends the novel: the love between Guerrero and his wife versus the rape of Nen by Felipe (a juxtaposition to which we return in more detail ahead).

The entire mood of the second half of the novel reflects the second, more violent tale of *mestizaje*. The events and narrative become increasingly chaotic as the two cultures clash in Tenochtitlán. The conquistadors commit the egregious offense of taking Moctezuma—the political and religious leader—prisoner (Solares 1994, 103); they defile the Aztecs' gods by destroying their icons and temples (98, 99); they introduce sickness and dizzying disorder. The chaos, which comes in many forms, culminates when the Spaniards prohibit the great festivals and ceremonies that are the heart of the Aztec calendar—at which point, for the Aztecs, all sense of purpose and temporal progression is lost. Nen, who has been preparing for the festival of Huitzilopochtli (the principal Aztec war deity), sums up the sense of loss and lack of direction:

> This year's festival could not be like previous ones. Everything around the Mexicans had become confused, and they no longer knew whom to worship.... They were not even sure they were allowed to celebrate that festival, which was of extreme importance to them. How were they to understand the rest of the year without that celebration?

[La fiesta de este año no podría ser como las anteriores. Todo alrededor de los mexicanos se había confundido y ya ni siquiera sabían bien a bien a quien adorar. . . . Ni siquiera estaban seguros de que les permitieran celebrar aquella fiesta, de una importancia extrema para ellos. ¿Cómo concebir el resto del año sin la celebración?] (87, 98)

Her work throughout the second part of the novel—the gathering of sacred materials, the delicate creation of effigies of the god, the exalted treatment and careful pampering of those effigies through rituals—is really her march toward death, for as the ceremony finally gets underway in the Templo Mayor, her premonitions merge with reality:

Upon seeing [Felipe] appear suddenly in the Templo Mayor—almost as part of the religious ceremony itself—she knew that her eyes were no longer her own and that he embodied the fatality she had always feared, that she had almost been his closest companion.

[Al verlo (a Felipe) aparecer de golpe en el Templo Mayor—casi como parte de la ceremonia religiosa misma—supo que sus ojos ya no eran sus ojos y que él encarnaba la fatalidad que siempre temió, que había sido casi su compañera más cercana.] (107)

The violation of the Templo Mayor—and of Nen—is about to begin. Because of her dreams, she has known this encounter to be her destiny all her life.

Here, as the narrative actively recalls *El laberinto de la soledad,* Solares melds his fiction with Paz's identity discourse. Seen through the enduring icons of *mexicanidad* set forth in *El laberinto de la soledad,* the scenes of festival preparation and orgiastic massacre demonstrate both the ritualistic and fatalistic character of Mexican society. The novel itself, in conjunction with the pronouncements of Solares concerning *mexicanidad,* reflects Paz's contention that Mexico is a nation that continually searches for its origin and for a means of self-expression.

Resolving the Dualism of the Mestizo Condition

The narrative of *Nen, la inútil* revises the history of encounter and tragedy of sixteenth-century Mexico by folding the past back into the present and then searching for a new expression of *mexicanidad* on both national and individual levels. Traditionally, Mexican history provides us with many binaries: Creole/peninsular, liberal/conservative, Spanish/indigenous, revolutionary/authoritarian. Although, as a result, dualism and binaries are common in Mexican identity discourses, Roger Bartra believes that they are the tools of nationalist unification programs. He writes, "The culture of duality is coming to an end: the theater of the institutional revolutionary or the semioriental mestizo is frankly bankrupt" ["La cultura de la dualidad está llegando a su fin: el teatro del revolucionario institucional o del mestizo semioriental está en franca quiebra"], and it will be replaced by democracy and multiplicity (1991, 18). However, Solares's previously quoted comment about his own dual identity—symbolized by the Dorados and Porfirio Díaz—demonstrates that his overall concern in terms of Mexican national identity is with its dualism, or the "otredad no resuelta," and the tragedy from which he believes Mexican mestizos are born.

Yet in *Nen, la inútil,* Solares achieves a remarkably rich ambiguity in terms of the characters who embody the ethnic or racial components of Mexico's *mestizaje.* Through their eyes, the encounter and conquest are rewritten and retold, creating a fuller picture of the past. The two protagonists not only represent differing perspectives of the historical events that transpire but they also set up—and upset—the two traditional facets of Mexican cultural and racial heritage: the indigenous and the Hispanic.[13] For example, the supposedly diametrically opposed characters, Nen and Felipe—the indigenous and the white, the Other and the self, the conquered and the conqueror, the margin and the center—come to reveal their confluent, parallel nature and therefore blur the commonly drawn lines between the stereotyped boundaries of indigenous and Spanish. In terms of current-day mestizo identity, the blurring of these lines and binaries consequently lessens the tensions between self and Other that many perceive as at odds in mestizo dualism. As we will see, it is through the simultaneous contrast and confusion of these two poles of Mexico's identity that Solares makes pointed statements about modern Mexican being.

First, Solares creates as one of the two principal characters Nencihuatl, "which meant woman who brings misfortune" ["que significaba mujer que acarrea desdichas"], or—as she is called—Nen, the useless (1994, 13). Nen is a young Aztec woman who had the misfortune of being born on one of the five leftover, nonritualized days in the Aztec calendar (the *nemontemi*), a circumstance that appears to be the cause of her uncanny clairvoyance and ability to see and dream the future. As a character, she demonstrates the blending of both historical "fact" and (one of Solares's writerly trademarks) the magical. Her visions revealing the apocalyptic auguries of conquest constitute telepathic or extrasensory dreams that "are extraordinarily accurate depictions of distant or future events, more or less as they actually occurred" (Hunt 1989, 113). She sees the fierce eyes and sporadic movements of unknown beasts—the first horses introduced to the New World by the conquerors—and she dreams of the *teules,* or gods, with their pale skin, beards, light hair, and silver-colored coverings (armor). Her ability to sense all of this yet unknown information constitutes a "trans-reality"[14] characteristic of Solares's fiction that is made very real through the narrative, occurring "in connection with the desire or need on the part of a character" (Brushwood 1989, 13).

The numerous signs and prophecies of Cortés's arrival and of the impending doom of the Aztec empire that today many believe that the Aztecs had are amply documented in chronicles of the sixteenth century and subsequent histories of Mexico and the conquest.[15] The eight primary omens that Moctezuma is believed to have received before Cortés landed on the eastern coast of his kingdom include a fire in the temple of Huitzilopochtli, a rain of sparks over Tenochtitlán, and a bird with a mirror in its head that reflected the heavens and the stars (Solares 1994, 52–53). In the novel, these "known" portents are supplemented by the horrifying dreams and visions that Nen has experienced since childhood.

Felipe, in contrast, is a practical sixteenth-century Spaniard who has come to the New World for adventure and wealth. The grandson of an impoverished *Hidalgo Señor* (Solares 1994, 50), Felipe enlists as a soldier when he fails to live up to the expectation that he make something of his life by serving in the clergy (20). He imagines the pure adventure of America:

> What terrestrial emotion could compare to crossing the great sea, planting their swords in the ardent banks of the new world, burning diabolical temples, demolishing idols, subduing idolaters, and spreading the word of Christ, something that had to be lived.
>
> [Qué emoción terrestre podía compararse con la de cruzar el gran mar, plantar sus espadas en las ardientes riberas del nuevo mundo, quemar templos diabólicos, derrumbar ídolos, sojuzgar a los idólatras, difundir la palabra de Cristo, algo que había que vivir.] (21)

And he admits his own personal agenda: "One of the attractions of the voyage—in no way the principal one, of course—was the possibility of returning to Spain with some money and dedicating myself to raising horses" ["Uno de los atractivos del viaje—de ninguna manera el principal, por supuesto—era la posibilidad de regresar a España con un poco de dinero y dedicarse a la cría de caballos"] (29). This dream, of course, would be possible only with the booty of conquest: gold (29). In addition, he is, in many ways, what one expects from a conquistador. He delights in situations that constitute metaphorical microcosms of the conquest: seeing animals suffer (33, 43), breaking horses to the bit (29–31), and possessing women—be they whores (26), married señoras of Seville (60), or indigenous women of New World (60, 111).

Thus, Nen and Felipe, who embody seemingly polar opposites, are stereotypical colonial subjects. She is an ethereal being trapped between the reality that she lives and the future that she feels, dreams, and knows will overtake her. He is a rational being in charge of his actions, poised to dominate all that crosses his path. Yet, upon closer examination, these opposites are not entirely what they seem. The protagonists share important characteristics that subvert their differences.[16] Although Nen and Felipe share similarities, their unresolved differences continue the indeterminacy inherent both in their unfixed borders and within the larger Mexican identity.

Because the culmination of the novel is the foreseen rape/intercourse between Nen and Felipe, it is important to note that the two characters not only experience sexual pleasure and terror in ways that deviate from societal and religious norms but also share extrasensory qualities that are linked to these pleasures. First, Nen is initiated into the realm of sexual experience through incestuous acts with her older brother, a taboo, as Nen's remarks reveal: "They were not supposed to do it, how could it be. You are my brother. That is called *netlapololtilztil*, and if their father were to find out, he would kill them" ["No debían hacerlo, cómo podía ser. Eres mi hermano. Eso se llama netlapololtilztli y si su padre se enteraba era capaz de matarlos"]. (Solares 1994, 38) Through these experiences, Nen learns that she is able to levitate from excitement or stimulation. She is able to achieve levitation in many ways—at a ritualistic dance (16), during orgasm (39), or while retelling a particularly exciting dream to the palace officials who use her as a seer (37). Once, while masturbating, she conjures up the faces of the men and beasts of her dreams until these fantastic images that she recalls for self-arousal include the terrifying and furious eyes of the conquerors' horses (as yet unknown to the Aztec empire). To a certain extent, her ability to sense the future plays into the heightening of her sexual pleasure and self-satisfaction.

Felipe not only acts on his heterosexual urges but also (while staying in a convent for a few days) discovers his propensity for deriving pleasure from self-flagellation. He begins by whipping himself on the backside with his own belt, from which he experiences "sweet satisfaction. . . . He felt euphoric, inside an intoxication that lead into a terrifying insomnia" ["dulce satisfacción. . . . Se sentía eufórico, dentro de una embriaguez que declinó en un absoluto y aterrador insomnio"] (Solares 1994, 45). This insomnia, however, produces the terrifying dream "that his injured buttocks were possessed by the tail—pointy and blazing—of an infuriated demon" ["que sus nalgas lastimadas eran poseídas por la cola—puntiaguda y ardiente—de un enfurecido demonio"] (46). Like Nen, he is terrified of this product of homo- and autoeroticism, and like her trans-real dreams of the images of the conquest to come, Felipe's flagellation is part of a greater attempt at mystical illumination. Participating in this self-mutilation in the hope of achieving some sort of religious revelation or transcendence (46–47), he is able to achieve supernatural perception in the convent and in his cell: "When the priest raised the host, Felipe seemed to feel an invisible presence" ["Cuando el sacerdote levantó la hostia, a Felipe le pareció adivinar una presencia invisible"] (44). Deviance for both Nen and Felipe is pleasurable and a bit mystical, while the important motif of supernatural eyes that are watching simultaneously arouses and inhibits them.

Throughout the narrative, therefore, Solares simultaneously upholds and unravels the traditionally held notions of Spanish and indigenous characters. Nen and Felipe, repectively, demonstrate such typical stereotyped traits as indigenous clairvoyance and vicious Spanish cruelty. Still, the protagonists overlap on issues of a sexual and spiritual nature. It is also important to note that Solares idealizes neither of the two societies portrayed. As noted in Chapter 1, the vilification of the Hispanic roots of Mexican society has often lead to the perception that all corruption and exploitation results from colonization and that the indigenous past is a paradise lost. Eduardo Matos Moctezuma comments, "That idyllic image of the pre-Hispanic world in which everything was, let's say, without a major problem is false" ["Esa imagen idílica del mundo prehispánico en que todo era, digamos, sin mayor problema es falsa"] (1996). Carlos Fuentes agrees: "The Aztec world was not at all a paradise; it was a repugnant autocracy in many ways. That a culture, a civilization, was interrupted is also true. But there are many things not worth celebrating" ["El mundo azteca no era un paraíso para nada; era una autocracia bastante repugnante en muchos aspectos. Que se interrumpió una cultura, una civilización también eso es cierto. Pero hay muchas cosas que no son dignas de celebrar"] (1996). Solares demonstrates that cruelty and barbarous ritual existed in both societies.

The Spaniards have long been known for the mass murder of indigenous people throughout the conquest and colonization of the New World, but Solares shows that the same inhumanity existed among the Aztecs. Many of Nen's childhood memories recall the human sacrifices she witnessed. The victims, almost always slaves, are treated as lesser beings. Nen is traumatized by the belief that the victims are alive not only as their hearts are being torn out on the sacrificial altar but even as their bodies are thrown down the temple stairs (1994, 25–26). She is also deeply disturbed by the ritualistic sacrifice of children, whose wails are said to please the gods. The children's fingernails are often torn out as they are sacrificed, in order to increase their cries (61–62). By demonstrating such similarities, Solares seeks to lessen the perceived conflicts between the two societies and facilitate their reinsertion into the Mexican national conscience.

Solares's project is particularly pertinent in Mexican society, where many believe that the negation of the country's cultural inheritance has gone on far too long. In 1950, noting that many Mexicans deny that *mexicanidad* is in any way connected to its Spanish or indigenous roots, Paz wrote, "The Mexican wants to be neither Indian nor Spaniard. Nor does he want to be descended from them. He denies them. . . . The Mexican and *la mexicanidad* are defined as rupture and denial" ["El mexicano no quiere ser ni indio ni español. Tampoco quiere descender de ellos. Los niega. . . . El mexicano y la mexicanidad se definen como ruptura y negación"] (1993, 96–97).[17] Paz's words echo those of the Muñoz character who is "¡puro mexicano!" Discomfort with these cultural roots is still pervasive, as is demonstrated by the anecdote about the statue of a conquistador, an indigenous woman, and their mestizo child in Coyoacán in Chapter 1. Here the extent to which the origins and inception of Mexican *mestizaje* have been traumatized becomes evident yet again.

Solares does not deny the traumatic inception of *mestizaje;* in fact, he acknowledges Mexicans as "hijos de una tragedia." Nevertheless, his text works against the tragedy as it simultaneously narrates it in all its cruelty and inhumanity—much the same way that his character development sets up and tears down traditional stereotypes of the conqueror/victim as it ostensibly seeks to assuage the conflict inherent in that paradigm.

Detraumatizing Mestizo Roots

As we have seen, Solares infuses the historical record of the sixteenth century with fictional characters, identity issues, and revised stereotypes. His central narrative project is to detraumatize mestizo origins despite the violent historical context in which they occurred. His narrative achievement of this goal is accomplished through a realistic retelling of the horror of conquest within which he develops a romance of destiny for Nen and Felipe. To this day, the conquest is a highly charged, contested, and painful issue in Mexico. In the words of Martínez, it is "a wound that remains vivid today" ["una llaga que aún permanece viva en México"] (1992, 10), and according to Solares, it is "something that could not have healed" ["algo que no pudo haberse cicatrizado"] (1996). Through graphic description and rapid-fire narrative, Solares's apt account of the shock and torment of this tragedy brings to life such realities as the Aztec sacrifice of children and slaves (1994, 61, 25) and the bloody massacre in the Templo Mayor (109). He has researched the past in order to "recreate, revive, not only cultural concerns but ways, customs, and habits that constitute a society" ["recrear, revivificar no sólo referentes culturales, sino formas, usos y costumbres que constituyen una sociedad"] (Pohlenz 1994, 5).

Yet Solares is also very forthcoming about both the source and the dilemma of his revision of the conquest:

> It is merely the fact that I would like Mexico to have been founded in an act of love. . . . Of course, had it been amorous, it would be a different country. It would have been something else; it would not have been a conquest. And certainly . . . the Other would have been part of us. So we Mexicans would be very different.

> [Es simplemente el hecho de que a mí me gustaría que México se hubiera fundado en un acto de amor. . . . Claro, la manera en que hubiera sido amoroso, hubiera sido otro país. Sería otra; no hubiera sido una conquista. Y efectivamente . . . el Otro hubiera sido parte nuestra. Entonces seríamos muy diferentes los mexicanos.] (1996)

This is the primary authorial goal of the novel: to resolve the conflictive character of the Cortés-Malinche paradigm through romanticization, thus transforming

Mexico's foundation into a love story. The analysis of *Nen, la inútil* herein gauges the text's adherence to and divergence from Solares's admitted objectives, although it is mindful that, as Umberto Eco puts it, "the response of the author must not be used in order to validate the interpretation of his text, but to show the discrepancies between the author's intention and the intention of the text" (1992, 73). Solares himself comments, "What interests me most about writing is the activity that goes from the unconscious to the paper without ever having to pass through consciousness" ["lo que más me interesa de la escritura es la actividad que va del inconsciente al papel sin pasar por el consciente"] (quoted in González 1995, 113). His insistence on the role of the subconscious in the act of creation or writing explains and lends credence to the phenomenon that Eco describes as a text's ultimate transcendence of authorial intent. As we will see, the narrative does, in fact, work toward the creation of an alternative history and the other Mexico that Solares so desires. Unfortunately, however, his characters and his novel's ending—a dramatically rewritten passage of the rape, in which both Nen and Felipe reach the afterlife—serve to foil his narrative project instead of successfully culminating it.

The novel continually clues readers that the traditionally violent tale of encounter has been rewritten within the romantic framework of a love story, as this discussion between Felipe and another Spanish conquistador demonstrates:

—Surprising the first Spaniard who lovingly dreamt about a Mexican Indian woman. Surprising the first Spaniard who found himself tied to a Mexican Indian woman forever, for all of eternity—said Felipe.
—No less surprising; or better yet, much more surprising, the first Mexican Indian woman who lovingly dreamt about a Spaniard. The first Mexican Indian woman who found herself tied to a Spaniard forever . . . —answered his partner.

[—Sorprendente el primer hombre español que soñó amorosamente con una india mexicana. Sorprendente el primer hombre español que se supo ligado a una india mexicana para siempre, por toda la eternidad—dijo Felipe.
—No menos sorprendente; o mejor dicho, mucho más sorprendente, la primera india mexicana que soñó amorosamente con un hombre español. La primera india mexicana que se supo ligada a un hombre español para siempre, por toda la eternidad . . . —contestó su compañero.] (Solares 1994, 12)

The text works to transform the tragic historical plot into the tale of imagined desire and love that the author wants to create. A number of narrative machinations—including the author's personal philosophy on fiction writing—aid Solares in his attempt to transform the past.

Although Solares bases the novel on the first Spaniard and indigenous woman to dream of each other lovingly and to be united forever, he does not, surprisingly, use Guerrero (the shipwrecked Spaniard who married into Mayan royalty on the Yucatan) to represent the amorous dreaming and eternal linkage of the indigenous and Spanish that is so central to this novel. The improbable nature of the revision he undertakes bespeaks the need for fictitious characters. Solares responds to the question of this apparent oversight as follows: "I didn't want to . . . take a historical character for this fable I was trying to write. It had to be an absolutely fictitious character." ["Yo no quería . . . tomar a un personaje ya histórico para esta fábula que quise hacer. Tenía que ser un personaje absolutamente ficticio"] (1996).[18]

Nonetheless, it is important to note once again that the second part of the novel begins on the Yucatan peninsula, where Cortés sent for Aguilar and Guerrero, the two shipwrecked Spaniards, to serve as interpreters. By beginning the second part of the novel with a reference to Guerrero (who is an important emblem of "successful" and productive adaptation and mixture), Solares sets the events that follow—the tragedy of the conquest and the rape of Nen by Felipe—within the framework of the futile desire for a metaphor that cannot work. In this way, his conscious choice of characters works against his intentions in the narrative. Although what happened in Tenochtitlán will never resemble Guerrero's life in the Yucatan, the text unwittingly contrasts the two in its attempt to rewrite the conquest as a mere encounter and to detraumatize the inception of *mestizaje*. Whereas Guerrero entered the Mayan world humbly, as a shipwreck survivor made a slave, the narrative fragments of *Nen, la inútil* tell of the conquistadors' brazen invasion of Tenochtitlán on many levels. While Guerrero adapts and integrates totally into the Mayan world, the Spaniards in Tenochtitlán have only one response to anything new: Destroy it. After slowly earning the trust of the Mayan people, Guerrero is given the prestigious title of warrior and the hand of a Mayan princess in marriage; meanwhile, the conquistadors simply seize everything they see and desire.

Guerrero's is, possibly, the only documented romantic tale of *mestizaje* to occur within the years of encounter and conquest in Mexico. Interestingly, moreover, it is the Western Guerrero who is absorbed into indigenous culture. Consequently, the story's shift of focus is one of the primary reasons that Solares's narrative fails to achieve true detraumatization of mestizo origins. Because Solares deals with Guerrrero's story only implicitly, the reader is left to contend explicitly with the Cortés-Malinche paradigm and the insurmountable obstacle of turning violent conquest into romantic love. As the Mexican literary critic Christopher Domínguez Michael writes, the novel "sticks to the most *mexicanista* of subjects: Cortés and Malinche, in this instance transfigured into an Indian girl who divines—Nen—and a Castilian soldier—Felipe—who fatally rapes her and wins her heart" ["se atiene al más *mexicanista* de los temas: Cortés y la Malinche, esta vez tranfigurados en una niña india que adivina—Nen—y un soldado castellano—Felipe—que fatalmente la viola y la enamora"] (1995, 41). But Domínguez Michael disregards not only the novel's detraumatizing narrative project but also the resultant textual struggle, incorrectly positing that the text merely reproduces the Cortés-Malinche paradigm without attempting to resolve it. The final scenes of the novel demonstrate both Solares's revisionist intentions and the novel's textual failings.

As previously noted, early in the story, the male protagonist, Felipe, muses about the first Spaniards and indigenous women to dream of each other lovingly. The novel provides an alternative to the Cortés-Malinche paradigm by ending with an attempt to move from dream and desire to romantic union despite the horrific scenes of the massacre in the Templo Mayor and the rape of Nen that precede. In the end, Solares tries to create a detraumatized and loving alternative to the historical rapes of the past (most notably that of Malinche by Cortés). The final passage, therefore, deserves careful analysis. Here, in the netherworld, or the *más allá,* Nen awaits Felipe, and upon meeting, Felipe tells us, the two caress each other and sensually consummate their passion. Their desire for each other is a combination of passion, violence, and death.[19] Their first encounter was marred by the unfettered violence of the conquest, which led to the death of Nen. Yet in the "second plane," when the two climax, it is meant to be sheer Eros, in contrast with the Thanatos of the earlier scene. The two no longer mutter incomprehensible words at each other; they create "a new language, just for us" ["un nuevo lenguaje sólo nuestro"] (1994, 131) just before the syncretic and sacred moment where Felipe says, "We fit together in the same groan, in the same ceremony of crosses and virgins and open chests atop a pyramid, in the liberation of the indestructible combined force that was gush and tear and sob and the sensation of elevating together, I swear, elevating together" ["Nos conjugábamos en el mismo quejido, en la misma ceremonia de cruces y vírgenes y pechos abiertos en lo alto de una pirámide, en la liberación de esa fuerza conjunta indestructible que era chorro y lágrima y sollozo y la sensación de elevarnos juntos, te juro, de elevarnos juntos"] (131). It is with these words that the novel comes to a close.

Nen and Felipe's celestial consummation mixes signifiers of the sacred and profane in both cultures. Sacrifice of their selves and liberation through combination result in total catharsis as the two achieve the union of *mestizaje* and levitate as one. This romanticization is, according to Solares, performed in order to create an ideal world and fulfill his wish that Mexico had been founded in an act of love.

In the utopian narration of Nen and Felipe's lovemaking, Solares equalizes the field between the two characters by excising conflict and, in the process, reflects the tenets of mestizophile thought, which presents *mestizaje* as unifying, harmonizing, even homogenizing. Since Solares's main concern is the inception or foundation of mestizo Mexico, it is important to return to his quotation: Founded in love, Mexico "would have been another country. . . . Then we Mexicans would be very different" ["hubiera sido otro país. . . . Entonces seríamos muy diferentes los mexicanos"] (1996). These "different" Mexicans would not continue to feel, or reproduce, the tragedy of the past or the contradictions of identity that Solares experiences so profoundly. Like Andrés Molina Enríquez—Mexico's greatest champion of *mestizaje*—they might witness the homogenization and ordering of society instead (Basave Benítez 1993, 13–15).

In her book *Foundational Fictions,* Doris Sommer points out that many nineteenth-century narratives that propose such heterosexual passion and eroticism as we find in the pages of *Nen, la inútil* function as allegories of hegemonic states (1993, 31)—which is, and has been, very much the case in Mexico. Mexico's mestizophile intellectuals, as shown in *México mestizo* by Agustín Basave Benítez, have provided the state with two centuries of discourse that have influenced education, agrarian policies, and many other aspects of life in Mexico. In this way, promotion of the mestizo state eclipses what may be called the indigenous state—or any other state for that matter—that may also exist within the nation. Mestizophiles believe not only that *mestizaje* is desirable but also that it makes Mexico unique through "uniqueness in mixture" ["la unicidad en la mezcla"] (Basave Benítez 1993, 141). Solares subscribes to this philosophy when he longs for the harmonic legacy of a love story rather than the conflictive heritage of the conquest. By revising the past, he seeks to rewrite identity and rethink the Mexican nation, for he believes that this romantic and passionate revision of the rape could have ramifications for Mexican national identity. In this way, Solares's text mirrors the harmonizing projects and nation-building desires of many of the nineteenth-century texts that Sommer analyzes. Moreover, Solares himself contends that, through fiction writing, imagined characters and events can take on a life of their own and in some circumstances can be perceived as more real than history itself. This, then, contributes to the realization of the possible nation that the narrative proposes in its pages.[20]

Nevertheless, in a most interesting and significant indication of how Solares's text transcends his intentions, his desire to imagine a different past and therefore to enshrine a different present remains unfulfilled in the text. First, we see that the last narrative fragment ends in the unmistakable voice of Felipe, an indication not that the two narrative perspectives have joined and become one but instead that Nen is now silenced, subsumed, and (as we will see) *chingada* once again. Next, it is important to consider the ramifications of the state of this narrative fragment as fictitious, imagined, and (to a certain extent) impossible rather than as integrated into the historical events of the novel. As previously noted, romantic narratives can be read as prescribing an ideal future for the nation. Normally, this is represented textually in the fruition of a union between characters. If they are fruitful and multiply, it denotes a fulfilled desire: the population of the country through the mixing of peoples. When Nen and Felipe unite in the *más allá* as an embodiment of Eros or the preservation of life, it must be noted that, because the union is imagined and they are dead, it is not productive; it fails. It is not the amorous new origin of the Mexican mestizo that Solares so ardently desires, because by failing to produce that mestizo, it unwittingly suggests to readers the falsehood of the mestizophile dream of harmony and homogeneity based in love.

Despite Solares's scrutiny of the origins of the mestizo, he is not able to inscribe the new mestizo in *Nen, la inútil*, and this textual failing is emblematic of the unfulfilled authorial intention. In view of Solares's aversion to traumatic origins, for example, it is logical for the two Spanish soldiers in the novel to express their fear of engendering offspring through conquest and rape: "What I don't want is to imagine the children of this nightmare or tragedy. That's why I sometimes try not to ejaculate inside the Indian women I possess. I mean, it's a minimal precaution" ["Lo que no quiero es imaginar a los hijos de esta pesadilla o tragedia. Yo por eso a veces trato de no eyacular dentro de las indias que poseyo. Digo, es una mínima precaución"] (1994, 119). If, however, in Solares's mind the desired originary moment of *mestizaje* should be one of willing abandonment (textually represented by Nen and Felipe's lovemaking in the *más allá*), then it makes little sense that in their moment of consummation Felipe says that he feels Nen's "will to be raped" ["voluntad de ser violada"] (131). Here the absurd notion that willingness cancels out the cruelty and conflict of a rape betrays the inability to successfully romanticize this origin.[21] Solares's choice of characters who reproduce the Cortés-Malinche paradigm, and here his choice of words, defeat the very textual goal for which he employs them: the detraumatization of mestizo origins.[22]

Although Solares succeeds in forcing readers to rethink the original drama of *mestizaje*, his text and its revisionist project are ultimately unable to break out of the Cortés-Malinche paradigm of mestizos as the *hijos de la chingada*, products of rape, seduction, treason, and tragedy. Nen is not the vindication of Malinche because "he who fucks never does it with the consent of the fucked" ["él que chinga jamás lo hace con el consentimiento de la chingada"] (Paz 1993, 85). The field cannot be leveled when it comes to the conquest, and as Domínguez Michael points out, "the vision of the conquered and that of the conqueror never meet in the novel" ["la visión de los vencidos y la del vencedor no se encuentran jamás en la novela"] (1995, 41). The insurmountable pain surrounding the tragedies of the conquest and mestizo origins has been tested and proven by Solares's narrative yet again. As much as it is rewritten, the "otredad no resuelta" that Solares so strongly identifies with *lo mexicano* is not harmonized in the text. This rewriting of the past may fulfill Solares's own desires, but it does not change modern Mexico's perception of itself, because it cannot assuage the conflicts of modern identity. This is especially the case for an assimilationist mestizo identity in which one component, the Other (the Western), subsumes another (the indigenous).

Significantly, however, just as Solares and other Mexican authors were rewriting the conquest as a means of confronting the crisis in nationalism of the 1980s and 1990s, the important shifts in the state's definitions of national culture mentioned in Chapter 1 began to reconfigure both official and popular notions of Mexican national identity. Despite the shortcomings of Carlos Salinas de Gortari's neoliberal economic policies in terms of generating wealth and development among the indigenous citizenry, his new official admission of a pluricultural nation based in indigenous origins was an attempt at recognizing Mexico's multiethnic population. The constitutional revision went a long way toward shattering the old, dualistic Janus-faced image of the Mexican mestizo, wherein the indigenous and the Spanish are seen as opposing, even conflicting, halves of a homogeneous whole. The constitutional amendment, then, allowed Mexico to accept, even embrace, the ethnically diverse reality for which the Zapatista uprising in January 1994 demanded both national and international recognition.

At the end of the millennium, as Mexico witnessed the crumbling of its political and economic pillars, many Mexican authors used the backdrop of the sixteenth century to pose poignant questions about the country's traditionally mestizophile national identity vis-à-vis Mexican social reality. Solares, for one, uses the motif of encounter to embark on a revisionist rewriting of the most painful and traumatic moments in the conquest of Mexico. The narrative fragmentation and dual perspectives highlight the textual importance of meetings and encounters, as Solares attempts to detraumatize Mexican mestizo origins. In addition, he simultaneously articulates and deconstructs the duality that Nen and Felipe constitute, setting them up as opposites only to undermine their differences in an attempt to draw them closer together on the continuum of human character. This strategy, in effect, lessens the narrative leap from tragedy to romance at the end of the novel, by means of which the author attempts to fulfill personal desires for national unity and equality through his narrative. However far from the mark the events of the final pages of the novel ultimately fall, their retelling is provocative, stirring thought about the deepest issues of identity in modern Mexico.

The textual failings of *Nen, la inútil* also demonstrate how very outdated and untenable mestizophile national identity was for Mexico at the end of the twentieth century. Despite Solares's attempt to resolve combative mestizo dualism and find the roots of national unity in mestizo origins, the search yields only violence and trauma. What Mexico needed to regain its sense of national unity was an inclusive ideology—an ideology such as multiculturalism or, at the very least, an ideology that recognized Mexico's pluriculture—not a figure such as the mestizo, whose search for historical roots brings realizations of rape and murder. By recognizing the nation's "pluricultural composition, sustained originally in its indigenous population," (*Political Constitution* 1994, 4) the Mexican constitution values diversity as the nation's origin, thus eliminating the need to harmonize or homogenize the nation's ethnic components. The concept of conflict may, indeed, manifest itself within this new pluralistic national identity at some point, but it is no longer intrinsic in the figure upon whom the weight of national identity and unity had been placed for the better part of the twentieth century: the dualistic mestizo.

Syncretism and the Spiritual Conquest of Mexico
before La Virgen de Guadalupe

If, in the twentieth century, the historical origins of racial *mestizaje* in Mexico were terribly traumatized, as we have seen, the reverse can be said about the origins of syncretic[23] religious beliefs during the corresponding historical period in New Spain, or what is today Mexico. In fact, the first decade or so of Christian evangelization (1519–1531) is largely downplayed, if not entirely overlooked, in Mexican national culture, with the Guadalupan events of 1531 taking a prominent role in modern Mexican national identity instead. The two conquests, sources of racial and spiritual mixture in Mexico, are of equal importance in the study of modern Mexican national identity. As Bartra has written, "The events of Tabasco in 1519 and of Tepeyac in 1531 were transformed, over the centuries, into two powerful symbolic cornerstones that ... have ended up being seen as the fertile seeds of Mexican nationality, sown in the founding womb of the motherland" ["Los sucesos de Tabasco de 1519 y de Tepeyac en 1531 se transformaron, con el correr de los siglos, en dos poderosos ejes simbólicos que ... han acabado por ser vistos como las semillas fecundas de la nacionalidad mexicana, depositadas en el vientre fundacional de la patria"] (1987, 174).

In 1531, it is believed, a dark-skinned Virgin Mary appeared to a humble indigenous man, Juan Diego, atop a hill at Tepeyac in Mexico. Speaking in Nahuatl, she asked him to tell the Mexican bishop, Juan de Zumárraga, to build a temple to her on that site (where, incidentally, there existed at that time a temple to Tonantzin, the Aztec mother goddess). The bishop paid Juan Diego no mind until he returned with a sign from the Virgin: At the Virgin's request, Juan Diego had gathered in his cloak a bunch of wildflowers that were growing, inexplicably, out of season. When Juan Diego dropped the flowers at the bishop's feet, the image of the Virgin was indelibly emblazoned on Juan Diego's garment. This cloak, known as the *lienzo de la Virgen de Guadalupe*, has been the cornerstone of the legend of the apparition and of the cult of the Virgin of Guadalupe. The garment is currently housed in the basilica built outside Mexico City as a shrine to the Virgin (Fig. 2.1).

It is commonly believed that the Virgin's appearance to Juan Diego at Tepeyac was followed by large-scale, rapid conversions of indigenous people. In popular legend and in Catholic teachings, the appearance of the Virgin of Guadalupe and her consequent widespread acceptance among Creoles, mestizos, and indigenous people alike raise none of the problematic issues of invasive evangelism that are associated with biological *mestizaje*. Rather, the Virgin of Guadalupe is one of the most recognizable, omnipresent, and enduringly positive symbols of Mexican national identity. She is credited with reconciling two opposing worlds (H. Johnson 1980, 192), defending the oppressed, winning the Mexican nation its independence, serving as mother to all Mexicans (Bartra 1996, 171), and representing

Figure 2.1. This image of the Virgen de Guadalupe, or the dark-skinned Virgin, was emblazoned on the cloak of the Aztec native Juan Diego in 1531, when the Virgin is said to have appeared to him. The Virgen de Guadalupe and her apparition play a vital role in Mexican national identity. Photo courtesy of George and Audrey DeLange.

the sociopolitical uniqueness of the entire Mexican population (Preston 1982, 5). She is, in the words of Eric Wolf, "a Mexican national symbol" (1958, 34). It is important to note that she is also a repository for and a reminder of the indigenous component of Mexican identity. Because of her Aztec features, the Virgin of Guadalupe is "the supreme expression of Mexican cultural identity and the patron saint of the continent" (K. Thomas 2000, F4).

Yet despite the current focus on Guadalupan events in the examination of the spread of Christianity throughout the Americas, early evangelization and conversion to Christianity in the New World were often as violent as the military campaigns of conquest. Upon Cortés's arrival on the coast of Mexico in 1519 and throughout his submission of the Aztec empire, he destroyed numerous religious temples and "idols" on the grounds that they were blasphemous. As Serge Gruzinski argues in *Images at War*, the process of annihilating Aztec religious "idols" and replacing them with Christian icons not only delivered this message despite a critical language barrier but also demonstrated to the Aztecs the superiority of the Spaniards, their weapons, and their Christian gods (2001, 47).

In 1524, when the first group of Franciscan friars, known as *Los doce apóstoles*, or the twelve apostles, arrived in Mexico to proselytize, their methods included (over and above teaching and preaching) the suppression of idolatry and the general use of force and authority (Braden 1930, 143). Because of linguistic barriers, the friars most often had to communicate by using signs (143). Although officially the indigenous population was not required to convert to Christianity, over the years, most clergy used whipping as a means of forcing the indigenous people to convert (169). Scenes of violent conversions and abjurations were commonly described in sixteenth-century texts.

In addition to what we know about these methods (and in contrast to the popular belief in rapid, widespread conversion), many modern scholars have written about the ways the indigenous population received the messages, icons, and god of Christianity. Three major currents of thought exist, each one speaking to a different level of acceptance and resistance among the Aztecs as they were confronted by Spanish Christianity. First, scholars who depict the evangelization of the Americas as having taken place within the cataclysmic or replacement mode believe that, when Christian missionaries violently laid waste to indigenous religions and replaced their "idols" with the Holy Trinity, the indigenous people simply adopted the new deities and practices in order to fill their spiritual void. Yet this cataclysmic or replacement interpretation suggests two quite different reasons for indigenous acceptance of Christianity: Either the indigenous people were so victimized that they had no choice but to accept or they converted instantly and seamlessly adapted to monotheism after they were surreptitiously convinced of the truth of Christian ways and beliefs.

The other currents of thought about conversion depict indigenous groups as much more resistant to Christian evangelization, deities, and teaching. The idols-behind-altars theory proposes that the indigenous people maintained their gods, their religious beliefs, and their practices by continuing their worship behind a thin veil of Christian practice. In fact, the sixteenth-century Spanish friar and expert on Aztec language and culture Fray Bernardino de Sahagún feared that early indigenous worshippers at the shrine to the Virgin of Guadalupe were, in fact, leaving offerings that paid tribute to Tonantzin (Burkhart 1993, 205). Similarly, in the theory of syncretism, elements of one religious system are fused with those of another to create hybrid gods, practices, and beliefs. Mother goddesses such as the Spanish Virgin Mary and the Aztec Tonantzin were worshipped as one, and similar practices (celebrations of fertility or harvest) survive the ages because they encompass the belief systems of both cultures. In her article "The Cult of the Virgin of Guadalupe in Mexico," Louise M. Burkhart explains, "From these dual roots [Nahua (Aztec) and Spanish Catholic religious traditions] was formed a new cult figure, whose existence both validated and personified the mixture of people and cultures that gave rise to the Mexican nation" (198). These three versions of the indigenous reception of the messages of Christianity affect modern Mexican national identity by altering the way that Mexicans view their past. They suggest scenarios that run the gamut from victimization to active resistance and even thoughtful cultural integration.

The syncretic model of religious assimilation serves as a perfect complement to cultural *mestizaje,* especially in terms of the aforementioned perceptions of racial *mestizaje* as harmonizing and homogenizing. Yet despite the vast imagery depicting amalgamated deities such as Virgin Mary/Tonantzin, the spiritual conquest, as we have seen, was no less violent than the military conquest. As a result, the allegedly serene meshing of Aztec and indigenous gods in Mexico's uniquely syncretic form of Catholicism is no less conflicted than the "hijos de una tragedia" depicted in Solares's novel.

La otra conquista: The Traumatic Road from Loss to Acceptance and Appropriation

The 1998 film *La otra conquista,*[24] directed by Salvador Carrasco,[25] depicts the Christian conversion of an Aztec man, Topiltzin, during the years between 1520 and 1531. Although the film demonstrates how all three of the theories of indigenous religious conversion discussed previously come into play in the originary moments of Mexican spiritual identity, it ultimately deconstructs the notion of syncretism as an accordant process. Although this issue is treated in more depth ahead, it is worth noting here that first the Spaniards destroy and outlaw Topiltzin's gods. Then, after Topiltzin continues to try to worship Tonantzin secretly, he finds that, for his own salvation, he must syncretically fuse Tonantzin and the Virgin Mary.

By tracing Mexican Christianity back to its roots in the years before Juan Diego's symbolic acts of devotion to the Virgin of Guadalupe, Carrasco demonstrates the violent subtext behind religious conversion that continues to vex modern Mexican national identity five centuries later. As Carrasco comments, when the Spaniards arrived, "the face of the American continent changed forever. . . . Many of the things that happened back then are still unresolved five centuries later. We are still seeking our identity" (quoted in Muñoz 2000, F4). Elsewhere Carrasco elaborates: "The truth is: The conquest is not over. And it's not perfectly clear who is doing the conquering" (Carrasco 2002, 167). Therefore, Carrasco contends that the unresolved nature of Mexican identity—which is akin to the combative duality of Solares's "otredad no resuelta"—results from the violent events of the sixteenth century, indigenous cultural resistance to Christianity, and an incomplete conquest of the indigenous peoples' souls. Even in his weakest moments, for example, To-piltzin yells to the Virgin, "Holy Mother, in your hands I deposit my body but never my spirit!!" ["¡¡Santa Madre, en tus manos deposito mi cuerpo, mas nunca el espíritu!!"] (Carrasco 1998). Although the film focuses on this *other* conquest—the spiritual conquest of Mexico—it also constitutes a journey to the religious roots of modern Mexican identity. In an attempt to better understand a national identity that Carrasco, like Solares, finds unresolved, he highlights the violent origins of Mexico's most cherished cultural and religious icon, the Virgin of Guadalupe, and accordingly the film echoes many of the themes found in *Nen, la inútil*. Carrasco returns to the inception of Mexico's religious beliefs to examine the unresolved nature of modern Mexican national identity—this time in terms of Mexico's syncretic religion, a paramount and key component of Mexico's mestizo culture.

Yet, unlike *Nen, la inútil*, *La otra conquista* returns to the conquest not to romanticize history but to visually represent the past in all its tragic splendor. Instead of romanticizing a traumatized origin, Carrasco's film traumatizes an idealized beginning. By doing so, the film works against the now untenable notions of *mestizaje* and syncretism as harmonious blends of different races and belief systems. As Carrasco notes, "I think we sometimes fall into the trap of exalting *mestizaje* and syncretism as if they were themselves values, as if they were more or less peaceful cultural processes, carried out within a framework of symmetrical power—as if Mexican identity fused two cultures of equal condition. . . . We wish to highlight . . . the violence implicit in such processes" ["Creo que, incluso, a veces hemos caído en la trampa de exaltar el mestizaje y el sincretismo como si fuesen valores en sí, como si fuesen procesos culturales más o menos pacíficos, llevados a cabo dentro de un marco de simetría de poderes—como si en la identidad mexicana se fundiesen armoniosamente dos culturas en igualdad de condiciones. . . . Deseamos subrayar . . . la violencia implícita en dichos procesos"] (quoted in Velazco 1999, 4).[26] Here Carrasco implies that the concept of transculturation better encompasses and explains modern Mexican identity and the foundational events that were taking place on Mexican soil in the sixteenth century.

Carrasco, then, bases *La otra conquista* on theories of transculturation more so than on those of *mestizaje. Transculturation*, as defined by Fernando Ortiz in his 1940 *Contrapunteo cubano del tabaco y el azúcar* (*Cuban Counterpoint: Tobacco and Sugar*), is an attempt to describe "the complex and multidirectional processes in cultural transformation" (quoted in Mignolo 2000, 167) that are integral to Cuban—and indeed all Latin American—history. Transculturation, then, combines the notion of acculturation (acquiring another culture) with violent deculturation (the loss or uprooting of a previous culture) and neoculturation (the consequent creation of new cultural phenomena) (Ortiz 1947, 102–103). Most important to Carrasco and *La otra conquista* is the notion of multidirectionality and the contention that every group, from the elite down to the most devastated of slaves, is "always exerting an influence and being influenced" (98). Although firmly based in the tragedy of conquest, transcultural processes demonstrate cultural resilience and adaptation among all sectors of a society. They also underscore the inherent imbalance of power in such processes.[27]

Carrasco's interest in and understanding of transculturation, therefore, allows *La otra conquista* to delve into myriad thorny issues that surround Mexico's current spiritual identity and to represent them from innovative perspectives. First, the film takes on the myth of harmony that surrounds Mexican cultural *mestizaje*, especially in terms of the origins of the syncretic cult of the Virgin of Guadalupe. Apparitions and spontaneous conversions are replaced with violent culture clashes,

Figure 2.2. Topiltzin, the protagonist in Salvador Carrasco's 1998 film *La otra conquista* (*The Other Conquest*) is first seen climbing the ruins of the Templo Mayor [Aztec Great Temple]. He has just survived the Spaniards' 1520 massacre of hundreds of Aztec men, women, and children. Courtesy of the photographer, Andrea Sanderson.

forced abjurations, and profound loss. Next, *La otra conquista* also posits evangelism and conversion as multidirectional pursuits wherein resultant syncretic beliefs affected the ways that both indigenous peoples and Europeans worshipped.

Although the film consciously treats the decade leading up to, but not including, the Guadalupan events, the Mexicans' devotion to her plays an important role as the subtext of the film. Because the Virgin of Guadalupe has been so closely associated with Aztec goddesses, especially Tonantzin, and because her cult in Mexico has been deemed "the prototypical example of religious syncretism" (Burkhart 1993, 198), she is a culturally mestizo figure, a new being sprung from two identifiable roots. Carrasco intends to interrogate and ultimately comment on the process by which the Virgin's profound hybridity was born. Just as the story of Guerrero sets up contrasting tales of *mestizaje* in *Nen, la inútil*, the Virgin of Guadalupe serves Carrasco's audience as a foil for Topiltzin's experience: surreptitious conversion versus total loss, free and unfettered devotion versus forced abjuration, harmonic syncretism versus painful mixed signs. In this way, Carrasco, refocuses Mexicans' sense of their religious beginnings on the violent culture shock and resultant destruction wrought by the Spaniards as they penetrated the Aztec empire.

Topiltzin: Symbol of Mexico's Orphaned Identity

La otra conquista tells the tragic and compelling tale of Topiltzin, an Aztec scribe who witnesses the unspeakable destruction of his people at the hands of the Spaniards. Topiltzin, a lone survivor, is first seen as he climbs from the ruins of the Templo Mayor after the 1520 massacre (Fig. 2.2). In every sense, his world is in ruins as he calls for his mother goddess, Tonantzin, with no response. In the wake of this trauma, Topiltzin dedicates himself to documenting his culture's downfall in detailed pictographic codices. As the camera moves from his paintbrush to the scene he is drawing, the pages of the sixteenth-century Aubin Codex literally spring to life on the screen to depict the death and annihilation of his people (Fig. 2.3).

Topiltzin's initial reaction to the Spaniards' hostile presence and motives for collaboration is intense resistance. He defiantly opposes his own brother, a collaborator, who tells him, "I am still the same person, but I have two halves inside of me: One belongs to lost time; the other has to adapt to survive" ["Sigo siendo el mismo, pero llevo dos mitades dentro de mi: Una pertenece al tiempo perdido; la otra tiene que adaptarse para sobrevivir"]. Topiltzin simply replies, "I am made of one single piece" ["¡Yo estoy hecho de una sola pieza!"] (Carrasco 1998). Yet Topiltzin is later captured and forced to renounce his culture and his gods through the burning of his feet as he is forced to face a statue of the Virgin Mary. After this cruel punishment, Topiltzin escapes death because he is the half-brother of Tecuichpo, Cortés's favorite courtesan. Tecuichpo informs the conquistador that

Figure 2.3. Topiltzin records the history and destruction of his people in a pictographic codex. This scene reinforces both the cultural and personal levels of one of the central themes of the film: loss. Courtesy of the director, Salvador Carrasco.

Topiltzin is an illegitimate son of Moctezuma and therefore an heir to the empire. Topiltzin's life is spared, but he is forced to convert to Christianity under the tutelage of the Spanish clergyman Fray Diego de la Coruña[28] in the Monasterio de Nuestra Señora de la Luz. Topiltzin's resistance continues but is thwarted at every turn. At last, he makes love to Tecuichpo in a desperate attempt to ensure the survival of their lineage. Cortés learns of the transgression and strangles Tecuichpo, killing both mother and unborn child.[29] At this point, Topiltzin's loss is total, and he begins the ambiguous and complex process of accepting and appropriating the Spanish Virgin Mary through debilitating fevers and hallucinations. Throughout Topiltzin's trials, Fray Diego has prodded, encouraged, and punished him. When Topiltzin commits his final act of assimilation or appropriation and dies under a statue of the Virgin Mary as it falls into his arms, the friar, believing his work is done, declares the scene "a miracle that reflects how two different races can be one through tolerance and love" ["un milagro que refleja cómo dos razas tan diferentes pueden ser una sola a través de la tolerancia y el amor"] (Carrasco 1998). The movie ends with the camera panning up and out the window of Topiltzin's cell on the dawning of a new day.

In addition to embodying the origins of modern Mexican faith symbolically through his spiritual journey, Topiltzin embodies many of the popular traditionally held beliefs about the Mexican national character. His identity is painfully unfixed—or unresolved, as both Solares and Carrasco have termed it—for he is conquered, victimized, Westernized, baptized, and renamed Tomás. As an illegitimate son of Moctezuma whose mother has been murdered by the Spaniards, he is a bastard orphaned son. Yet he also encompasses many of the positive myths of *lo mexicano*: As an heir of Moctezuma, he is a proud representative of the glorious indigenous past. He is a resistant but punished rebel, much like Cuauhtémoc, the last Aztec emperor, who also suffered the torture of having his feet burned by Cortés. Although we understand that, as an indigenous protagonist, he does not entirely encompass modern Mexico's mestizo identity, he does embody one aspect of that identity: the indigenous. His actions and experiences will therefore ultimately speak to the place of the indigenous in modern Mexican consciousness, how it came to be, and the reasons that Carrasco believes that Mexican national identity remains unresolved.

Like *Nen, la inútil,* which was organized around the principal of encounter between the Spanish and the indigenous, *La otra conquista* bases its tale of culture shock and religious conversion on a principal concept: the indigenous population's total loss. Topiltzin's physical and spiritual worlds have been laid to waste in a matter of years. His ultimate appropriation and difficult acceptance of the Virgin Mary can be understood only within the context of these losses. Significantly, Carrasco points to the source of this concept: "I think [Octavio] Paz is right in suggesting that la Virgen de Guadalupe is the answer to the orphaned state of the indigenous after the conquest" ["Creo que (Octavio) Paz tiene razón al sugerir que la Virgen de Guadalupe es la respuesta a la situación de orfandad en que quedó el indígena después de la conquista."] (quoted in Velazco 1999, 4).[30] Paz's depiction of orphanhood as the incarnate emblem of loss appears in *La otra conquista* as early as the textual prologue, which reads in part, "After two years [of the Spanish penetration into Tenochtitlán], the Aztec civilization found itself in a state of orphanhood, and the survivors were trying to adapt themselves to a new world without families, homes, language, temples . . . and gods" ["Al cabo de dos años (de la penetración de los españoles en Tenochtitlán) la civilización azteca se hallaba en estado de orfandad y los sobrevivientes trataban de adaptarse a un nuevo mundo sin familias, hogares, lengua, templos . . . ni dioses"] (Carrasco 1998). Of note in these opening words is the use of the word *orfandad* [orphanhood], where one might expect to read *ruina* [ruin]. Here, yet again, we see the stubborn resurgence, the pervasiveness of Paz's thinking with respect to the interpretation of Mexican history and national identity.

From the very first scenes of the film, Topiltzin's losses characterize him as an orphan, yet as a positively cast, resistant orphan. In the aftermath of the Templo Mayor massacre, Topiltzin regains consciousness, finds himself surrounded by murdered compatriots—among them, his mother—and screams out to his mother goddess, "Tonantzin!" (which is translated in the English subtitles as "Mother!").[31] Although the depiction of Mexicans—or at least their indigenous ancestors—as orphans supports Paz's or Carrasco's contentions that transculturation, syncretism, and *mestizaje* followed profound loss and victimization among the Aztecs, it is my contention that to a certain extent it serves to infantilize them. The characterization of the indigenous as orphans frames their experience within the rubric of childhood and highlights their status as abandoned victims. Unfortunately, this infantilization undermines the indigenous capacity for cultural and military resistance, a function that works against Carrasco's filmic intention to show the evangelization of the New World as a difficult and unfulfilled project thanks to indigenous tenacity.

Still another encapsulation of the film's theme of loss appears prior to the prologue, when the screen is filled with the graphic emblem of the movie: a skull superimposed on a Christian cross. It is important to note that this graphic emerges from one of the film's first images. We see a codex page with a skull centered on two intersecting red lines (which form a simple cross with four arms of equal length) (Figs. 2.4 and 2.5). The combination of the two, to Western eyes, conjures thoughts of death (the crucifixion) and Christianity, perhaps suggesting the crucifixion and resurrection as a symbol of transculturation. The visual symbol might even evoke a syncretic reading of a Christian cross and an indigenous *calavera* (skull), suggesting either the ultimate sacrifice that was paid by Mexico's indigenous population during Christian evangelization or the promise of life everlasting (the cross as victory over death) that enticed the indigenous to convert. Yet contemplated from an indigenous point of view, the two symbols—especially the cross of equal arms—represent death as spread throughout the four corners of the earth, the cross indicating the four cardinal points of the compass. The four cardinal points also represent the four sons of Omecíhuatl, or Tonacacíhuatl, (Caso 1988, 9–10) and thus the truncation of Tonantzin's lineage.

These early images, then, prepare the audience for the tragic events that follow and for the need to read the film's visual signs from a variety of perspectives. Yet Carrasco's intention is not merely to produce a sad tale of Mexico's distant history (though he does so artfully and accurately).[32] Carrasco has set out to explain the cultural process of syncretic transculturation in real human terms. As he has commented, "We have tried to imagine what this fascinating period of our history could have been like, full of complexities and ambiguities; how an indigenous man, faithful to his beliefs and traditions, would have reacted to the series of losses brought by the conquest, and how his cultural resistance would affect those around him" ["Hemos tratado de imaginarnos cómo pudo haber sido este período tan fascinante de nuestra historia, lleno de complejidades y ambigüedades; cómo pudo haber reaccionado un indígena fiel a sus creencias y tradiciones a la serie de pérdidas que trajo consigo la conquista, y cómo su resistencia cultural afecta a quienes le rodean"] (quoted in Velazco 1999, 4). Carrasco envisions this process of loss and resistance as the cornerstone of indigenous willingness to accept and adore a Spanish Virgin and therefore as the basis of Mexican national identity. He does not, however, limit his film to a representation of the difficult and incomplete conquest of the indigenous spirit. When he deals with transculturation, Carrasco

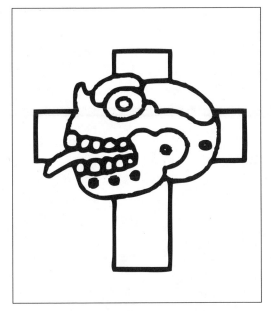

Figure 2.4. The skull atop a Christian cross is a graphic emblem of the film. It not only echoes the theme of loss but also suggests the transformational nature of syncretism, where elements of two religions mesh to form a hybrid belief system. The Virgen de Guadalupe in Mexico has been described as a syncretic mixture of the Spanish Catholic Virgin and the Aztec goddess Tonantzin. Courtesy of the director, Salvador Carrasco.

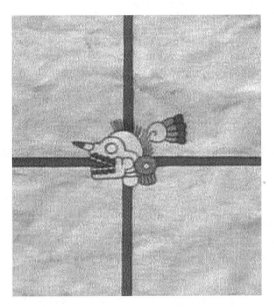

Figure 2.5. The Aztec skull atop two intersecting red lines is an image from the pages of an indigenous codex that lends itself to interpretations that range from hopeful to despairing. These interpretations, in turn, reflect the ambivalence with which many Mexicans view the sixteenth-century conquest. Courtesy of the director, Salvador Carrasco.

also treats the transformation of Fray Diego as a result of his experiences in the New World.

The two protagonists, Topiltzin and Fray Diego de la Coruña, are symbolic of not only the indigenous and Spanish components of Mexico's early syncretic Christianity but also Mexico's mestizo heritage. They also demonstrate the popularly held version of how modern Mexican faith was born. Despite the initial trauma, Topiltzin converts by becoming Tomás (his baptismal name) and by accepting Catholic beliefs. Yet, as mentioned earlier, the film complicates this popular but simplistic vision of early evangelization and strives to represent multi-directional transculturation rather than harmonious syncretic mixing. Fray Diego is also "converted" by Topiltzin and by his close contact with Aztec culture. Fray Diego not only learns to speak Nahuatl but also visits Cihuaccóatl, an indigenous *sacerdote* (priest), to seek guidance about Topiltzin's failing health. Upon Topiltzin's death, Fray Diego delivers a benediction in Nahuatl: "Now that you have left us, wake up. May our venerable mother keep you forever with dignity" ["Ya pasaste rápidamente a dejarnos. Despierta. Espero que nuestra venerable madre te guarde dignamente"] (Carrasco 1998). Although the spiritual evolution of Fray Diego's character is not treated in the same depth as is that of Topiltzin, it is, at least, consistent. In the opening scenes that depict Topiltzin's death in 1558, Fray Diego's colleagues discover a hidden piece of Topiltzin's codex stashed secretly in the tome that Fray Diego clings to so tenuously on his deathbed. A piece of Aztec history therefore survives in Fray Diego, and he has been changed by it.

Yet, just as Solares does in *Nen, la inútil*, Carrasco depicts as similar in important ways his two polar opposite protagonists and the societies from which they come. The first notable similarity between Topiltzin's and Fray Diego's worlds is behavioral. Early in the film, Topiltzin and his surviving family members have clandestinely arranged a human sacrifice to Tonantzin. At the moment that the human heart is raised as an offering, the Spaniards arrive, covered in metal suits of armor, and Fray Diego gasps, "Truly you come from another world" ["De verdad venís de otro mundo"] (Fig. 2.6). The Spaniards are shocked by the cruelty of the sacrifice, but they respond by imprisoning and brutally murdering the Aztecs, causing Fray Diego to lament, "You are behaving just like them!" ["¡Estaís comportando a la altura de ellos!"] (Carrasco 1998). The violent behavior of both societies highlights for the audience the relativity of their culturally held beliefs.

On an individual level, both Topiltzin and Fray Diego demonstrate deep spirituality and cultural pride. After arguing about the bloodthirsty practices of both cultures—Aztec human sacrifice and such Spanish military massacres of civilians as the massacre at the Templo Mayor—Topiltzin says to the friar, "You and I, deep inside, share the same beliefs, Fray Diego, even though we come from worlds so different. We live in all places and in all times" (Carrasco 1998). This culturally relativistic attitude on Topiltzin's part is, however, one of a series of mischaracterizations of Aztec and Spanish culture that serve only to subvert Carrasco's attempt to underscore the trauma of the spiritual conquest and Mexico's early Christian roots.

First, Topiltzin's allegation that he and Fray Diego share similar cultural beliefs allows the audience to draw a dangerously facile assumption. By omitting discussion of the sacred and ritualistic aspects of human sacrifice, the film oversimplifies Topiltzin's conversion process. He is no longer being asked to renounce all that is sacred and meaningful to him but simply to change one violent society for an-

Figure 2.6. When the Spaniards come upon this human sacrifice, Fray Diego mutters, "Truly you come from another world" ["De verdad venís de otro mundo"]. The Spaniards then imprison and brutally murder the indigenous people, causing the friar in their midst to lament, "You are behaving just like them!" ["¡Estaís comportando a la altura de ellos!"]. Courtesy of the director, Salvador Carrasco.

other. Moreover, although the treatment of Topiltzin's journey toward acceptance of the Spanish Virgin Mary is poetic and provocative, it does not address troublesome issues such as monotheism that Aztecs who converted to Christianity faced. If Topiltzin and Fray Diego share a similar spiritual fervor, we can understand that Topiltzin's conversion to Christianity might be of comfort to him in that it at least affords him a chance to worship in some way. Yet despite the polytheistic nature of Aztec religion, Topiltzin is characterized as virtually monotheistic in his devotion to Tonantzin. By the same token, Topiltzin does not confront the difficult concepts of the triune god (the trinity), or the concept of a soul, or the ways that European or Christian thought conflicts with his own culture.

The film therefore not only eases much of the spiritual conflict that Topiltzin would have faced but also attempts to characterize him in broadly Christ-like strokes. Like Christ, for example, Topiltzin is betrayed by those closest to him: first by his brother and then by his mentor. His brother turns him over to the Spaniards for captivity, and Fray Diego turns him over to Cortés for punishment (thus unwittingly causing the death of Tecuichpo as well). Bringing to mind Jesus' words on the cross, "Father why have you forsaken me?" Topiltzin also screams to the heavens, after the massacre of his people, "Sun god, why have you abandoned us?" These characterizations serve only to confuse the audience. Topiltzin is no longer the orphaned symbol of Mexican national identity but a strange parallel to the

Christian savior. He will indeed be sacrificed in the end, but his redemption and resurrection, as we will see, are uncertain.

Fray Diego and Topiltzin in combination, then, are meant to represent the two components of Mexican spiritual mixing in contact and in conflict. Topiltzin, for his part, represents a lost Mexico, and, through his experiences over the course of the movie, embodies the spiritual conquest in real human terms. Through Topiltzin, viewers experience one of the major processes by which current-day Mexico was born. Although the two protagonists demonstrate the give-and-take relationship of transculturation, they do not go as far as Nen and Felipe do toward representing the components of mestizo identity—perhaps as an indication that spiritual mixing is less essential to the Mexican essence than is biological mixing or perhaps as an indication of the incomplete nature of the spiritual conquest. Certainly, however, they mirror the imbalance of power present in the transcultural path toward Mexico's syncretic form of Catholicism.

As Carrasco demonstrates, the process of Topiltzin's transculturation borrows elements from all three theories of indigenous reception of the Virgin (the cataclysmic, or replacement, theory; the idols-behind-altars theory; and the syncretic theory). Topiltzin, we find, experiences and exhibits all three processes in varying degrees before his last gesture and the ending to the film. As the film progresses from the first scenes of the massacre at the Templo Mayor, Topiltzin is isolated from his spiritual touchstones, demonstrating the cataclysmic model of religious conversion. As part of this process, his brother bemoans the fact that the Spaniards have forbidden them to be with their gods. While Topiltzin clandestinely consecrates to Tonantzin (in a sacred human sacrifice) the codices that depict the carnage of the conquest, the Spaniards interrupt him and (succinctly representing their "images at war," as Gruzinski phrases it) destroy the stone image of Tonantzin. Fray Diego tries to supplant native goddesses with the Christian Virgin (as in the replacement model of evangelization), when he tells Topiltzin to behold the image of the Virgin Mary instead of Tonantzin: "Look at her closely. Maria, mother of God. Yours is nothing more than a pile of rocks" ["Miradla bien. María, madre de Dios. La vuestra es nada más que un puñado de piedras"] (Carrasco 1998). Later, in the monastery, after Fray Diego has been charged with Topiltzin's conversion, he also instructs him that Mary is the "new word" ["nueva palabra"]. Spiritually, Topiltzin has been emptied of the ritual practices, the physical representations, and the symbolic mother figure that are all central to his religion.

As a demonstration of the syncretic mode, near the end of the film, Topiltzin appears to resist conversion resolutely and successfully—that is, at least until the statue of the Virgen de la Luz is delivered to the convent. Then he experiences strange hallucinatory dreams concurrent with the arrival of the blonde Virgin, which seem to signal his spiritual capitulation. In one vision, fearing that he will be branded with the sign of the cross by a conquistador, Topiltzin sees the statue of the Virgin and child being lowered into the chapel by a rope. The Christ child is jarred from her grasp and falls into Topiltzin's arms, magically transforming into a flesh-and-blood infant (Fig. 2.7). Thus, it appears that Topiltzin has received Christ as a gift from the Virgin and must respond by becoming Christian. Perceiving himself as a high priest, Topiltzin then poises to sacrifice the Virgin as his grandmother whispers to her, "You are the chosen one." The Virgin's face transforms into that of Tonantzin, and Topiltzin awakens. This dream seems to be a simple and straightforward depiction of Topiltzin's transition into the realm of syncretism. One goddess's image blends into another as their respective signs become blurred. The image of the Aztec sacrifice of the Virgin implies that the cult of the Virgin will, in fact, feed and sustain Tonantzin's worship. The Virgin has, in a way, saved Tonantzin, and Topiltzin, upon embracing the Christ child (or the Christian savior crucified), keeps Christianity alive. With this, however, his own culture has been sacrificed, just as Christ will be crucified, and in the end he will be crushed.[33]

This dream's jumble of images, however straightforwardly syncretic it may seem, does not quite represent the blending of components that occurs in syncretism. Instead, the images reaffirm the overlapping of various theories on religious reception (Fig. 2.8). For example, the Virgin Mary appears as a façade that conceals Tonantzin (as in the idols-behind-altars model), for as the Virgin's face transforms into that of Tonantzin, Topiltzin can be seen as merely accepting the Virgin as a stand-in for his Aztec mother goddess and thus worshipping the "idol" behind the Virgin on the altar. The Virgin also appears to be the answer to Topiltzin's

Figure 2.7. Hallucinatory visions signal Topiltzin's spiritual capitulation, or conversion. Here the Christ child falls from the arms of a statue of the Virgin. Topiltzin catches him, and the baby is transformed into a flesh-and-blood child. Courtesy of the director, Salvador Carrasco.

Figure 2.8. Facing the statue of the Virgen de la Luz, Topiltzin may be adoring his new mother goddess, the Virgin, or merely accepting her as a replacement for his lost mother goddess, Tonantzin. The scene artfully reflects the ambiguity of Topiltzin's religious conversion. Courtesy of the photographer, Andrea Sanderson.

orphanhood. As such, the images of the Virgin-goddess suggest that he accepts the replacement of Tonantzin by Mary (according to the cataclysmic/replacement model). Still another reading of this ambiguous dream supports the view of the Virgin as a syncretic icon, because she embodies a mixture of feminine figures and deities that include his grandmother, sister, and mother goddess. Despite its ambiguous meaning, the dream sequence clearly shows that, as the bloodline of Moctezuma ends with Tecuichpo's death, the Virgin offers the indigenous people new life and a new identity. Topiltzin, holding the living Christ child, is transformed into a son of the Virgin, or *hijo de la virgen,* when he accepts her—and Christ—in Tonantzin's place. Instead of demonstrating the fusion that syncretism connotes, *La otra conquista* ultimately represents Topiltzin's conversion as based on replacement and on the total decimation or loss of his past cultural identity.

Often in creative works, dream-like, surreal narrative perspectives serve to highlight the very scenes that contain the author's most provocative and potent message. It is important to note that not only is this the case in *La otra conquista*[34] but also the dreams or hallucinations occur just as Topiltzin's spiritual and familial losses culminate. His last act of resistance, in fact, involves an incestuous return to his roots as he and his half-sister, Tecuichpo, attempt to conceive a child who will continue their royal Aztec line, maintain their people's traditions, and symbolically herald the survival of the indigenous people in the New World. But Cortés strangles Tecuichpo, killing her and Topiltzin's child. Topiltzin's hallucinations, then, are most likely caused by a sexually transmitted disease—or the *mal de amor* introduced to the New World by Europeans—that Tecuichpo contracted through Cortés. In addition, in a manner similar to the unproductive union of Nen and Felipe, Topiltzin and Tecuichpo's unproductive coupling and truncated bloodline again signal the falsehood of indigenous survival in modern Mexican national identity.

This pessimistic view of the place of the indigenous in modern Mexican identity and consciousness extends, similarly, into the religious and spiritual realms, as analysis of the film's ending will show. In addition to Topiltzin's problematic conversion and the tragic termination of his lineage, the ambiguous and open ending that follows is a tinderbox of signifiers and symbols. Recall that, in the film's last scene, Topiltzin pulls the statue of the Virgin Mary to him in his cell—embracing her from behind—and falls, thus crushing himself with her likeness. Even with the detailed analysis of the film contained herein, this last gesture and Fray Diego's commentary on it remain vexing.

¿*Todos somos Topiltzin?* Indigenous Presence —Past and Present—in Mexico

In light of Carrasco's intention to speak to and elucidate the conflictive nature of modern Mexican national identity, the film's ending is of paramount importance in understanding its key argument. The ending scene, I contend, refocuses and explains the unresolved nature of Mexican national identity. Through an exploration of transcultural processes, Mexicans' sense of their religious beginnings can encompass the violent, the syncretic, and the resistant. Topiltzin brings that all to life. However, Carrasco fails to capture in the ending scene one aspect of Mexican spirituality: the open-ended sense that the conquest is incomplete. Because it drastically undermines the film's overarching message, this shortcoming is of utmost significance.

With respect to the film's ending, Carrasco contends that Topiltzin is "on a personal crusade to conquer her in whose name inconceivable things have been done. If he absorbs the Virgin's powers, if he fuses with her, redemption will follow. For Topiltzin, to conquer is not to destroy but to appropriate the main symbol of his oppressors in order to regain what he had lost" (Carrasco 2002, 167–68). Yet the viewer is nowhere clued in to either these individual intentions of Topiltzin or the redemption that the director attempts to demonstrate.[35] Instead, the audience is faced with a pessimistic ending that signals—perhaps unintentionally—the absence of the indigenous in modern Mexican spirituality and identity, for if individual Aztecs appropriated the Virgin into their lives in order to regain a lost Tonantzin, we understand that they did so in an ardent effort to continue to worship. Topiltzin *dies* in the process. If he is, then, redeemed and his mother goddess is, in fact, regained, then the visual representation of this process makes no sense. His death merely signals the annihilation of Topiltzin as an individual, the subsuming of Aztec culture as a whole, and the absence of the indigenous in Mexican spirituality today.

Finally, upon finding the two motionless figures, Fray Diego sends for Cortés so that he too might witness "a miracle that reflects how two very different races can become one through tolerance and love" ["un milagro que refleja cómo dos razas tan diferentes pueden ser una sola através de la tolerancia y el amor"] (Fig. 2.9). These poetic words inexplicably echo the mestizophile ideal of harmonic fusion. To Fray Diego's Western eyes, Topiltzin's end embodies love, tolerance, and fusion, yet it is clear that the visual reality reinforces a message of death, cultural loss, and the silencing of the indigenous. With respect to this ending, Carrasco has written, "Providence, God, fate, historical necessity, or life's mutability—whatever one calls that mysterious force that holds the strings of our existence—chooses *mestizaje*, the fusion of indigenous and European bloods. And thus, from unhealed wounds, a new nation is born, leaving Indians bleeding on the fringes, trapped in a state of cultural orphanage" (Carrasco 2002, 168). In light of the image we are left with, however—and if, indeed, the film represents and Carrasco believes that cultural

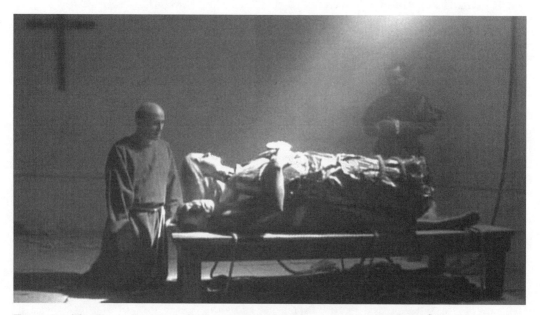

Figure 2.9. The film ends enigmatically with Fray Diego staring at Topiltzin, who lies dead under the Virgen de la Luz. The scene may be a metaphor for *mestizaje* or for the annihilation and silencing of the indigenous race. Courtesy of the director, Salvador Carrasco.

annihilation occurred, leaving the indigenous in a state of "cultural orphanage"—it is puzzling that Carrasco can speak in terms of real cultural mixing (whether it is syncretism or *mestizaje*).

Carrasco is well aware of the controversial nature of his film and the opposition it produces by taking on the most sacred and essential aspects of Mexican national identity. The conquest of Mexico has been mythified, as we have seen, to provide Mexicans with a well-crafted tale of good and bad. Carrasco himself contends that "the official history of the conquest was not meant to be questioned because of the embarrassing things that it might say about the situation of Mexican Indians today" (Carrasco 2002, 167). Embarrassing, indeed. Carrasco set out to explore the reasons for Mexico's conflictive identity. His film reveals the profound loss experienced as the indigenous people were forced to adapt to the new invading culture and religion. Embarrassingly enough, the film also turns popular myths about unproblematic religious conversions on their ear. Even more embarrassing for Mexico in the 1990s was the question of what had become of the indigenous population as a result of the conquest. The 1994 Zapatista uprising was an answer that few Mexicans wanted to hear. The Zapatistas not only called on the nation to recognize centuries of exploitation and abuse of indigenous cultures, lands, and rights; they also demanded an increased role in national politics and more sovereignty in terms of their own local governance.

These same questions about the state of indigenous peoples in Mexico, how the Virgin of Guadalupe was accepted in the Americas, and the future role of indigenous groups in Mexican society were also being posed across the Atlantic. In the Vatican, Pope John Paul II decreed that Juan Diego Cuauhtlatoatzin, the Chichimeca man who first brought the news of the Virgin's appearance to Zumárraga, would be canonized in Mexico City on July 31, 2002.

The elevation of Juan Diego to sainthood—making him the first indigenous American saint ever—was profoundly relevant for a number of reasons. First of all, "it put an end—at least for the Catholic church—to the polemic over the historicity of the Virgin of Guadalupe's witness in 1531" ["puso fin—cuando menos para la Iglesia católica—a la polémica sobre la historicidad del vidente de la Virgen de Guadalupe, en 1531"] (Roman and Vargas 2002, 1). In addition, in his homily during the three-hour ceremony at the Basílica de Guadalupe in Mexico City, Pope John Paul II took the opportunity to send to Mexicans a strong message about the plight of the indigenous: Lending the church's support to "the indigenous people in their legitimate aspirations" ["los indígenas en sus legítimas aspiraciones"] (quoted in Loaeza 2002, 3), he intoned, "Mexico needs its indigenous people, and the indigenous people need Mexico!" ["¡México necesita a sus indígenas y los indígenas necesitan de México!"] (quoted in Roman and Vargas 2002, 1). Juan Diego, he said, served as a model because by embracing the Christian message, without renouncing his indigenous origins, Juan Diego became the protagonist of the "new Mexican identity," and ... his life must continue to drive the construction of the nation, promote brotherhood among all his children and contribute more and more to the reconciliation of Mexico with its origins, its values, and its traditions.

[al acoger el mensaje cristiano, sin renunciar a su orígen indígena, Juan Diego fue protagonista de la "nueva identidad mexicana" y ... su vida debe seguir impulsando la construcción de la nación, promover la fraternidad entre todos sus hijos y favorecer cada vez más la reconciliación de México con sus orígenes, sus valores y sus tradiciones.] (quoted in Roman and Vargas 2002, 1)

One reporter wrote that John Paul II "wanted, before he died, to canonize Juan Diego. Making the indigenous man a saint, was, perhaps, a way of 'sanctifying' all indigenous Mexicans in the eyes of the government" ["quiso, antes de morir, canonizar a Juan Diego. Hacer santo al indígena, era, tal vez, una forma de 'santificar' ante los ojos del gobierno a todos los indígenas de México"] (Loaeza 2002, 3). Another reporter believed that "the canonization of Juan Diego has the character, one could say, of a technological revindication and relevant pastoral letter, although late, for all indigenous Latin Americans on Rome's behalf" ["la canonización de Juan Diego tiene el carácter, cabría suponer, de una reivindicación teológica y pastoral pertinente, aunque tardía, de los indígenas latinoamericanos por parte de Roma"] ("Quinto viaje" 2002, 1). The *New York Times* reported that the canonization "stirred considerable debate in Mexico: about whether Juan Diego was a real man or a convenient marketing tool for the Catholic faith, and about whether the church, in trying to court indigenous people, was actually offending them" (Bruni and Thompson 2002, A6).

The same issues and debates are echoed in *La otra conquista*. In its depiction of the trials and tribulations of Topiltzin, the film also seeks to valorize the historical indigenous role in and contribution to Mexico's unique form of Catholicism. Although Carrasco demonstrates the real costs, in both human and spiritual terms, that a conversion such as Juan Diego's entails (as we have seen) in the end, the film's visuals appear so disconnected from the message that they leave the audience hopelessly befuddled as to the final value of such a radical process.

The same can be said for Juan Diego's canonization ceremony. Despite the Pope's poetic and symbolic words, the powerful visuals presented to the public betrayed what some saw as institutional racism and governmental erasure of the indigenous. Criticisms about the small number of indigenous people at the ceremony poured in, as evidenced by the headline, "The Canonization of the Indian Juan Diego without the Indigenous" ["La canonización del indio Juan Diego, sin indígenas"] (Mejía 2002b). In a separate article, the same commentator drew still more profound conclusions about Mexico's relationship with its indigenous people:

"This is a country that makes use of its indigenous past only to put its historical discourse in order but in fact does not participate with them in ecclesiastical communion" ["Este es un país que se sirve de su pasado indio únicamente para formalizar su discurso histórico pero de facto no participa con ellos en la comunión eclesiástica"] (Mejía 2002a, 1).

The most troubling observation, however, concerned the painting of Juan Diego that was presented to the Pope for canonization. One outraged reporter wrote, "It must be said before the elevation of the Tepeyac Indian to the altars that the Vatican has altered the image of the soon-to-be saint, who is now presented as an individual with Caucasian features and white complexion. The europeanization and whitening of the figure of Juan Diego cannot be understood as anything but a gross expression of racism, which taints basic Christian values and distorts the indigenist tone of the canonization process" ["No puede omitirse que antes de la elevación del indio del Tepeyac a los altares la oficialidad vaticana ha realizado una alteración de la imagen del iminente santo, el cual es presentado ahora como un indivíduo de rasgos caucásicos y piel blanca. La europeización y el blanqueo de la figura de Juan Diego no pueden entenderse sino como expresiones de grosero racismo que desvirtúan los valores cristianos básicos y distorcionan el sentido indigenista del proceso de canonización"] ("Quinto viaje" 2002, 1). Indeed, the *New York Times* reported that "straight hair, a full beard and an angular face . . . did not seem to reflect an Indian ancestry" (Bruni and Thompson 2002, A6). Once again, powerful attempts to return to the origins of Mexico's national identity and romanticize or revalue them can easily be undone by a few words (as in the case of *Nen, la inútil*), editorial cuts (as in *La otra conquista*), or an inaccurate artist's rendition (as in Juan Diego's likeness).

The works examined in this chapter demonstrate two of the core flaws of mestizophile ideology as a basis for modern Mexican national identity. First, despite efforts to construct mestizo identity and culture (especially syncretism) around positive, even romantic, origins, forging harmony from the violence of the conquest of Mexico is virtually impossible. Second, the silencing of the indigenous—no matter how romantic or heroic their last actions—bespeaks the reality of *mestizaje* as assimilation. As a result, it is understandable that the mestizo as the emblematic Mexican and a modern Mexican national unity based on mestizophile ideology might be fair targets for attack among writers of this era.

3

Moving toward Multiculturalism

Examining the Makeup of Mexican Mestizo Identity

Mexico's collective revisiting of the roots of its mestizo national identity in the late 1980s and early 1990s meant grappling with some difficult contradictions. How could *mestizaje,* seen by some as a harmonic mixture, reconcile its violent origins in conquest and forced religious conversion? Although Ignacio Solares and Salvador Carrasco make great strides in examining this important question, the indigenous characters in both *Nen, la inútil* and *La otra conquista* come to a silent fatal end, ultimately demonstrating the assimilationist consequences of mestizophile ideology and the high price paid by Mexico's indigenous people.

The texts by Carmen Boullosa and Carlos Fuentes examined here also search for answers to identity questions in Mexico's official national history. The incomplete nature of history fuels the creativity of both authors, as they, respectively, debate history's claim to privilege and fill in historical gaps. Their contribution to Mexican identity discourse, in addition, lies in the fact that they both discard the essentialist notion of Mexico as a mestizo (Spanish and indigenous) nation and they both advocate tolerance and understanding—pillars of multiculturalism—in modern Mexico. Both authors delve into the foundational colonial history and the components of mestizo Mexico; in the end, however, Boullosa laments Mexico's lost indigenous past and Fuentes attempts to ascribe plurality to *mestizaje* in a pan-Hispanic context.

Although they were written several years apart, to a certain extent Boullosa's 1989 novel *Llanto: Novelas imposibles* (see Boullosa 1992) coincides with Fuentes's story "Las dos orillas" (1993a) when it comes to a redefinition of Mexican national identity. Boullosa's characters succeed in exhibiting an understanding of the Other, thus enabling them to admit the true makeup of Mexican national identity and to understand the roots of Mexican culture. Fuentes ascribes an even broader cultural and ethnic plurality, informed by theories of multiculturalism, to Hispanic culture worldwide. He proposes the same sort of admission and tolerance of plurality and even posits its role in turning Hispanics into leaders in the twenty-first century. Yet where Boullosa's text ends with a despairing view of the future, Fuentes's story comes to an upbeat close. This chapter examines how both authors use history and debate the past, how they redefine modern Mexican national identity, and how they view the various components that constitute a modern Mexican identity.

Llanto: Novelas imposibles, by Carmen Boullosa

Since the 1991 publication of *Son vacas, somos puercos,* Carmen Boullosa,[1] one of Mexico's most celebrated young writers of the 1990s, has been experimenting with the historical record in a variety of ways. Where her previous works labored under a profound personal poetics and the enclosed interior worlds of children, the historical novels that she published in the 1990s, tapping into the omnipresent wealth of the past, focused mainly on Mexican and Caribbean histories of the sixteenth and seventeenth centuries.[2]

Llanto: Novelas imposibles (published in 1992) was Boullosa's second published historical novel; however, the fact that it had actually been written and corrected by 1990 makes it her first work of historical fiction. Of the works of Boullosa examined herein, it is also, chronologically, the first work penned. *Llanto* provides a most valuable and salient intermeshing of many of the historical issues and narrative concerns that we have seen thus far. As the title of the novel suggests, *Llanto*'s narrative projects are doomed "impossible novels" ["novelas imposibles"]. A description of the ends toward which they strive clarifies why: First, the truncated novel itself tells the story of three contemporary Mexican women who, after a night out partying in 1989, find that Motecuhzoma[3] (the ninth *tlatoani*), has reappeared, brought back to life in Mexico City's Parque Hundido. Second, the novel is *about* its own writing and creation, for in the nine "novel fragments" ["fragmentos de novela"] we follow numerous narrators/writers who debate their own ability to recreate Moctezuma fictively in various anecdotal plots, since so little useful information about him exists in historical documents.[4] Third, the narrative attempts to recover much of the mythic indigenous infrastructure of Mexico's past in an effort to revive Moctezuma and thus to explore Mexican identity.

Boullosa's writing in *Llanto* constitutes a fitting and, in many ways, challenging approach to historical sources, to attitudes toward the conquest, and to the novelistic search for modern Mexican origins. Instead of engaging, as do many historical novels, in a totalizing narrative that seeks to recreate the past, *Llanto* lays bare the unacceptable incompleteness of historiography and actively debates the usefulness of history as a narrative source.

As noted, for Boullosa, the writing of *Llanto* meant a creative leap into historical fiction. According to the author, the novel emerged from "the need to think about our public history, or collective history, our impersonal history, to put it that way" ["la necesidad de pensar nuestra historia pública, o nuestra historia colectiva, nuestra historia impersonal, por decirlo así"] (1996). Once again, the unique weight of Mexico's past and the urgency with which Mexican authors revisit and revise it becomes evident. The novel strategically recovers Moctezuma in order to vindicate him from centuries of slander, which alternately characterize him as a ruthless dictatorial emperor and a superstitious coward who, in both instances, is fully to blame for the fall of Mexico and the three centuries of colonial domination that followed. Boullosa's narrative agenda therefore employs a number of the revisionist strategies that abounded during the Quincentennial debates.

Yet the public collective and impersonal narrative material (historical events) that Boullosa employs is wholly transformed in *Llanto* to form an enchantingly intimate view of the past. Although the narration is a fragmented and at times incoherent discourse (which can have a profoundly confusing effect on the reader), Boullosa achieves a narrative intimacy on two counts: First, she personalizes the narration of a moment in her nation's history by employing friends and family as characters and narrators who take part in the novel's creation. The three main characters in *Llanto*—Laura, Luisa, and Margarita—are versions of Boullosa's childhood friends and schoolmates (Jesusa Rodríguez, a writer and actor; Ana Luisa Liguori, an anthropologist; and Magali Lara, a painter).[5] Although in the second "fragmento de novela," one of the narrators reveals her intention to write a novel around similar protagonists, the character-reality connections are not explicit in *Llanto*. Moreover, among the nine narrators, Boullosa herself and her companion of many years, Alejandro Aura (also a writer), are identifiable as the narrators of the second and third fragments, respectively. Although these details may be of interest to readers (especially those acquainted with current Mexican literary circles) and they confirm Boullosa's confession that "there are other personal, intellectual 'histories' intertwined in the novel" ["hay otras 'historias' personales, intelectuales, entreveradas en la novela"] (1995b, 218), those who are unaware of the narrative intimacy cannot miss the tender personal atmosphere that the novel creates throughout.

Second, because *Llanto* strives to recreate Moctezuma's world and thus explain his mind-set, Boullosa researches and documents the novel thoroughly. Her narrators confirm this, saying, "The confession of Moctezuma the young must be made within the framework of his culture in order to be comprehensible" ["La confesión de Moctezuma el joven tiene que ser hecha en el marco de su cultura para ser comprensible"] (1992, 39). Alvaro Enrigue's "Llanto," a review of the novel, indicates some of Boullosa's narrative techniques that work toward the re-creation of this lost era: twenty chapters, the number indicating "the days of a month on a divinatory Nahuatl calendar" ["los días de un mes del calendario adivinatorio nahua"]; nine novel fragments "that obviously represent the nine levels of the netherworld" ["que obviamente representan a los nueve escalones del inframundo"]; and language that makes the text "deeply hermetic (and confusing at times): the phrasing is structured by its devotion to the translations of classic Nahuatl discourse" ["profundamente hermético (a ratos confuso): el fraseo está estructurado a las traducciones del discurso náhuatl clásico"].[6] Boullosa herself attests to this linguistic stage setting, saying, "*Llanto* is the impossible language of an emperor who is reborn into a world that no longer belongs to him" ["*Llanto* es la lengua imposible de un emperador que renace en un mundo que ya no le pertenece"] (Ibsen 1995, 56). Each of these narrative techniques constructs a familiar atmosphere into which the ninth *tlatoani* reappears. The narrative treats Moctezuma's character within an intimate fairy tale during his return to his lost city, a city that is now entirely hostile to him.

In addition, the characterization of Moctezuma paints an affectionate, reverent portrait of one of Mexico's most controversial and maligned historical figures. When the three contemporary characters finally comprehend that they are, in fact, in Moctezuma's presence, they lay their sweaters and jean jackets at his feet, forming a pathway for his steps and saying, "Forgive us, your highness; we had not recognized you; step right this way" ["Perdone su señoría, no lo habíamos identificado, pise usted por aquí"] (Boullosa 1992, 63). Later Laura carefully plays Antonio Vivaldi's eponymous operatic tribute to the emperor and lovingly bathes him before making love to him (100–102). Elena Poniatowska hails this novelistic treatment of Moctezuma, writing, "I wish our heroes received that same treatment and were taken up again from feminine angles so history would not simplify them" ["Ojalá y nuestros héroes recibieran ese trato y fueran retomados desde ángulos femeninos para que la historia no los acartonara"] (1993, 28). Then she confesses, "I always had an enormous sympathy for Moctezuma" ["Siempre le tuve una simpatía enorme a Moctezuma"] (27).

At times, however, the narrative tenderness in the novel borders on an infantilization of the Aztec emperor. When the three women first find Moctezuma in the park, Laura becomes quite possessive, picking him up to carry him and saying, "I take him with me wherever I go. He is mine" ["Lo llevo conmigo, donde yo vaya. Es mío"] (Boullosa 1992, 48). Similarly, in the car, she describes him as a "child god" ["niño dios"] (50) "on the brink of tears" ["a punto de llorar"] (51). She "arranged all of the clothes he wore. . . . She spoke to him as you would to a small child" ["acomodó toda la ropa que él vestía. . . . Le habló como a un niño chiquito"] (52), and when he cried, she wiped away his tears, hugging him and singing to him as if to a baby (53). The affection of the narrative is, however, directly related to (and a means of compensating for) the "failure" or impossibility of its own creation.

Because the novel sets as its goal the vindication of Moctezuma—but cannot achieve this end, as it cannot fictively reconstruct him—*Llanto* launches its own sympathetic but vociferous version of the past, proffering opinions and assertions of forceful forthrightness. Boullosa engages in debate over the historiographic perspective best suited to update sixteenth-century events, and the result is a highly inventive view of the conquest and its ramifications for modern Mexico and Mexicans alike.

Llanto: An Identity Discourse Profoundly Based on Historical Narration and Historiography

One answer to the question of Boullosa's purpose for the fragmented form of her novel and its focus on Moctezuma lies in the sources included in her acknowledgments [agradecimientos] on the last page of the text. The sources and, indeed, the intertexts ground the novel squarely in Mexican history and historiography. First mentioned is Fray Bernardino de Sahagún and his extraordinary coauthors, the trilingual indigenous scribes who together composed the *Códice Florentino,* found in the *Historia de las cosas de la Nueva España,* which inspired the novel's multiple narrative voices. Next cited is Tzvetan Todorov's *La conquête de l'Amérique, la question de l'autre.* As we will see, Boullosa closely—almost uncritically—follows Todorov's writings on the conquest. Through a study of the methodologies and conclusions of these texts, we see how Boullosa—by adopting the optic of Sahagún and his aides, while mirroring Moctezuma's confused perspective, which Todorov proposes as part of a discourse of the Other—thematically and formally inscribes a multiplicity of voices into the writing of *Llanto.*

To begin, Sahagún's voluminous work (the *Códice Florentino* comprises merely four of the twelve volumes of the *Historia de las cosas de la Nueva España,* the last volume of which is entitled *Historia de la conquista de México*) resulted from years of experience with indigenous people in the Americas and countless hours of interpretation and translation of the bases of pre-Hispanic cultures. It is an encyclopedic attempt to document everything from the creation myths of different indigenous groups to their "idolatrous" religious beliefs, their institutions, their histories, and their own versions of the invasion and consequent conquest by the Castilians. Like Sahagún's *Historia, Llanto* depends largely on the transcribing and interpreting of past accounts. In *Llanto,* Boullosa thoroughly documents her work to assert its historicity (although she simultaneously discusses its fictiveness). Whereas Sahagún labored to document the worldview of the indigenous Mexicans through work with symbolic pictorial glyphs and narratives in many languages,[7] Boullosa transcribes, interprets, and recreates the historical record from an incomplete, cryptic historiography of the past.

In the novel, Boullosa also consults, quotes, and acknowledges such contemporary scholars of the ancient world as Alfredo López Austin and Eduardo Matos Moctezuma, who—much as the trilingual aides did for Sahagún—act as cultural bridges for her endeavor. Her novel originates from the desire to piece together a coherent vision of ancient Mexico by combining Nahuatl images and icons (found in *Llanto*'s "La aparición" and "Una estampida de imagenes" [1992, 11–34]) with indigenous and Spanish perspectives on Moctezuma. However, her insurmountable distance from her subject causes her narrators to abandon the attempt to rework history and to vindicate Moctezuma. The sources, they proclaim in frustration, are insufficient, and their subject is inaccessible: "Futile enterprise: Tenochtitlán has died, and its memory is confused" ["Empresa inútil: Tenochtitlán ha muerto y su memoria es confusa"] (39). Unlike other writers, who consider it possible to recreate the past, Boullosa declares the project impossible, emphasizing yet again the questionable value of a textualized past and therefore the possibility of historical knowledge.

In addition, just as Todorov dedicates his work to analyzing the conquest through the discourse of the Other, *Llanto*'s narrators struggle to narrate the Other (Moctezuma) despite the fact that he has no satisfactorily documented referent. Like the writer yearning for divine inspiration, in the days of Hernán Cortés's arrival in Mexico, Moctezuma tried in vain to read the messages that he required from the gods in order to take appropriate action. Todorov postulates:

> When the country's leaders want to understand the present, they naturally seek not experts on men but those who communicate with the gods, with the masters of interpretation.

> [Cuando los dirigentes del país desean entender el presente, se dirigen con toda naturalidad no a conocedores de hombres, sino a los que practican el intercambio con los dioses, con los maestros en interpretación.] (1989, 81)

This, Todorov concludes, was a grave mistake, as the responses that Moctezuma chose were based on a human-to-world relationship and not on the increasingly urgent and life-threatening human-to-human relations that were developing between the Spaniards and the Aztecs. Just as Moctezuma searched for ritualistic answers to his dilemma, *Llanto*'s writers reveal the same need for a traditional mythic inspiration—symbolized in the text by a muse-like, narrative-inspiring, dusty wind—in order to write.

In *Llanto*, as a result of a common lack of information, both the narrators and the Aztec emperor (we imagine) also share a truncated, fractured perspective through which they view events. As we have seen, Moctezuma's ritualized information base was not entirely appropriate for his needs. He was thus, again according to Todorov, incapable of perceiving the Spaniards as traditional Others because "the Spaniards' identity is so different, their behavior is unpredictable to such an extent that it shakes the very system of communication" ["la identidad de los españoles es tan diferente, su comportamiento es a tal punto imprevisible, que se sacude todo el sistema de comunicación"] (1989, 81). If true comprehension of these beings was impossible for the emperor and their actions utterly surprising, then his communication with them was doomed as well. The messages and gifts that he sent to the Spaniards in an effort to deter them from marching to Tenochtitlán all failed because they were *rituals* used to appease *gods* rather than communiqués meant to uncover or understand the Spaniards' intentions.[8]

The narrators of *Llanto* demonstrate an equally puzzled and frustrated perspective as they watch the fictive narrative fail from the complete lack of historical references. One narrator laments the loss of ancient Mexico's cultural framework, concluding that Moctezuma is illegible to us because

> we have what we need to know what Philip II or Carlos V felt, thought, or believed, but in contrast with Motecuhzoma no evidence remains. No bones, no indications as to what he thought, nothing.

> [tenemos con qué saber qué sintió, pensó, opinó Felipe II o Carlos V, pero en cambio de Motecuhzoma no quedaron indicios. Ni huesos, ni señas de cómo era su pensamiento, ni nada de nada.] (Boullosa 1992, 75)

Like the misguided rituals that Moctezuma applied to the Spaniards, the historical narrative of the conquest neither informs nor helps in *Llanto*'s re-creation and fictionalization of the Aztec emperor, his thought process, or his mind-set. *Llanto* had hoped to fill with imagination and fictionalization the informational void that surrounds the figure of Moctezuma, but the narrator, deeming this an impossible task, asks:

> What would I care if truth went to hell? But since he, Motecuhzoma, was a real figure and was a person at an especially sensitive historical moment, one of connection, of crossroads, of battlefields, I couldn't do it.

> [¿Qué me hubiera importado mandar qualquier verdad a la porra? Pero como él, Motecuhzoma, fue un personaje cierto, como él fue una persona y está en un punto histórico especialmente sensible, de entronque, de encrucijada, de campo de batalla, no lo pude hacer.] (96)

Thus, *Llanto* creates a perspective that directly imitates that of Moctezuma upon the arrival of the Castilians. Moctezuma is plagued with incomprehension, unable to discern ritual from real or symbolic from empirical, and *Llanto*'s narrators are similarly confused by the unavailability of a sufficiently documented past. The two also demonstrate failed communication. Moctezuma dealt with gods (not people) and may have even revered the Spaniards as deities, whereas Boullosa's narrators succeed only in planning a narrative (not writing one) and thus "fail" in their attempt to revive the ninth *tlatoani*. Thus, the fragmentary nature of the narrative serves as a metaphor for the piecemeal work that such chroniclers as Sahagún performed in the name of documentation. Moreover, the utter incomprehension that frustrates both writers and characters alike in *Llanto* mimics that of modern Mexicans who peer back in time at the Others (sixteenth-century beings) who played out the conquest on the same spot some five centuries ago.[9]

In *Llanto* numerous narrative sources and narrative voices create a polyphony that amply reflects Boullosa's own beliefs about literature and about historical fiction in particular. Books, to Boullosa, are hardly mere narratives or physical objects. Rather, they are resources that actively participate in what she calls "the dialogues that take place all day in the universal library, so to speak, [which] never stop and . . . nourish all humanity, even those who don't read or write" (Reid 1995, 147). This view of writing as a collective, universally beneficial endeavor also appears at the end of *Llanto,* where Boullosa's list of acknowledgments provides useful clues for deciphering the novel. At the bottom of the list, she calls further attention to the creative collectivity that she believes is at work in literature, by confessing that she cited the references "because together with them I wrote this novel" ["porque junto con ellos escribí este libro"] (1992, 122).

This collective creativity, moreover, appears to have been inspired by, or at least sparked by, the crises of Mexican national identity and nationalist discourse that began in the late 1980s, which accounts for the appearance of numerous creative works that rewrite the same fifty years of Mexican history. Thinking back, and reflecting on the past years of crisis in Mexico, Boullosa also contends, "Mexico was nearing an enormous crisis, and . . . we all felt the need to rewrite ourselves from the first foundational moment as the homeland we are, as a mestizo homeland" ["México se acercaba a una crisis enorme y . . . todos sentimos la necesidad de reescribirnos desde nuestro primer momento de fundación como la patria que somos, como patria mestiza"] (1996). After a decade of crises that shook Mexico's economy, political institutions, and sense of itself as a nation, narratives that emerged spoke to the fear that *mexicanidad* was, in some way, a curse that destined the nation to failure. Boullosa, then, takes a bold stand with respect to Mexico's colonial past, the value of its historiography, and the possible originary figure of modern Mexico.

We now turn to an examination of how *Llanto: Novelas imposibles* constitutes an identity discourse. We begin by attempting to assemble the pieces of shattered, fragmentary narrative to demonstrate the process through which the novel was written. The desire to develop a single anecdote (the return of Moctezuma in 1989 Mexico) then evolves into an effort to vindicate Moctezuma, while the novel—motivated by national concerns over official history and its representations of the past—lays bare the shortcomings and inconsistencies of sixteenth-century historical narration.

The Creative Progression of *Llanto*:
Narrative and Historical Perspectives

The multiple narrative projects in *Llanto* and its fragmented form can have quite an overwhelming and confusing effect on readers. Yet the novel's metafictitious element (narrators actively debating the very novel's creation) functions as a map that plots the creative process—or processes—by openly discussing its own writing. The narrators in the "fragmentos de novela" demonstrate *Llanto* to have originated in an anecdote: three contemporary Mexican women find Moctezuma alive in the Parque Hundido.[10] Boullosa herself confirms this, stating, "I decided to use my fantasies to write the novel. I saw, I swear, Moctezuma appear one day in the Parque Hundido" ["decidí usar mis fantasías para escribir una novela. Vi, lo juro, un día aparecer a Moctezuma en el Parque Hundido"] (1995b, 218). Years after its writing and publication, however—viewing this same anecdote as a source of the novel's shortcomings—she laments:

> With *Llanto* I made a mistake from the very beginning, a narrative error: I imagined a very small and stable anecdote—like a portrait—in a way, not a real anecdote that would evolve. The story is about Moctezuma appearing in the Parque Hundido, but it is a story that comes to an end when it happens. . . . In the case of *Llanto*, there is a narrative paralysis from the start.

> [Con *Llanto* cometí un error desde el principio, un error narrativo que fue: Me imaginé una anécdota muy pequeña y estable—como un retrato—por así decirlo, no una verdadera anécdota que fuera evolucionando. La historia es que aparece Moctezuma en el Parque Hundido, pero es una historia que llega a su término cuando ocurre. . . . En el caso de *Llanto* hay una parálisis narrativa desde el principio.] (1996)

Yet although the original anecdote may, in fact, have been a static one, it is precisely the impossibility of its elaboration that gives rise to the rich questioning and debate that makes *Llanto* such a valuable voice in the dialogues of the "universal library."

One of the narrators realizes the urgency and value of *Llanto*'s scrutiny of the historical record, noting that the very novel demands its own telling: "The novel pushes me to continue with the story, to advance for the sake of the endless movement of what occurred that sunny morning, the thirteenth of August of the year one thousand nine hundred eighty-nine. The novel pushes me" ["Novela me fuerza a continuar con la historia, a avanzar por el móvil sinfín de lo que ocurrió en el amanecer de un soleado trece de agosto en el año mil novecientos ochenta y nueve. Novela me fuerza"] (Boullosa 1992, 113). Narrative necessity is maintained throughout the novel by a unique muse. Before each fragment of the novel, the narrators of *Llanto* are invited, inspired, and informed by a mysterious messenger wind that is full of a fine, sandy dust—said to be the remains of an Aztec woman traveling through time with Moctezuma. *She* is the messenger: "She must have been the dust-messenger who knew how to narrate the novel worthy of Motecuhzoma's appearance. It is not conjecture: she would have known how" ["Ella habría sido el polvo mensajero que hubiera sabido cómo contar la novela que mereciera la aparición de Motecuhzoma. No es conjetura: ella hubiera sabido cómo"] (95). She represents the narrative link to the revival of the personage of the great Aztec emperor—and thus the unrecorded past.[11]

Moctezuma's revival, of course, would provide the stage upon which to debate the historiography that defines him for modern Mexicans. Boullosa herself states, "He came so we would rethink his persona, because what they have sold to us benefits neither him nor our memory" ["Vino para que se repensara su figura, porque la que nos ha vendido de él no le convenía ni a él ni a nuestra memoria"] (1995b, 218). As we have seen, the conquest and colonial times in Mexico have been quite problematic in the nation's "official story." During the controversies over the *Libros de texto gratuitos,* these historical moments again proved to be underrepresented (if not wholly misrepresented). In his article summarizing the texts of the Carlos Salinas de Gortari administration, Ignacio Ramírez writes, "Furthermore, the emphasis with which they insist on the Indians' submissive character during the Conquest is worrisome. To them, the figure of Cuauhtémoc warrants only two and a half lines" ["Es preocupante, además, el énfasis con que se insiste en el carácter sumiso de los indios durante la Conquista. La figura de Cuauhtémoc sólo les merece dos renglones y medio"] (1992, 6). In the 1992 fifth-grade text *Mi libro de historia de México*, the conquest is given all of four pages (the majority of which is occupied by illustrations). Moreover, if Cuauhtémoc fares poorly with only two lines, Moctezuma fares worse: He is mentioned only three times, in reference to (1) his gifts to Cortés, (2) his public reception of Cortés in Tenochtitlán, and (3) his status as a prisoner of the Spaniards (36–39). Nowhere are his actions explained; nowhere is his death treated. Daniel Cazés further scornfully notes that schoolchildren have no exposure to instances of indigenous resistance: "They will learn nothing about resistance from the texts that narrate the official history of so-called social neoliberalism" ["De la resistencia nada aprenderán de los textos en los que se relata la historia oficial del neoliberalismo llamado social"] (1992b, 15).

The 1994 revised *Historia: Quinto grado* devotes six pages to the conquest and states that although Moctezuma was "an experienced warrior . . . now he was dominated by indecision and fear" ["un guerrero experimentado . . . ahora estaba dominado por la indecisión y el temor"] (149). It also remarks that Moctezuma was superstitious and that he "decided to obey Cortés" ["decidió obedecer a Cortés"] (149). His death is framed by the fact that "the people no longer listened to the *tlatoani*: when he tried to speak to them, he received a shower of stones and he was wounded" ["el pueblo ya no escuchó al *tlatoani*: cuando intentó hablar recibió una lluvia de piedras y resultó herido"] (151). The history texts posit two possible (and traditionally held) scenarios for his death: "He died a few days later; it is unknown whether this was as a result of his wounds or because he was assassinated by the Spaniards, to whom he was no longer useful" ["Murió unos días después, no se sabe si a consequencia de sus lesiones o asesinado por los españoles, a quienes ya no era útil"] (151). These encapsulated official representations of Moctezuma demonstrate the real need to rethink the figure who serves as a link—if a lost one at that—between the ancient world and the beginning of the modern world.

Because Boullosa realizes the capricious nature of the conquest's textual history, *Llanto* launches a variety of caustic and interrogative attacks on sixteenth-century historical narration and its (mis)representations. Not only does Boullosa's text blur the heretofore rigid distinction between history and literature by challenging historiography's accuracy; it also asks where privilege lies, if, in fact, it exists. *Llanto* begs the question "If all literature is historical and all history is literary, what privilege can the notion of history or the historic have at all?" (Smarr 1993, 17).

One of the most evident means by which *Llanto* discredits the notion of history's privilege is the stark juxtaposition of historiographic sources. *Llanto* does not assimilate its historical intertexts: Whole blocks of documents from Hernán Cortés's *Cartas de relación;* Bernal Díaz de Castillo's 1992 *Historia verdadera;* and the Aubin, Florentino, and Ramírez Codices are pasted between the fragments of the novel, allowing the texts to speak for (and contradict) themselves. Boullosa remarks of her research for the novel:

> I began to read with an innocence I no longer give [the texts]. But when I realized that they contradicted themselves, for example, I began to search obsessively for a description of Moctezuma's death.

> [Empecé a leer con una inocencia que ya no les doy (a los textos). Pero en el momento en que me di cuenta que todos se contradecían entre sí, por ejemplo, empecé a buscar con obsesión nada más el momento de describir la muerte de Moctezuma.] (1996)

This technique of focusing on a single event and the discrepancies that surround its narration—as the texts openly contradict each other, causing utter disillusionment and distrust in the author and in her narrators—highlights just how unreliable even historical narration can be.

Because the contradictory and juxtaposed texts included in *Llanto* represent as many of the voices of the past as possible, they tap into various categories of the abundant historiography concerning the conquest. Boullosa considers each entry in the list of pertinent texts for the early phase of the conquest that Todorov enumerates in *La conquista de América*: "the reports from Cortés himself; the Spanish chronicles, the most notable of which is by Bernal Díaz del Castillo; and last, the indigenous narratives, transcribed by the Spanish missionaries or written by the Mexicans themselves" ["los informes del propio Cortés; las crónicas españolas, la más notable de las cuales es la de Bernal Díaz del Castillo; y por último, los relatos indígenas, transcritos por los misioneros españoles o redactados por los propios mexicanos"] (1989, 59). A brief study of the texts grafted onto the pages of *Llanto* and their contributions to the historical textuality of the conquest of Mexico during the years from 1519 to roughly 1526 highlights the circumstances under which they were written and thus explains, to a small extent, their differing perspectives—especially the perspectives on the death of Moctezuma.

First, Cortés's *Cartas de relación*, written as a series of letters to his sovereign, is a well-crafted version of the events from 1519 to 1526 whose raison d'être heavily influences its narrative. In short, Cortés commanded this expedition in defiance of Diego Velázquez, the governor of Cuba. He was authorized only to explore and trade; he had no authority to settle or colonize. Thus, Cortés's letters to King Carlos V are part of an attempt to justify autonomy from his superiors and to seize legitimate authorization to conquer and settle the lands and wealth that he encountered in Mexico.[12] These *Cartas* further politicize and manipulate events to bolster Cortés's legitimacy as sole conqueror. In this "official" story, he asserts that "Muctuzuma" died as a result of a stone thrown at his head by his own subjects. However, as J. H. Elliott notes, "For all Cortés's eager insistence that he was providing a 'true' relation, he displayed a masterly capacity for suppression of evidence and ingenious distortion" (1986, xx).

Díaz del Castillo, an infantry soldier on Cortés's expedition, also took pen to paper in a self-affirmed true account of the conquest. He wrote his *Historia verdadera de la conquista de la Nueva España* in Guatemala in the 1560s as a corrective response to Francisco López de Gómara's allegedly inaccurate version of the tale. Evidently, López de Gómara wished to "exalt the fortunate captain Hernán Cortés ... reducing exceptional facts down to the actions of a hero" ["engrandecer al venturoso capitán Hernán Cortés ... reduciendo los hechos excepcionales a la acción de un heroe"] (Pereyra 1968, 19). Díaz del Castillo wished for a more pluralistic view of the events in Mexico—notably, one in which he played a much larger role—because, as he puts it, "I have no fortune to leave my children and descendants, except this my true and notable account, as you will see ahead" ["no tengo otra riqueza que dejar a mis hijos y descendientes, salvo esta mi verdadera y notable relación, como adelante en ella verán"] (1992, 15). Díaz del Castillo too describes Moctezuma's death as from wounds acquired at the hands of his own people; thus, the European version of the event lays the blame for Moctezuma's demise on his own subjects.

Llanto also makes use of Antonio de Solís's seventeenth-century work *Historia de la conquista de México*. Because the writing of this *Historia* was officially commissioned, Solís sheds a positive light on Cortés's actions, and he views Díaz del Castillo's criticism of Cortés as heretical and audacious. Analysis of this text demonstrates how Cortés's own *Cartas*—which couch his failures in victorious narratives—served as the basis for later rewritings of the conquest, which presented the conquest as even more epic, heroic, and favorable to the Spanish conquistadors than had the original chronicles.

In addition to these narratives, *Llanto* employs a variety of codices that attempt to record the indigenous view of the crisis. First, two examples of what can be accomplished through the cooperation of Spanish missionaries with their indigenous interpreters are Fray Bernardino de Sahagún's *Códice Florentino* (discussed earlier) and Fray Toribio de Benavente Motolinía's *Memoriales: Libro de las cosas de la Nueva España y los naturales de ella* (which includes information that was most likely originally intended for two separate works). The texts in the next category of codices are examples of multilingual recordings of pre-Hispanic cultures whose circumstances of creation are unknown. The *Códice Ramírez*, for example, is an untitled sixteenth-century manuscript found in a monastery in the nineteenth century. Because of, among other things, "the deviation and even the contempt with which [the author] speaks of Motecuhzoma when he describes his tragic death, attributing it to the Spaniards themselves" ["el desvío y aún el desprecio con que habla (el autor) de Motecuhzoma al describir su trágica muerte, atribuyéndola a los españoles mismos"] (Alvarado Tezozómoc 1980, 9–10), the codex is thought to have been written by an indigenous scribe and translated from the Nahuatl. The *Códice Aubin*, in contrast, consists solely of "ideographic glyphs and a memorized oral tradition, transmitted through generations" ["glifos ideográficos y una tradición oral memorizada y transmitida a través de generaciones"] (*Codex Aubin* 1963, 13). Its glyphs are accompanied by varying degrees of interpretation in Nahuatl, and the codex itself—"taken with certain carelessness from previous codices and annals but all of them after the year 1540" ["tomado con cierto descuido de códices y anales anteriores, pero todos posteriores al año 1540"] (13)—is thought to have been compiled around the year 1562. Each of these indigenous texts stipulates that the Aztec emperor was already dead when the crowd threw the stone or when his body was thrown from the temple that doubled as a Spanish fort.

Boullosa has placed blocks of these historical texts throughout her novel's narration. Each text narrates either the circumstances of Moctezuma's death or the way his body was subsequently treated by his subjects and by the Spaniards. Although the historical narratives do not create a precise interplay with the novelistic fragments that directly precede and follow them—that is to say, they do not echo the issues or narrative material that most closely surrounds them in the novel—

they are ordered in a way that highlights contradictions. Pieces of the Ramírez, Florentino, and Aubin Codices—which show that Moctezuma was already dead when he was stoned by his subjects—appear first (it is worth noting that, because of their primacy, these narratives are privileged by the author). Without much detail or explanation, the codices also narrate the fury of the Aztec people over Moctezuma's death and the reluctance of many indigenous communities to receive his body for incineration. Spanish versions of the events then lie in open contradiction to the codices. Cortés himself states that the stone was the cause of Moctezuma's death, and Solís reports that Spanish conquistadors mourned the death of the Aztec emperor as openly as did the Aztec people themselves. Solís's text contradicts itself in its portrayal of Moctezuma as both an insecure leader whose authority was not ensured and the ultimate ruler of a people who depended on him greatly. In this way, the two groups of texts (the codices and chronicles) further muddle the reader's sense of who Moctezuma was: a prisoner put to death by his captors, an ambiguous leader whose unremarkable death caused confusion among his subjects, or a beloved ruler assassinated by and mourned by his people.

This cross section of historical narration evidences the rich textual diversity of narratives that concern the conquest of Mexico, and the blocks of historiography included in the novel reflect the narrative contest in which various versions of this history engage. As the narrative voice in the section "Aquella voz" states, "We quarreled amongst ourselves to trap the version that we held to be true in time. We quarreled; we heard truths buzz around at unimaginable speeds" ["Entre todos nosotros nos peleábamos por atrapar a tiempo la versión que se sostenía por cierta. Nos peleábamos; oíamos las verdades cruzar zumbando a velocidades impermisibles"] (Boullosa 1992, 106–7). The various versions in *Llanto* highlight a single historical moment: Moctezuma's death. There are, in essence (as noted in Mexico's revised 1994 fifth-grade history textbooks), two views of what happened to the Aztec emperor and, as we have seen, sixteenth-century Spanish and indigenous sources oscillate between the two versions of his death. This bipartisanism forms the basis of the novel's disillusionment with historiography, but it does not shut down the narrative. Instead, it sets the stage for the creation of a new version of Moctezuma's life.

Llanto's narrative projects (the anecdote, the revival of Moctezuma, and the scrutiny of historical referents) culminate in a textual vindication of the Aztec emperor—despite the fact that this vindication is the first piece of narrative that we read. As the novel opens, "In a Stampede of Images" ["Por una estampida de imágenes"] (Boullosa 1992, 15–33) narrates fictive scenes and experiences from Moctezuma's life. We come to realize through our reading of the rest of the novel that these images constitute a portion of the novel that *Llanto*'s narrators planned to write. Had the narrative "succeeded," Moctezuma would have been revived and thus enabled, through personal testimony, to vindicate himself from the historiographic label as superstitious coward. The "failure" of Boullosa's static narrative anecdote and the impossibility of reviving the lost Aztec perspective in that anecdote, however, have left only fleeting images of this narrative. Yet it is not until we reach the end of the novel that we understand the importance and significance of the "estampida de imágenes."

In fact, all three of the novel's narrative projects are borne out in *Llanto*'s early narrative scenarios. The images succeed in developing Moctezuma's character, they are based in historiography (yet surpass it with imagination), and they attest to Moctezuma's nobility. First, the narrator of the seventh "fragmento de novela" strategically contradicts "documentary" historiography, declaring, "I abandoned the man who died by stoning, because I do not think the *mexica* people would have dared to raise a hand against their *Tlatoani*" ["Deserté del hombre que murió de una pedrada porque no creo que el pueblo mexica se haya atrevido a alzar la mano contra su Tlatoani"] (Boullosa 1992, 96). Consequently, the images of the "estampida" show Moctezuma as a wholly revered, cherished leader from an early age. As a boy, his nursemaids would not allow him to wade in the ocean, protectively plucking their royal charge from the water's edge (16), and later in his life he enjoys the company of his "favoritas," a harem of adoring young women entirely devoted to the emperor's pleasure (15, 18). The same narrator writes:

> I abandoned the idea of the suffering man, indecisive, terrified, and irresolute, because I think Moctezuma is seen as vacillating or cowardly in terms of a Western idea of a coward and a man who vacillates before a war he had no reason to understand.

> [deserté de la idea del hombre atribulado, indeciso, aterrorizado y vacilante porque creo que se ve a Moctezuma vacilar o actuar como un cobarde desde la idea del Occidente de lo que es un cobarde y un hombre que vacila ante una guerra que él no tenía por qué entender.] (97)

These modifications of traditional representations of the *tlatoani* take numerous forms. First, a youthful Moctezuma demonstrates his bravery when, unlike his compatriots, he refuses to fear earthquakes, volcanic eruptions, and fires, because he is in training to become a warrior king (17–18). Next, in one scenario, he scolds a child for screaming out needlessly, and the children learn that Moctezuma is far from being an indecisive leader; in fact, "the word of Motecuhzoma is pronounced in order to bring order to heavens' foundations" ["la palabra de Motecuhzoma es dicha para poner el orden en los cimientos del cielo"] (26).

The issue of Moctezuma's alleged superstition also arises and is contested. The narrator of the seventh fragment discards the image of a *tlatoani* who cowered when he received auguries foretelling the horrific downfall of his kingdom. When the water of the lakes surrounding Tenochtitlán begins to "boil," instead of proclaiming imminent apocalypse, the sages explain how the salts from the lake's sediment create this effect (Boullosa 1992, 30). Although Moctezuma secretly fears that the event may foretell some future disgrace for his people, he is neither terrorized nor incapacitated by the auguries. This reflects the narrator's contention:

> It does not seem to me that the omens occurred during his time but instead were invented later . . . so that history would not seem a cradle of cadavers.

> [No me parece que los presagios hayan ocurido en su tiempo sino que fueron inventados después . . . para que la historia no pareciera cuna de cadáveres.] (96)

In the "estampida," Moctezuma admits the possibility that some minor auguries announce "something terrible against which it was difficult to fight" ["algo terrible contra lo que era difícil batallar"] (30). Yet he concludes that it is "impossible to fight . . . because I had not initiated the war" ["imposible pelear . . . porque yo no había iniciado la guerra"] (30), thus implicitly contrasting the all-out, take-no-prisoners warfare of the expanding Spanish empire with the traditional Aztec battles for territory. The mention of an incomprehensible war hearkens back to Todorov's theory about the misunderstandings that occurred during the conquest, one being the difference between unmitigated, absolute Western warfare and ritualistic Aztec warfare.

In the first "fragmento de novela," the narrator explores discrepant styles of fighting, declaring, "To let them enter, bestow gifts upon them and house them like noble guests in the lord's palace are actions that have been erroneously read as signs of submission and cowardice" ["Dejarlos entrar, obsequiarlos, albergarlos como nobles huéspedes en el palacio del padre son acciones que han sido erróneamente leídas como signos de entrega y de cobardía"] (Boullosa 1992, 37). In fact, Moctezuma's gestures signal his adherence to the etiquette of Mesoamerican warfare wherein "one had to respect the steps that needed to be followed, the ritual, the tradition of war, and, having done so, one had the right to all violence" ["había que respetar los pasos a seguir, el rito, la tradición de la guerra, hecho lo cual, se tenía acceso a toda la violencia"] (37). Cortés and his men, in contrast, act erratically: They accept Moctezuma's gifts but then respond "with gratuitous violence, without respecting the rules of war, like barbarians: War began with the attempt to come to an agreement . . . the comparison of and balancing of forces so the fight would be equitable and the gods could intervene in determining the victor" ["con violencia gratuita, sin respetar las pautas de la guerra, como bárbaros: Hacer la guerra comenzaba con intentar llegar a un acuerdo . . . comparar las fuerzas y equilibrarlas para que la lucha fuera pareja y los dioses pudieran intervenir en la decisión del ganador"] (38).

Last, and most important, *Llanto* proffers a new version of the circumstances that surround Moctezuma's death. Moctezuma's first-person account of his own murder recounts the unconscionably cowardly way in which the Spaniards ended his life by assassination: "I cannot jump; the shackles make it impossible, and two men hold me while turning their faces away so that I cannot recognize them. . . . When I feel pain in my soft flesh, I feel a dagger destroy me" ["No puedo brincar, los grillos me lo impiden y entre dos me sostienen retirando sus rostros del mío para que yo no pueda reconocerlos. . . . Cuando siento el dolor en mis carnes huecas, siento la daga destrozándome"] (Boullosa 1992, 27). Orders are given to leave the body intact so that they can "display" it, and in another section a baffled (indigenous) voice asks why so many sacred Aztec rules have been broken: "Why do they let his blood fall on the ground? . . . What destiny awaits him in death with a demise like that?" ["¿Por qué dejan regar su sangre al piso? . . . ¿Qué destino le espera en la muerte con una forma de muerte así?"] (23). This is another example of the Spaniards' violation of Aztec rituals: They do not value the emperor's blood (an Aztec offering to the gods), and they murder instead of sacrifice. In the last section of the "estampida," entitled "The Cadaver of the Emperor" ["El cadáver del emperador"], the Spaniards parade Moctezuma's dead body in front of his subjects, with "his city writhing in fury, abandoned, broken" ["su ciudad revuelta en ira, abandonada, descompuesta"] (33). Their ire and abandonment are attributed to the actions of neither the Spaniards nor the emperor, lacing *Llanto*'s version with ambiguity. Yet because the Spaniards have neglected to play the music that always prefigures the emperor's appearance, the Aztecs know that what they see is merely the corpse of their emperor. Moctezuma's conscience believes that the stone that is thrown "is not for me but for Hernán Cortés" ["No es para mí, es para Hernando Cortés"] (32), but it is not entirely clear whether his perceptions of the farcical parade are accurate, leaving the mood of the Aztec people in question and lending indeterminacy to even this version of his death.

Thus, *Llanto*'s narration comes full circle. From its desire to rethink the figure of Moctezuma and valorize the ancient Aztec perspective has arisen a probing search for that figure and that perspective. Despite the fact that the novel's narrative project never comes to fruition (or perhaps as a result of its frustration), *Llanto* engages in a series of profound assessments of the historical record, concluding that historiography's incomplete sources and unfortunate representations render the past unknowable. This finding, in turn, affects the national identity discourse of a nation that relies heavily on its historical past. *Llanto*'s only recourse is to piece together paltry images in the "estampida de imágenes," adopting a format emblematic of the very history that purports to represent the past. In the scripting of a new life for Moctezuma, *Llanto* enshrines a new version of the past—albeit one grounded and documented—thus continuing history's intertextual discourse. Yet, as we will see, the narrative failure and frustration result in a profoundly useful but pessimistic search for national identity.

Forging a Historical Identity: The Antihero as Self Not Other

Late in the novel, *Llanto*'s despair with its own impossibility takes the narrative in a new direction. As a direct result of the difficulty the narrators of *Llanto* face in textually reviving Moctezuma, they begin to question the alleged mestizo character of the Mexican nation, thus opening their debates to an identity discourse. Although neither Boullosa nor the narrators state the intention to formulate a soul-searching identity discourse, the failure of the novel itself necessarily leads to a treatment of national identity. By raising difficult quandaries and questions, the novel's narrative is both a historical revision and an identity discourse: If the past functions as the basis for the present, and we are unable to recover the Aztec past satisfactorily, how can that element be considered part of Mexico's present? More important: How, then, can Mexico call itself a mestizo nation?

Boullosa believes, as do many Mexican intellectuals, that the past is uniquely present in Mexico. In one of her essays, she prefaces a mention of the discovery and excavation of the Templo Mayor with the following statement:

> Yesterday, in this city, is present today. If the passing of time heals wounds, in Mexico it opens them. If the passing of time buries what happened, in Mexico the passing of time brings to light what other years buried.
>
> [El ayer, en esta ciudad, forma parte presente del presente. Si el paso de los años cierra cicatrices, en Mexico las abre. Si el paso de los años entierra lo ocurrido, en México el paso de los años saca a luz lo que otros años enterraron.] (1995a, 9)

Boullosa again makes the connection between the past (history), literature, and the present (identity) in the following statement:

> Why not walk with your head turned around . . . search in the past for where the genealogy of emotions themselves can ferment and truly take the shape of a fantasy? . . . We could (why not?) begin to forge another, better version of ourselves.
>
> [¿Por qué no caminar con la cabeza girada hacia atrás . . . buscar en el pasado el pasaje donde la genealogía de los propios sentimientos pueda fermentar y cobrar forma válida de fantasía? . . . Podríamos (por qué no) empezar a fraguar otra mejor invención de nosotros mismos."] (13)

Many identity discourses, such as the ones analyzed here, pose the very same queries and respond by enshrining new versions of the past that attempt to encapsulate their own interpretations of *mexicanidad* or Mexican identity.

Many Mexican intellectuals see the conquest as the origin of *mestizaje,* the birth of the Mexican nation, and the beginning of modern Mexican history. In *Llanto* the narrators add that the sixteenth-century events played out in Tenochtitlán directly mirror today's world. Yet *Llanto* brings a sense of tragedy and pessimism to its narration (which is also, at times, extremely tender and loving). In addition, through the comparison of the sixteenth and twentieth centuries, *Llanto* reworks our perspective on the past as it rethinks the concepts of victor and vanquished.

Llanto's basic theme or pretext is the reappearance of the ninth *tlatoani* in current-day Mexico City. In this way, the novel undermines the reader's concept of the unilinear progressive passage of time by bridging the twentieth century and the sixteenth century. The past five hundred years are denied their progressive character and are, instead, turned into a cyclical *re*currence (nine times fifty-two years) when a detailed argument that draws comparisons and similarities between the two eras weaves the narrative fragments together toward the closing of the novel.

Needless to say, our Western concept of time as linear and ever progressing is upset by Moctezuma's revival, because it reveals a past that can invade the present. This, according to one narrator, proves that "time can shatter" ["el tiempo puede romperse"] (Boullosa 1992, 45). The fractured worldview (in this case, the Western concept of time) as a theme or plot is in no way gratuitous, as it directly parallels the shock of the ancient Aztecs when the Spaniards appeared to them. The West's invasion destroyed the Aztecs' certainty about the repetitive nature of time and the value of the past as a reliable harbinger for both the present and the future.[13]

In an effort to draw parallels between the sixteenth and twentieth centuries, the narrator of the seventh novel fragment explains how Moctezuma watched uncomprehendingly as the Westerners turned the valley of Tenochtitlán into a "cuna de cadáveres" (Boullosa 1992, 96), thus exterminating the Aztec empire and its manner of seeing the world. In this sense,

> that time resembles our twentieth century. They lost their gods.... Ours, our one, has died. We did not have a conquistador: our world has been overcome by us.... We feel we are going to perish; we painfully see that the end of human beings is near and it will be at the hand of human beings themselves.... Our shadows scoff at us; our shadows are in the shape of atomic weapons. We have devoured a large part of our planet with the made-up mouth of civilization.... We are our own conquerors.

> [esa época se parece a nuestro siglo veinte. A ellos se les murieron los dioses.... Los nuestros, el nuestro, ha muerto. No tuvimos conquistador: nuestro mundo ha sido rendido por nosotros mismos.... Sentimos que vamos a perecer, vemos con dolor que se acerca el fin del ser humano a manos del ser

humano. . . . Nuestras sombras se burlan de nosotros, nuestras sombras tienen forma de armas atómicas. Hemos devorado gran parte del planeta con la boca aquillada de la civilización. . . . Nuestros conquistadores somos nosotros.] (97)

A modern view of our world therefore mirrors that of Moctezuma in its apocalyptic pessimism. Clashes, be they from antiquity or modernity, always result in heavy losses. Where in the sixteenth century an entire civilization and its worldview were lost, now the threat of global extermination looms.

A common theme among students of the discovery and conquest of the Americas is a different loss: loss of the indigenous perspective. Because victors are known to write history, little is understood of how the indigenous populations viewed events. Throughout her work, Beatriz Pastor has shown how the Eurocentric worldview—narrating the discovery and conquest through silence, omission, and absence—in essence, silenced all others (1992, 122). In his book *The Mexican Dream: Or the Interrupted Thought of Amerindian Civilizations* (which Boullosa cites in her acknowledgments), J. M. G. Le Clézio contends that "the coming together of two worlds . . . was the extermination of an ancient dream by the frenzy of a modern one" (1993, 3). In its revision of Moctezuma, *Llanto* too carries the motif of apocalyptic loss, because the Aztec emperor "did not understand that it had to do with the end of the *mexica* empire. It was about the end of a way of seeing the world. The extermination of a way of life. Their culture was facing that extermination" ["no vio que se trataba del fin del imperio mexica. Se trataba del fin de una manera de concebir el mundo. Del exterminio de un modo de ser. De la frontera de su cultura con tal exterminio"] (Boullosa 1992, 97). Yet to the narrative in *Llanto,* the most important aspect of this loss is not the absence of the Aztec worldview but what that absence means in real terms to modern Mexican identity. For Boullosa, Moctezuma's textual inaccessibility signals far more than just her failed narrative. In her novel, this lack shows that the fundamental cause of Mexican identity's irresolution is its basis in untruth—incomplete documentation.

As the novel comes to a close, the ninth and last "fragmento de novela" continues both the narrative's identity discourse and its lamentation for an absent Moctezuma. It considers the absence, loss, and silence of the "Indian memory" ["memoria india"] in more general terms as well, reflecting on Mexican history (and therefore Mexican identity) as being marred by "a broken root" ["una raíz rota"] (Boullosa 1992, 117). The impossibility of narrating through the indigenous perspective causes the narrator to question whether this indigenous perspective is, in any way, present in Mexican identity. The conclusion is that it is not:

Indigenous memory is indelible and impossible to avoid, unrecoverable and unreachable, the memory of a dominion of the world that cannot be imitated today, a dominion that no longer is, that can no longer be practiced.

[Es una memoria india imborrable e imposible de evitar, irrecuperable e inalcanzable, el recuerdo de un dominio del mundo que hoy no puede tener imitación, un dominio que ya no está, que ya no se puede practicar.] (118)

Although the narrator concedes that this memory is preserved among Mexico's modern indigenous groups—"a multitude preserves it, as it was, identical to and outside of its time, perverted and pure in the framework of an era not its own" ["una multitud la conserva, como fue, idéntica y afuera de su propio tiempo, pervertida y purísima en el marco de una era que no le pertenece"] (118)—its unavailability to Mexico's mestizo population fosters a radical revision of national identity. Without access to this cultural base, this essential root, *Llanto* states, "the root turns to pure venom and exuberant vitality in all Mexicans, certainty negated and inhabited, an unrecognizable essence, an impossible *mestizaje*, a root that is at once your own and foreign" ["la raíz se torna veneno puro y vitalidad exuberante en todo mexicano, certeza negada y habitada, de esencia irreconciliable, de mestizaje imposible, raíz propia y ajena"] (118). The broken root, then, shows that the idealized (and oftentimes official) version of *mestizaje* as a harmonic mixture is a sham, suggesting instead that there are many Mexicos, not least among them both a Western mestizo Mexico and an indigenous Mexico.

The lamentation for the lost indigenous world, then, leaves the narrative to make the surprising announcement that it is, indeed, Fernando (Hernán) Cortés who is considered to be the first Mexican: "Fernando was the first Mexican, as the word we use today, Mexican, is a Castilianized form of *mexica* and was therefore stripped from its ancient owners" ["Fernando fue el primero de todos los mexicanos, como hoy se usa la palabra mexicanos, castellanizando el mexica y arrebatándolo a sus antiguos poseedores"] (Boullosa 1992, 117). The narrative identifies Cortés as the founder of the new nation and its "history that has among its roots a broken one" ["historia que entre sus raíces tiene una rota"] (118), thus affirming the Western character of Mexican mestizo culture and also imputing to Cortés's conquest the effective extinction of the indigenous worldview.

Yet, in this way, the novel challenges our traditional notions of victor and vanquished. Whereas Cortés most commonly occupies the role of antihero, in *Llanto*—because Boullosa sees him as the first Mexican—he is assimilated into the Mexican national conscience as an (if not the) originary figure. Her definition of *mexicanidad*, of course, differs greatly from that of Solares. It approaches the concept of multiculturalism in admitting many Mexicos and advocating comprehension of the Other. The ninth novel fragment ends with the following affirmation:

Like all the inhabitants of the world, we are children of understanding, gestation, and crime, in our particular case because Cortés understood, he listened to the signs of another culture and knew how to interpret them.

[Como todos los habitantes del mundo, somos hijos de la comprensión, la gestación y el crimen, en nuestro caso concreto porque Cortés comprendió, escuchó los signos de otra cultura y supo interpretarlos.] (Boullosa 1992, 119)

This same contention appears in Todorov's study of the conquest, when he notes that Cortés's first priority was reading signs and searching for information (not gold) (1989, 107).

Obviously, this characterization of Cortés—the same conquistador credited in Chapter 2 with decimating indigenous temples and religious practices—as understanding of other cultures is highly controversial and problematic. In fact, it needs to be tempered by the assertion that he used this information to his own advantage and to the supreme disadvantage of the indigenous people. Yet the figure of Cortés continues to provoke dramatically discordant opinions in Mexico. Ironically, in his well-known book *Los grandes momentos del indigenismo en México*, Luis Villoro deems Cortés Mexico's first indigenist, as one who believed that "the [indigenous] civilization has every right to survive. It must be respected as much as possible. . . . He didn't come to brutally impose one culture, making a clean slate of the other, but to face both in an exchange of values" ["tiene la civilización (indígena) perfectos derechos a sobrevivir. Debe respetarse hasta donde sea posible. . . . No viene a imponer salvajemente una cultura, haciendo tabla rasa de la otra, sino que enfrenta a ambas en un intercambio de valores"] (1950, 21–22). In a nation where Cortés has long been vilified for his historically documented mistreatment of the indigenous population, this quotation and Boullosa's difficult admission of his role as a seminal figure in Mexican national identity again reveal the malleable nature of national heroes examined in Chapter 1.

Despite the tragic consequences of Cortés's comprehension of indigenous Mexico in *Llanto*, the understanding of another culture's signs is a highly visible motif and metaphor for Boullosa's revision of modern Mexican national identity. Throughout the novel, instances of these cultural bridges abound. In the scene where the three women try to authenticate Moctezuma as the true *tlatoani* and not just a disoriented indigenous man, they telephone Alfredo López Austín, a renowned Mexican anthropologist and historian. He carries on a conversation with the *tlatoani* in classical Nahuatl (Boullosa 1992, 86) and later views many of the artifacts that Moctezuma wore or carried as a means of reading the signs of the past and interpreting or confirming them for the present.

Llanto itself as a narrative also functions as a cultural link in much the same way. As we have seen, this narrative mirrors the work of Sahagún, who (with the help of his trilingual aides) "reproduces the discourse as it is dictated to him and *adds* his own translation, instead of substituting the discourse with the translation" ["reproduce el discurso tal como se lo dicen, y *agrega* su traducción, en vez de sustituir el discurso con la traducción"] (Todorov 1989, 238). Instead of replacing existing historiography with its own version of events, Boullosa reproduces the historical discourse, interprets and debates it, and then adds her version of the past. The novel serves, then, as a metaphorical representation (with all the consequent difficulties and impossibilities) of the type of comprehension of various cultural discourses that Boullosa deems a core value of modern Mexican society.

In this way, *Llanto* demonstrates many of Boullosa's own theories of literature, identity, and history. First, she believes that novels "have to be open spaces and should create more questions and start a dialogue that never shows people where to go, what to do, just be a way of rethinking things" (Reid 1995, 146). This novel both produces and provides dialogue not only with history but also with its own readers. The problematic, but nonetheless textually supported, promotion of the Westerner, Cortés, as the first Mexican on the basis of his open mind reflects Boullosa's thoughts on the commemoration of the Quincentennial. In an article about the festivities, she writes:

> May the Quincentennial festivities help us to accept our pluralities . . . and let us think about the *tlatoani* of inexplicable behavior in order to broaden our understanding with our mind set on enriching ourselves and finding new ways to conceive of civilization, culture, and our own inventions of ourselves.

> [Que sirvan los festejos del Quinto Centenario para aceptar nuestras pluralidades . . . y pensemos en el tlatoani de comportamiento inexplicable, para estirar la liga de nuestra comprensión con miras a enriquecernos con la mirada puesta en otras maneras de fincar la civilización, la cultura, nuestra propia invención de nosotros mismos.] (1991b, 38)

Tolerance and comprehension are therefore the key to modern Mexico—as is, I would add, Boullosa's early admission of multiethnicity in Mexico. Here *Llanto*'s narrative takes a chance by evaluating many sides of the debate. Ironically, the novel ultimately discards commonly held notions about the ethnic makeup of Mexico and opts to incorporate the Other (Cortés) as an integral part of its Self, thereby enriching the narrative perspective, historical debate, and identity discourse along the way.

History Revised and Retold in "Las dos orillas," by Carlos Fuentes

In his book *El naranjo, o los círculos del tiempo*—in which five stories retell tales of discovery, conquest, and colony in an effort to examine the cyclical nature of history and the many peculiar ironies of the past—Carlos Fuentes[14] takes on history in a markedly different way. Compared to Solares—who, for the most part, faithfully rewrites historical events on a fictive stage, toying only with the imagined and magical interstices of events—Fuentes plays more with history and historical discourse. By focusing on numerous empires and colonies, separated both temporally and spatially, the stories in *El naranjo* demonstrate how the "historical fact" of a colonial past has contributed to the very fabric of the modern world.

As we see in the closing words of "Las dos Américas," the final story in *El naranjo*, Fuentes puts forth his theses on the circularity of time and the plurality of Hispanic—and universal—identities:

> Time circulates like the tides, uniting and relating all, conquerors of yesterday and today, reconquests and counterconquests, besieged paradises, pinnacles and decadences, arrivals and departures, appearances and disappearances, utopias of memory and hope. . . . The constant in this back-and-forth is the painful movement of peoples, immigration, escape, hope, yesterday and today.

> [El tiempo circula como las corrientes y todo lo une y relaciona, conquistadores de ayer y de hoy, reconquistas y contraconquistas paraísos sitiados, apogeos y decadencias, llegadas y partidas, apariciones y desapariciones, utopías del recuerdo y del deseo. . . . La constante de este trasiego es el movimiento doloroso de los pueblos, la emigración, la fuga, la esperanza, ayer y hoy.] (1993a)

The author's use of the motifs of time and identity are important components of both his fictional and nonfictional writing.

It can be argued that as early as 1970, in *Tiempo mexicano*, Fuentes developed the organization of his narrative around a specific concept of time. There he wrote, "Among us . . . there is not a single time: all times are alive; all pasts are present. Our time presents itself as impure, charged with resistant agonies" ["Entre nosotros . . . no hay un solo tiempo: todos los tiempos están vivos, todos los pasados están presentes. Nuestro tiempo se nos presenta impuro, cargado de agonías resistentes"] (1992b, 9). Fuentes views time as multiple, and he conceives of history as not only circular, cyclical, and repeating but also decidedly unfixed. In the stories of *El naranjo*, Fuentes transforms the historical record by "rescuing" a number of figures that have traditionally been underrepresented in historiography, because he believes that "the novelist lends a voice to those who still do not have one and a name to those who are anonymous" ["el novelista da una voz a quienes todavía no la tienen y un nombre a quienes son anónimos"] (quoted in Torres Fierro 1992, 55). The inclusion of these figures is just one method that Fuentes employs as a means of actively modifying the past and its consequences, or resultant identities.

To Fuentes, writers wield the power to invent (not just imagine) the future as they interweave three temporalities—past, present, and future—into their creative perspectives: "I think that the past occurs today in our memory and that the future occurs today in our desires. . . . that all times occur today, that we have a past because we remember and that today we have a future because we wish" ["Creo que el pasado ocurre hoy en la memoria, y el futuro ocurre hoy en el deseo . . .

que todos los tiempos ocurren hoy, que tenemos pasado porque recordamos, y hoy tenemos futuro porque deseamos"] (quoted in Zeran 1994, 33). The urgency that Fuentes demonstrates in projects that concern the past, the future, and identity hinges on his ephemeral position in the present: He feels that it is his task to complete these constructions of events before they become part of someone else's past or memory.

Although it is complex, this philosophy of time is important to understand because of its primacy in *El naranjo, o los círculos del tiempo* and other works by Fuentes. *El naranjo,* in fact, constitutes the latest addition to what Fuentes calls "the age of time" ["la edad del tiempo"], a type of narrative cycle that orders his works not along chronological time but according to certain thematic *edades* (ages) therein.[15] In addition to circles of time, "la edad del tiempo" explores romantic, revolutionary, political, and actual time. To date, virtually all the narrative works by Fuentes—especially those that explore temporal discourses—are included in this cycle. In the case of *El naranjo,* circular time fuels the exploration of historical issues that are directly related to our perceptions of modern identity.

Mestizaje versus Multiculturalism in the Works of Carlos Fuentes

It is important to note that the 1993 publication of *El naranjo* followed closely the 1992 international publication of *El espejo enterrado,* an essayistic work written by Fuentes in commemoration of the Quincentennial of Columbus's voyage as his contribution to the extant debates on history and identity. *El naranjo* represents imaginatively many of the historical and cultural theories put forth in *El espejo enterrado* [The Buried Mirror], a book "dedicated . . . to the search for cultural continuity with which to transform and transcend the economic discord and political fragmentation of the Hispanic World" ["dedicado . . . a la búsqueda de la continuidad cultural que pueda transformar y trascender la desunión económica y la fragmentación política del mundo hispánico]" (1992a, 11). Roger Bartra even deems *El espejo enterrado* "a contribution to the project of putting in order the house of culture" ["una aportación a (la) tarea de poner orden en la casa de la cultura"] (1993, 13). During the Quincentennial, Fuentes himself sheds light on the driving forces behind his writings on culture when he notes that "1992 is perhaps our last opportunity to tell ourselves: this is who we are, and this is what we will give the world" ["1992 es quizás nuestra última oportunidad de decirnos a nosotros mismos: esto somos y esto le daremos al mundo"] (1993b, 43). He contends that 1992 and the impending close of the millennium "oblige us to stop and reflect about our place in time and our work in history" ["nos obligan a detenernos y a reflexionar sobre nuestro lugar en el tiempo y nuestro trabajo en la historia"] (49). Significantly, in trying to speak for all of Latin America, Fuentes seeks out the uniform, not the multiform, in Hispanic culture. Although the need to affirm and fix Hispanic identity is a constant in his works, in the early 1990s Fuentes was particularly absorbed by it for historically pertinent reasons.

In *El espejo enterrado* and his other contemporaneous writings, Fuentes puts forth his project of cultural awareness, which speaks not only to issues of Mexican identity but also to issues of identity for all Latin America. Two goals of his efforts are (1) to widen our perceptions of the ethnic spectrum of Latin American identity and (2) to vindicate Spanish cultural contributions to the Americas. In the late 1980s—although the second goal was extremely controversial, as Fuentes was aware—he insisted on a responsible attitude toward Spanish cultural heritage, proposing (among other things) that a statue of Cortés be placed in Mexico City. Amid the uproar provoked by this proposal, Fuentes confirmed, "I would like to see Hernán Cortés in a plaza in Mexico City to rid ourselves of that complex. . . . There is no need to reject the father or the mother, or the brother; we accept everything we are" ["Yo quisiera ver a Hernán Cortés en una plaza de la Ciudad de México para quitarnos ese complejo. . . . No hay por qué negar ni al padre ni a la madre, ni al hermano, aceptamos todo lo que somos"] (quoted in Ochoa Sandy 1992, 46). By way of answering critics who would rather continue to hold Spain responsible for the atrocities committed during the conquest and therefore amputate the Spanish root from the cultural tree, Fuentes argues that Latin America—a name invented by the French in the nineteenth century—should, in fact, be called "Indo-Afro-Ibero-America" (1990, 10) to highlight the hybrid multiplicity of cultural influences. He thus not only revalues indigenous and Iberian roots equally but also acknowledges African influences. Thus, Fuentes insists on the unique reality that is America to establish that the Spaniards culturally enriched the region through imperial expansion.

Going beyond the controversial efforts of his widely published attempts to reinsert Hispanic cultural identity objectively into not only Mexican but also wider Latin American consciousness, Fuentes contends that Latin American *mestizaje* began even before its colonial inception on American soil. He points to the fact that the population of the Iberian peninsula in the fifteenth century was already largely culturally mixed: "We were immediately mestizos. . . . We are the face of a striped West, as the Mexican poet Ramón López Velarde said, of Moor and Aztec—and, I would add, of Jewish and African, of Roman and Greek" ["Fuimos, inmediatamente, mestizos. . . . Somos el rostro de un occidente rayado, como dijo el poeta mexicano Ramón López Velarde, de moro y de azteca—y, añadiría yo, de judío y de africano, de romano y de griego"] (1993b, 56).[16] Fuentes also comments on the Spanish practice of *mestizaje* in the New World: "Sexual contact and integration were, surely, the norm in Iberian colonies, in contrast with the racial purity and puritanical hypocrisy of English colonies" ["El contacto y la integración sexuales fueron, ciertamente, la norma de las colonias ibéricas, en oposición a la pureza racial y la hipocresía puritana de las colonias inglesas"] (1992a, 155). Here Fuentes calls attention to one of the most important material differences between Iberian and British imperialism. Yet although societies that were produced by the Spanish practices of miscegenation and the British formation of settler colonies differ greatly, the long-standing and urgent issues of race occupy national consciousness across the board. Fuentes refocuses the Latin American debate on *mestizaje* by claiming that the multifaceted cultural mixture of Latin America springs not from the violent rape of the conquest but from preexisting multicultural conditions on the Iberian peninsula. Although his point with respect to Iberian *mestizaje* is well taken, the equation of Muslim and Spanish imperialism is an erroneous oversimplification.

In *El espejo enterrado* and *Tres discursos para dos aldeas*, Fuentes observes that cycles of history, migration, and cultural *mestizaje* continue to repeat themselves: "Well, the world to come will be as ours has been: a world of *mestizaje*, a world of migrations, but now they'll be instantaneous, not in caravels but in jets" ["Pues el mundo por venir será como ha sido el nuestro: un mundo de mestizaje, un mundo de migraciones, pero esta vez instantáneas, no en carabela, sino en *jet*"] (1993b, 70). Here it is important to note the indiscriminate use of the terms *mestizo* and *mestizaje* by Fuentes in these quotations. By employing the terms as he does in *El espejo enterrado* and in the stories of *El naranjo*, Fuentes undermines, in a number of ways, his own attempts to affirm cultural plurality.

First, he disregards the homogenizing effect of the terms. By definition, *mestizo*—whether it is used in reference to race or culture—means a new, third, element produced by the combination of two original components. Fuentes's search for the continuity within the Hispanic world, despite his celebration of its multifaceted nature, is a homogenizing pursuit. The use of such terms as *mestizo* and *mestizaje* is then emblematic of this contradiction in the author's intellectual framework. Terms better suited to his argument would be *heterogeneous*[17] (to describe multiethnic societies) and *transculturation* (to describe the historical processes that made them so). The troubling contradictions and terminological confusion, nevertheless, mirror current debates in multicultural societies worldwide. Whereas proponents of cultural pluralism advocate the maintenance of cultural identities, assimilationists believe in the amalgamation of all groups into the mainstream (Janzen 1994, 9). To what extent an amalgamated mainstream upholds the ideals of diversity and cultural tolerance, however, is an issue that has been satisfactorily articulated by neither assimilationists nor Fuentes himself.

Second, his use of the terms *mestizo* and *mestizaje* conjures up the decades-old homogenizing national identity of Mexico. Especially since the Revolution, Mexican governments have relied on *mestizofilia* to unite an ethnically diverse population under the banner of a single national culture by deeming the nation mestizo. But, whereas mestizophiles believe that "the goal is a country of cultural uniformity, which, of course, does not rule out racial diversity" ["la meta es un país con uniformidad cultural, lo cual desde luego, no excluye la diversidad racial]" (Basave Benítez 1993, 27), Guillermo Bonfil Batalla argues convincingly in his *México pro-*

fundo that "in a society that recognizes itself as plural and wants to be so, thinking about a national culture means abandoning the idea that it be uniform" (1996, 168).[18] Indeed, the concept of a single national culture depends not on an attitude of multiculturalism but on integrating the many into the whole.

Finally, the terms *mestizo* and *mestizaje* carry with them burdensome sexual baggage. As Silvia Spitta writes, "For Latin America, mestizaje, or miscegenation, often used synonymously with transculturation and/or translation, carries precisely those sexual connotations absent in the latter terms and yet crucial to explain the dynamics of cultural and sexual 'encounters'" (1995, 28 n. 58). Guillermo Bonfil Batalla agrees, arguing that using the term *mestizaje*, "is an inappropriate way to understand non-biological processes, such as those that occur in the cultures of different groups in contact, within the context of cultural domination" (1996, 17). Fuentes, like Mexican intellectuals of the 1940s and 1950s, tries to refocus the Latin American debate on culture by claiming that today's heterogeneous Latin America springs not from the violent rape of the conquest but from preexisting multicultural conditions on the Iberian peninsula. Unfortunately, his use of terms that consistently reference the sexual and the violent work against the goals of harmonic inclusion proposed in his text.

The history of conquest told in the first of the *El naranjo* stories, "Las dos orillas," is narrated through the filter of the author's philosophies of circular time and continual cultural *mestizaje*. By rewriting the past, Fuentes creates his own version of what happened and, in doing so, speaks to us of the present identities of the Americas—and of Mexico in particular—that will in turn enable the continent to determine its future. Fuentes, like Salinas de Gortari, uses his identity discourses and cultural valuations to guide Mexicans toward a progressive future. Through the enmeshing of memory and desire, past and future, Fuentes works to reconstruct notions of identity at a key commemorative moment in the history of the Americas.

Narration: The Power of Language and Communication

In "Las dos orillas," the early events of the conquest of Mexico are told through the eyes of Jerónimo de Aguilar, who was shipwrecked with Gonzalo Guerrero for eight years on the Yucatán and who later served Cortés and his troops as a translator on their march toward Tenochtitlán. Although—or perhaps because—Aguilar left no known writings, Fuentes manipulates his voice to reveal untold intrigues of the conquest. Aguilar is thus rescued from historical oblivion, given a narrative voice, and characterized as understanding both sides of the sixteenth-century encounters: Spanish and indigenous.

In this story, Aguilar speaks from the grave, bearing witness to his actions and experiences in the conquest of Mexico in a backwards chronology from the fall of Tenochtitlán to his "rescue" by Cortés's men on the Yucatán peninsula. His narration of the conquest is based loosely on the writings of Díaz del Castillo, whom Fuentes considers to be the first novelist of the Americas because of his use of "novelists' modern memory" ["la memoria moderna de los novelistas"], which narrates through such dramatic devices as characterization, detail, gossip, theatricality, and intrigue (1990, 80).[19] The privileging of Díaz del Castillo's text as foundational, however, is not exclusive, as Fuentes believes that "the Hispano-American novel is found (and finds itself) and is recognized in its foundational texts: the Chronicles of the Indies" ["la novela hispanoamericana se conoce (a sí misma, por los demás) y reconoce en sus textos de fundación: Las Crónicas de Indias"] (47). Fuentes therefore deems the texts seminal to modern Mexican reality.

In order to make sixteenth-century chronicles of conquest and colony speak to today's Latin America, Fuentes carefully rewrites them to serve his own ends. For example, Aguilar's narration closely parallels Fuentes's notions of memory recreating the past and desire formulating the future. As Aguilar recounts the events of the conquest, he also insists on the role that language plays in the construction of reality and the formation of the future. The central importance of language then lends itself to discussions about not only identity but also power, reality, and what Julián Ríos calls "la historia futurible" (1996, 231). Emphasis on the circularity of time segues with the narrator's observations on ironies and revisions of the past. By combining circular time, irony, and historical revisionism, Fuentes bolsters his refashioning of the historical record with his own personal literary and philosophical theses.

As both a historical figure and the narrator of "Las dos orillas," Aguilar personally represents the poignant role of language and communication at crucial moments in history, especially those of the conquest. Margo Glantz, a Mexican writer and critic, has written extensively on the conquest and colony, on their writings and on their figures. She notes that "language is, thus, one of the key elements of the Conquest" ["la lengua es, así, uno de los puntos esenciales de la Conquista"] (1994, 45).[20] Because Aguilar was bilingual (he spoke both Maya and Spanish) Cortés rescued him from the Yucatán so that he might serve as the translator—or literally, "la lengua"—for two worlds as they collided on Mexican soil. Todorov has also studied the role of the first translator in Mexico. In an analysis of Todorov's well-known and widely translated *La conquista de América: El problema del otro*, post-colonial theorists Bill Ashcroft, Gareth Griffiths, and Helen Tiffin write that

> the role of the first interpreter in the colonial contact is a profoundly ambiguous one. The ambivalent interpretive role and the significance of the interpretive site forms one of the major foci of the process of abrogation and appropriation. The interpreter always emerges from the dominated discourse. (1989, 80)

Aguilar, however, does not emerge from the dominated discourse. He is essentially Spanish, but he was immersed in Mesoamerican culture for eight years. Where his loyalties lie is anyone's guess, and Fuentes taps this uncertainty fully.

Aguilar is therefore a profoundly ambiguous narrator and translator in *El naranjo*. His services appear to contribute a great deal of understanding and clarity to Cortés's exchanges with the indigenous people. Before Aguilar's services were enlisted, the only means of communicating was signing (as in pantomime) with indigenous guides who spoke little Spanish. Yet in "Las dos orillas," Aguilar points to his absolute control over both the content and meaning of all communiqués as an opportunity to translate irresponsibly and incorrectly. First, on the coast of Tabasco, Aguilar demonstrates how he twists Cortés's proclamation that the Spaniards come in peace. He notes, "No one there knew that I lied as I translated for the conqueror, and yet I also told the truth. Hernán Cortés's words of peace, translated by me into words of war, provoked a shower of arrows" ["Nadie allí podía saber que traduciendo al conquistador yo mentía y sin embargo yo decía la verdad. Las palabras de paz de Hernán Cortés, traducidas por mí al vocabulario de la guerra, provocaron una lluvia de flechas"] (Fuentes 1993a, 40). His creative and subversive use of insinuation evolves into outright fabrication, especially in the meeting between Cortés and Cuauhtémoc, the last Aztec emperor. Aguilar admits:

> They could not understand one another. I translated as I pleased. I did not tell the defeated prince what Cortés really said; I instead placed a threat in the mouth of our leader. . . . I added, inventing on my own and mocking Cortés. . . . I translated, I betrayed, [and] I invented.

> [No podían comprenderse entre sí. Traduje a mi antojo. No le comuniqué al príncipe vencido lo que Cortés realmente le dijo, sino que puse en boca de nuestro jefe una amenaza. . . . Añadí, inventando por mi cuenta y burlándome de Cortés. . . . Traduje, traicioné, (y) inventé.] (18)

Bearing out the adage "traditore traduttore" (translation is traitorous),[21] Aguilar deems misrepresentation a simple game. Soon, however, he is shocked that the words he invents become reality and the threat he invents results in the torture of Cuauhtémoc:

> In a cruel comedy, the one I invented . . . the young emperor was the king of fools, dragged by the conquerors' chariot, crowned with cactus and finally hanged upside down, from the branches of a sacred silk cotton tree, like a hunted animal. Things occurred exactly as I falsely invented them.

[Comedia cruel, la misma que yo inventé . . . el joven emperador fue el rey de burlas, arrastrado por la carroza del vencedor, coronado de nopales y al cabo colgado de cabeza, desde las ramas de una ceiba sagrada, como un animal cazado. Sucedió exactamente lo que yo, mentirosamente, inventé.] (19)

Aguilar thus realizes that language is an extremely powerful tool because words construct reality. In this sense, Aguilar is a Spaniard awed by the native because, as Ashcroft and colleagues point out, the worldviews of oral cultures have always endowed words with "the power to bring into being the events or states they stand for, to embody rather than represent reality" (1989, 81). The constitutive power of his words causes Aguilar fright and guilt, but this very same power confirms Fuentes's contention that literature, specifically the manner in which one narrates the past or the future, contributes to our reality—whether or not the narrated events ever actually take place.[22]

Aguilar discovers the slippery nature of language and power when his translating abilities converge with those of Malintzin, the indigenous woman given to Cortés as a slave. Because she speaks both Maya and Nahuatl (called *mexicano* in the story, much as Solares referred to the Aztecs as *mexicanos*), she completes a communicative triangle with Cortés and Aguilar, which allows better communication with the Nahuatl-speaking subjects of the Aztec empire. She nevertheless represents a risk, because she too has the power to invent. At the outset, this does not worry Aguilar because, he says, "the Castilian version that reached the ears of the conquistador was always my own" ["la versión castellana que llegaba a oídos del conquistador, era siempre la mía"] (Fuentes 1993a, 32). When the competition and the politics between the two translators turns sexual, however—Malintzin, baptized as Marina, rejects advances by Aguilar and becomes Cortés's lover—Aguilar begins to use his words to willfully construct and manipulate certain historical events and outcomes.

He once again realizes, "Language was more than dignity; it was power, and more than power it was life itself that bolstered my intentions" ["La lengua era más que la dignidad, era el poder; y más que el poder era la vida misma que animaba mis propósitos"] (36), and he sets out to convince Moctezuma to save his empire from certain ruin through an opportune attack on Cortés and his men. Aguilar therefore reveals to Moctezuma that Spanish troops have arrived and are looking to capture Cortés, who is considered to be in open rebellion of the Spanish king's orders.[23] Here, Aguilar tries to humanize Cortés as an insignificant and disobedient subject to another sovereign, not a deity [*teul*]. The treacherous translator acknowledges, "I gave the King the secret of Cortés's weakness, in the same way that Doña Marina had given Cortés the secret to the Aztecs' weakness: the discord, the envy, the struggle between brothers, which affected Spain as they did Mexico" ["Le di al Rey el secreto de la debilidad de Cortés, como doña Marina le había dado a Cortés el secreto de la debilidad Azteca: la división, la discordia, la pugna entre hermanos, que lo mismo afectaba a España que a México"] (27). Yet he realizes the futility of his intentions, because "Moctezuma listened only to the gods; I was not one" ["Moctezuma sólo escuchaba a los dioses; yo no lo era"] (31). Moctezuma's unwillingness or inability to act and to defend his empire from the Spaniards is thus textually rendered as a misunderstanding. As we saw earlier, in *La conquista de América: El problema del otro*, Todorov describes Moctezuma as having a largely ritual perspective wherein his most important communication took place with deities rather than with mortals. Although Todorov presents a well-argued thesis, no real documentation exists with respect to why Moctezuma acted—or failed to act—the way that he did. Fuentes employs Aguilar's fictive narrative voice to consecrate a new version (and therefore a new reality) of unrecorded historical events. In a situation in which Aguilar lacks access to, and therefore power over, the communiqués to Cortés, he turns coat and tries to manipulate Moctezuma with his words.

Indeed, the clearest illustration of the link between word and power comes at the moment in which Aguilar discovers that Marina has learned Spanish and become trilingual, thus managing to monopolize all translation duties and curtail any need for Aguilar's services. His reaction is one of pure rage, fed by the shame and impotency of his powerlessness:

I realized that Jerónimo de Aguilar was no longer needed [because] the diabolical female was translating everything; Marina daughter of a whore and a whore herself had learned to speak Spanish; the scoundrel, the traitor, the expert in sucking, the conquistador's concubine had stolen my professional singularity from me, my indisputable function, my—to coin a word—monopoly over the Castilian language.... Malinche had ripped the Spanish language from Cortés's sex, she had sucked it out of him, [and] she had castrated him of it without his knowing, confusing mutilation with pleasure.

[Me di cuenta de que Jerónimo de Aguilar ya no hacía falta, (porque) la hembra diabólica lo estaba traduciendo todo, la tal Marina hideputa y puta ella misma había aprendido a hablar el español, la malandrina, la mohatrera, la experta en mamonas, la coima del conquistador, me había arrebatado mi singularidad profesional, mi indiscutible función, vamos, por acuñar mi vocablo, mi *monopolio* de la lengua castellana. . . . La Malinche le había arrancado la lengua española al sexo de Cortés, se la había chupado, (y) se la había *castrado* sin que él lo supiera, confundiendo la mutilación con el placer.] (Fuentes 1993a, 34)

His tirade demonstrates the urgent struggle for power and control that ensues when two languages vie for dominance. Aguilar reacts so harshly not because Marina has learned Spanish, the dominant language, but because she now *controls* all means of communication.

Interestingly, Aguilar's rage reflects many of the issues of power and language scrutinized by postcolonial studies. For example, stripped of his work, his importance, and his evidently phallic "lengua," Aguilar mourns, "Poor me, Jerónimo de Aguilar, dead all this time with a split tongue, forked, like the plumed serpent. Who am I, [and] what am I good for?" ["Pobre de mí, Jerónimo de Aguilar, muerto todo este tiempo con la lengua cortada a la mitad, bífida, como la serpiente emplumada. ¿Quién soy, (y) para qué sirvo?"] (Fuentes 1993a, 35).[24] His identity, then, hinges on his language, a symbolic parallel for his sexual member and all the concomitant issues of power that they wield. Whereas the colonizer traditionally controls the communicative processes and production, here a native—a woman, no less—takes over. The verbal interplay with the word *tongue* [*lengua*] and the documented sexual nature of the relationship between Cortés and Marina also introduces the well-worn issues of seduction and betrayal, often equated with *malinchismo*, or selling out. Octavio Paz contends that *malinchistas* are "the proponents of opening Mexico to the outside world: the true children of Malinche, who is the Chingada in person" ["los partidarios de que México se abra al exterior: los verdaderos hijos de la Malinche, que es la Chingada en persona"] (1993, 95). Aguilar blames Malinche for his shame, which is augmented by her status as a slave and a woman. He feels the cultural rape that many postcolonial writers express symbolically.

Usually, in cases of conquest, a written culture colonizes a formerly oral one and rapidly silences native memory and voice. The pen as the key to power—in the form of knowledge—serves as the phallus in this cultural rape (Ashcroft et al. 1989, 85). In the case of "Las dos orillas," however, Aguilar reveals how Marina's purely oral language manipulated events *before* written versions were penned, and calls into question the veracity of colonial chronicles.[25] Her tongue, not her pen, becomes an instrument of the deception and violence perceived by Aguilar. Her sexual access to Cortés links seduction and carnal pleasure to the betrayal felt by Aguilar, and her singular ability to wield a communicative weapon allows her to commit the worst violence against Aguilar's manhood: castration—albeit cultural and linguistic.

Aguilar, thus unable to maintain his position as translator, becomes, in his words, a failure "in my efforts to make Cortés fail" ["en mi intento de hacer fracasar a Cortés"] (Fuentes 1993a, 53). In an attempt to compensate for his shortcomings, Aguilar once again calls on language's power to construct reality. He decides to launch a *postmortem* communicative project to modify history. Narrating from the grave, he recounts his memories of the past and his desires for the future—thus creating the text that we read and the version that we remember. He begins his tale and the story by noting, "I have seen it all. I would like to tell it all. But my appearances in history are severely limited by what was said of me" ["Lo he visto todo. Quisiera contarlo todo. Pero mis apariciones en la historia están severamente limitadas a lo que de mí se dijo"] (12). He has been marginalized from history because Marina ultimately eclipses him as translator, and all that is known of him stems from Díaz del Castillo's mention of him a mere fifty-eight times (by the count of the fictional Aguilar) in *Historia verdadera de la conquista de la Nueva España*.[26] By reinserting Aguilar into the history of the conquest, Fuentes creates a new vantage of sixteenth-century events. Aguilar unapologetically narrates with Cortés's thirst for power and with the advantageous hindsight of Díaz del Castillo. Yet Aguilar's version of the past is also decidedly modern. He acknowledges that he is an impossible narrator riddled with self-doubt. The narrative takes place in a state of tension, as Aguilar is unable to rest in his grave, haunted by guilt-ridden memories of Aztec gold being shipped to Spain in heavily laden boats (15) or the crying face of Cuauhtémoc (17). These images serve as sources of shame to Aguilar in view of his failure to save the Aztec world. These scenes and what he calls the ironies of history disturb his eternal rest—"my eyes cannot close in peace" ["mis ojos no llegan a cerrarse en paz"] (15)—and he must therefore narrate in order to regain both his position and his potency.

In narrating and naming anew, Aguilar reconstitutes what is commonly known of the past, this time through the looking glass of language. Because he emphasizes the roles played by him and by Marina in manipulating the communicative processes of the encounter, we come to see that history is constructed by word more than by deed. Aguilar's tale therefore undermines the traditional historical record as it reinvents various temporalities—past, present, and future.

Aguilar, who has already retold his active attempts at subverting history, shows how his telling of history—his story—is a constructive process as well. Aguilar begins to signal this aspect of his storytelling as he recounts the Mayan myth of creation, where "the world was created by two gods, one named Heart of Heaven and the other Heart of Earth. Upon meeting, between them they made all things fertile by naming them" ["el mundo fue creado por dos dioses, el uno llamado Corazón de los Cielos y el otro Corazón de la Tierra. Al encontrarse, entrambos fertilizaron todas las cosas al nombrarlas"] (Fuentes 1993a, 52).[27] Humans are, therefore, created to maintain the world through use of the word: "And thus men were born, with the purpose of maintaining divine creation on a daily basis in the same way that the earth, the heavens, and everything therein came to be: through the word" ["Y así nacieron los hombres, con el propósito de mantener día con día la creación divina mediante lo mismo que dio orígen a la tierra, el cielo y cuanto en ellos se halla: la palabra"] (52–53). Words, and especially teleology, therefore, not only name but also call into existence (as seen in Aguilar's disastrous encounter with Cuauhtémoc). Aguilar ponders this:

> I wonder if an event is not narrated, whether it actually occurs. What is not invented is only recorded. One more thing: a catastrophe (and all wars are) is disputed only if it is narrated. The telling outlasts the war. The telling disputes the order of things. Silence only confirms that order.

[Me pregunto si un evento no es narrado, ocurre en realidad. Pues lo que no se inventa sólo se consigna. Algo más: una catástrofe (y toda guerra lo es) sólo es disputada si es narrada. La narración la sobrepasa. La narración disputa el orden de las cosas. El silencio lo confirma.] (58)

Having been a man of words—"the transitory master of words" ["el amo transitorio de las palabras"] (53)—Aguilar must speak up; he must narrate from the grave in order to regain his place in the past but also in order to use language and the word to instruct his audience.

At the end of his narration, he comments on and defends the trite use of "the form of this narration, which is a story told in reverse" ["la forma de este relato, que es una cuenta al revés"] (Fuentes 1993a, 59) by saying, "I like using it today, starting with ten to arrive at zero, with the goal of pointing out perpetual beginnings of stories perpetually unfinished, but on the condition that they are presided over by the word, as in the Mayan story of the Gods of the Heavens and the Earth" ["Me gusta emplearla hoy, partiendo de diez para llegar a cero, a fin de indicar, en vez, un perpetuo reinicio de historias perpetuamente inacabadas, pero sólo a condición de que las presida, como en el cuento maya de los Dioses de los Cielos y de la Tierra, la palabra"] (59). His final insistence on language and narration again lays bare the circular workings of time in the work of Fuentes.

The Reverse of the Conquest and the Construction of a Different Past

The organizing principal of *El naranjo,* as we have seen, is a circular, cyclical conception of time. In the ancient cultures of Mesoamerica, time was conceived of as a cycle that needed constant renewal. Humans were responsible for offerings and sacrifices to appease gods who could ensure that the sun would continue to rise and rain would nourish crops.[28] As Aguilar notes in the story "Las dos orillas," Moctezuma, the Aztec emperor, had one principal responsibility: "His obligation consisted of always being the first man to ask, in the name of us all: Will the sun come up again? . . . Will it rain again, will the maize grow, will the river flow, [and] will the beast bellow again?" ["Su obligación consistía en ser siempre, en nombre de todos, ese primer hombre que pregunta:—¿Volverá a amanecer? . . . ¿Volvería a llover, a crecer el maíz, a correr el río, (y) a bramar la fiera?"] (Fuentes 1993a, 30). Aguilar also describes encountering this cyclical concept during his experience with the Mayan culture:

I will always remember the first funeral ceremony we attended, because in it we were able to distinguish a celebration of origins and the continuity of all things, identical to what we celebrate when we are born. Death, proclaimed the faces, the gestures, the musical rhythms, is the source of life; death is the first birth.

[Recordaré siempre la primera ceremonia fúnebre a la que asistimos, pues en ella distinguimos una celebración del principio y continuidad de todas las cosas, idéntico a lo que celebramos al nacer. La muerte, proclamaban los rostros, los gestos, los ritmos musicales, es el origen de la vida, la muerte es el primer nacimiento.] (51)

Thus, as he speaks from the grave, with this perspective on what he has witnessed, he regards history—especially the history of the conquest—as a cycle that is repeated and renewed globally ad infinitum. Cycles of alternating submission and dominance, conquest and colony, appear transformed and transfigured across centuries and continents in each of the five stories of *El naranjo*. The renewed cycles show history to be repetitive, further undermining our notion of time as progressive.

For Fuentes, as we know, memory creates the past—or history as we know it—and literature gives verbal reality to an unwritten part of the world. Aguilar reconstitutes what we know of the conquest by retelling it from his perspective—whether or not it actually occurred as such. Yet Fuentes also contends that desire creates and formulates the possible future ["la historia futurible"]. Aguilar's growing desire to save the indigenous people from certain annihilation by the Spaniards spurs "una historia futurible"—a modification of the "reverse of the conquest." According to Fuentes, the "reverse of the conquest" originated as a question posed by Francisco de Vitoria at the University of Salamanca in the sixteenth-century debate over Spanish atrocities in the New World: "What would you have thought if, instead of conquering the American Indians, they had conquered Spain and treated us the way we treat them?" ["¿Qué habrían pensado ustedes si en vez de conquistar a los indios americanos, son éstos los que conquistan España y nos tratan a nosotros como nosotros los tratamos a ellos?"] (1993b, 60). Thus, at the end of his backwards story, Aguilar narrates how, from the tomb, he inspires Guerrero "to answer conquest with conquest" ["para que contestase a la conquista con la conquista"] (Fuentes 1993a, 53). The last segment of the story, numbered "0," tells of a Mesoamerican cycle of conquest on the Iberian peninsula, deepening the sense of historical déjà vu as it narratively mirrors and parallels the first segment, numbered "10."

In these two segments, respectively, Aguilar bears witness to the similarities and differences of conquest exhibited as the Spanish conquerors overtake Mexico and the Mayan conquerors then overrun Spain. He tells of the fall of two great cities, one Aztec and the other Andalusian. He sees the Spanish cannons and Mayan fire throwers ignite both the waters of Tenochtitlán's lagoon and the Guadalquivir River. Pagan temples are destroyed—in Tenochtitlán for being pluritheistic and in Cádiz and Seville for being monotheistic. The day after this destruction, new temples are erected with the very stones from the rubble. The Templo Mayor is reborn as a Christian church and the Giralda of Seville is reborn as a "temple of four religions, inscribed with the word of Christ, Muhammad, Abraham, and Quetzalcoátl" ["templo de las cuatro religiones, inscrito con el verbo de Cristo, Mahoma, Abraham y Quetzalcoátl"] (Fuentes 1993a, 54).[29] Where the Spaniards destroyed and outlawed the objects and the practices that they found to be repugnant in the Aztec world—most notably human sacrifices—the Maya take action against the members of the Santa Inquisición, "burning them in the public plazas from Logroño to Barcelona. We burned their archives too, along with the laws of purity of blood and ancient Christianity" ["quemándoles en las plazas públicas de Logroño a Barcelona. Sus archivos los quemamos también, junto con las leyes de pureza de sangre y cristianismo antiguo"] (54). The Maya combat an image problem similar to the Spanish "leyenda negra" and Aguilar defends their sacrifices of Spaniards as "misunderstood by all of the humanist poets, philosophers, and Spanish Erasmians" ["mal comprendida por todos los humanistas poetas, filósofos, y erasmianos españoles"] (55).

Finally, Aguilar responds to modern history's attempt to explain the unthinkable conquest of the Aztec empire by a ragtag troop of five hundred Spaniards through the use of their secret weapon, the horse. He contends instead that the secret weapon of the Maya was surprise: "In Mexico, the Spaniards, that is to say, the white gods, bearded and blond, were expected. Here, in contrast, no one expected anyone. It was a complete surprise" ["En México, los españoles, es decir, los dioses blancos, barbudos y rubios, eran esperados. Aquí, en cambio, nadie esperaba a nadie. La sorpresa fue total"] (Fuentes 1993a, 56). Such details demonstrate that a "reverse" conquest would not have been a true reversal but rather a repetition of the cycle of discovery, conquest, and colonization, albeit with slight changes in nuance.[30]

At various other points in his narration, Aguilar pauses to reflect on these cycles of empire. As he and Guerrero spend time on the Yucatán peninsula, they contemplate the Mayan ruins of "the splendid cities, that resembled the biblical descriptions of Babylon, that kept watch over the details of everyday life in the village" ["las grandes ciudades, parecidas a las bíblicas descripciones de la Babilonia, que como centineles vigilaban la minucia del quehacer diario en la aldea"] (Fuentes 1993a, 48). They decide that great and powerful peoples "like all great powers, depended on the weakness of the people, and they needed to fight other strong nations in order to convince themselves of their own power. We were able to deduce that the Indian nations destroyed each other" ["como todos, dependían de la debilidad y necesitaban, para convencerse de su propio poder, combatir a otras fuertes naciones. Pudimos deducir que las naciones indias se destruyeron entre sí"] (49). This in-fighting and division is what Cortés uses against the Aztec empire to divide and conquer it. Aguilar had tried to alert Moctezuma to the fact that the very same weakness could be used against Cortés, when he noted "division, discord, envy, the struggle between brothers, that affected Spain just as it did Mexico: half of the country perpetually dying at the hands of the other half" ["la división, la discordia, la envidia, la pugna entre hermanos, que lo mismo afectaba a España que a México: una mitad del país perpetuamente muriéndose de la otra mitad"] (27).

Another historical event that Aguilar narrates—through great hostility, because it illustrates his own misfortune—is that of the role of Marina in this (hi)story of power, control, and intrigue. According to Aguilar, Marina turned Cortés away from any counsel but her own, isolating him and controlling all exchanges between Spaniards and indigenous people. That an enslaved indigenous woman could have determined the course of history as profoundly as Aguilar claims in "Las dos orillas" is both improbable and unlikely. Still, recent revisions of Marina have been largely vindicatory, showing her to possess great intelligence and a penchant for strategic plotting. Fuentes, aware of the fact that Marina's stigma as a simple traitor is being reworked in Mexico, described her in an interview as "a rebellious woman, a gestating woman, an independent woman, a woman who decided that she, knowing herself to be fatal, was going to construct something, a history, a child, a nation, a language. . . . She is a founder, a bearer. She is not a traitor" ["una mujer rebelde, una mujer gestadora, una mujer independiente, una mujer que decide que ella, que sabe que es fatal, va a construir algo, una historia, un hijo, un país, una lengua. . . . Ella es una fundadora, una gestadora. No es una traidora"] (quoted in Zeran 1994, 32). Yet Fuentes also undermines the value of her vindication when he says outright, "What happens in Mexico is that Malinche is the country's founding mother, but since she is Cortés's whore and a traitor, well, it's terrible to descend from a traitorous whore. . . . But there is a movement now—I think many women are participating in it—toward giving Malinche her place as a woman and understanding her circumstances" ["Lo que pasa en México es que la Malinche es la madre fundadora del país, pero como es la puta de Cortés, y la traidora, pues, qué terrible descender de una puta traidora. . . . Pero ahora hay un movimiento—yo creo que muchas mujeres participan de él—de darle su puesto de mujer a la Malinche y de entenderla en su circunstancia"] (1996).

Although attempts have been made to further understand the figure of Marina, her treatment in "Las dos orillas" reflects the extent to which she is still judged. Here Aguilar employs a double-edged narrative with reference to Marina. His enumeration of Marina's names signals a number of the ways she has been represented: "Her name was Malintzin, which means 'penitence.' That same day the Mercederian Olmedo baptized her 'Marina,' making her the first Christian woman in New Spain. But her people called her 'La Malinche,' the traitor" ["Se llamaba Malintzin, que quiere decir 'Penitencia,' Ese mismo día el mercedario Olmedo la bautizó 'Marina,' convirtiéndola en la primera cristiana de la Nueva España. Pero su pueblo le puso 'La Malinche,' la traidora"] (Fuentes 1993a, 41).

Ironically, by calling attention to her status as the first Christian in New Spain, Aguilar also points to her dubious sexual purity, as it was common Spanish policy to "baptize women before they sinned with them" ["bautizar a las mujeres antes de pecar con ellas"] (Frost 1994, 119). Marina's names—each given to her, not chosen by her—tell of a life marked by transgression, redemption, and condemnation. As we have seen, these names construct her by calling into being or consecrating certain visions of her., Depending on the context and his feelings toward her, Aguilar uses all three names in referring to her. He muses pityingly:

> Poor Marina, abandoned by her conquistador, carrying a fatherless child, stigmatized by her people with the mark of betrayal, and, because of all that, mother and origin of a new nation, which could be born and grow only against the burdens of abandonment, illegitimacy, and betrayal. . . . Poor Malinche but rich Malinche too, who with her man determined history.

> [Pobre Marina, abandonada al cabo por su conquistador, cargada con un hijo sin padre, estigmatizada por su pueblo con el mote de la traición y, sin embargo, por todo ello, madre y origen de una nación nueva, que acaso sólo podía nacer y crecer en contra de las cargas del abandono, la bastardía y la traición. . . . Pobre Malinche pero rica Malinche también, que con su hombre determinó la historia.] (Fuentes 1993a, 43)

Aguilar alternately pities Marina as a suffering Christian and feels unabated jealousy toward Malinche, reflecting the negativism in the *malinchista* equation of Malinche-traitor.

In the story, Aguilar also alternates between admiration and contempt, attraction and repulsion for Marina's actions. When she learns Spanish without Aguilar's help, demonstrating her linguistic abilities, she is berated by Aguilar as a "daughter of a whore and a whore herself" ["hideputa y puta ella misma"] (Fuentes 1993a, 34). She proves her value as a linguist, a strategist, and a cultural liaison when she reveals the secret of Aztec weakness to Cortés: division. This could be deemed either an act of loyalty to her master or as the betrayal of "her" people.[31] The case of Marina presents us with other contradictions as well. Her power as a translator conflicts with her status as a slave; her importance as Cortés's lover defies the unimportance of woman in the male activities of conquest; and, finally, her native ethnicity complicates her categorization as victor [*vencedora*] or vanquished [*vencida*]. Aguilar demonstrates the dual nature of Marina's role in the conquest, judging her to be a woman who "bore the deep pain and resentment, but also the hope, of her state; she had to risk everything to save her life and have descendants" ["acarreaba el dolor y el rencor profundos, pero también la esperanza, de su estado; tuvo que jugarse toda entera para salvar la vida y tener descendencia"] (31). Although he tries to understand her actions, he condemns Marina for what he perceives to be her shortsighted and egocentric view of her role in history. Despite recent currents of revisionism, Marina, still caught between the images of rebel and whore, more often than not is deemed the latter.

Fuentes views Marina as the mother of Mexico, the woman who "established the central act of our multiracial civilization, mixing sex with language" ["estableció el hecho central de nuestra civilización multirracial, mezclando el sexo con el lenguaje"] (1992a, 125), valorizing her role in the ethnic and cultural makeup of the emergent society. But the fact remains that in "Las dos orillas" Aguilar sarcastically condemns her for her lack of vision. He accuses her of *malinchismo*, because he alone professes to understand both sides: Mexico and Spain. He even fancies himself the first indigenist, as he tells how he came to love the Maya for their "sweetness and dignity" ["dulzura y dignidad"] (Fuentes 1993a, 48) and for their ecological commitment to the earth. Having come close to losing his ability to speak Spanish after eight years among the Maya, Aguilar literally becomes a Maya (44): He hopes for and works toward an indigenous victory against the Spaniards (28), he tries to prevent Cortés's progress toward Tenochtitlán (38), and he considers Mexico his "adopted homeland" ["patria adoptiva"] (31). Aguilar's multicultural perspective, which valorizes the indigenous, differentiates him not only from the other Spaniards in this story but also from those in other novels by Fuentes, most notably in his encyclopedic *Terra Nostra*. Fuentes himself comments that the Spaniards in *Terra Nostra* "could think of nothing else than to destroy the unknown. . . . One must become the other; only in this way can one achieve the unity of his being" (1980, 415). Aguilar, better than any, demonstrates the achievement of the unity of being that faces today's Latin Americans, whose lineage is rooted on both shores. As a narrator, moreover, he signals the movement in Fuentes's work, from *Terra Nostra* to *El naranjo*, in which a more pluralistic voice embraces Otherness.

Moving toward Multiculturalism

Because of the multiplicity of his perspective and sensibilities in "Las dos orillas," Aguilar envisions a future for Marina and for himself that he believes would have radically altered the historic events and makeup of Mexico. When he first sees her, his desire for her is so strong that his gaze literally tells her, "I speak your Mayan tongue, and I love your people; I don't know how to combat the fatality of what is happening; I cannot stop it, but perhaps you and I together, Indian and Spaniard, can save something" ["Yo hablo tu lengua maya y quiero a tu pueblo, no sé cómo combatir la fatalidad de cuanto ocurre, no puedo impedirlo, pero acaso tú y yo juntos, india y español, podamos salvar algo"] (Fuentes 1993a, 41). He also envisions having a son with her so that "together she and I, Marina and Jerónimo, masters of languages, could also become masters of the land, an invincible couple because we understood the two voices of Mexico, that of men and also that of the gods" ["juntos ella y yo, Marina y Jerónimo, dueños de las lenguas, seríamos también dueños de las tierras, pareja invincible porque entendíamos las dos voces de México, la de los hombres pero también la de los dioses"] (42).[32]

The fact that she rejects his advances and by the next day has become Cortés's lover means that his dream of harmonious cultural *mestizaje* evaporates, never to be realized.[33] Aguilar's imagined world of words is, in reality, unattainable. As a narrator, however, he effects a degree of cultural *mestizaje* in Guerrero's "reverse of the conquest." Because Aguilar's dream of saving the ancient world with Marina's help is truncated by her lack of participation, he drops her from his narration of the possible future, or "historia futurible." Thus, she remains a mere presence in "Las dos orillas." She has not been written into history this time either but remains a being constituted only by secondhand quotations describing her person and her actions. She is therefore neither the focus of nor a factor in the last fantasized story segment concerning the cycles of conquest.

Instead, "Las dos orillas" progresses toward a more universal and generalized prescription of plurality in Latin American cultures. This textual project reflects the views of Fuentes on both plurality and inclusion—his continued use of such terms as *mestizo* and *mestizaje* to describe them notwithstanding. As noted earlier, in *El espejo enterrado* (1992a) and *Tres discursos para dos aldeas* (1993b), Fuentes focuses on the repetition of cycles of history, migration, and cultural *mestizaje*. Another Mexican writer, Víctor Flores Olea, echoes this sentiment when he notes that, as a result of the constant and most recent migrations, "by definition, culture is always the result of *mestizaje,* child of the combination of similar elements yet contradictory and opposed" ["por definición, la cultura es siempre el resultado de un mestizaje, hija de la combinación de elementos afines y aun contradictorios y opuestos"] (1995, 77). Cultural mixing has been a part of Latin American reality for at least five centuries and will be a beneficial strength and an absolute necessity for the continent, contends Fuentes. In *El espejo enterrado,* he writes:

Is there anyone better prepared than we, the Spaniards, the Hispanic Americans, and the Hispanics in the United States, to deal with the central theme of encounter with the other under the modern conditions of the coming century? We are indigenous peoples, blacks, Europeans, but, above all, mestizos. We are Greeks and Iberians, Romans and Jews, Arabs, Christians, and Gypsies. That is to say: Spain and the New World are centers of incorporation and not exclusion. When we exclude, we betray and impoverish ourselves. When we include, we enrich and find ourselves.

[¿Hay alguien mejor preparado que nosotros, los españoles, los hispanoamericanos y los hispanos en los Estados Unidos para tratar este tema central del encuentro con el otro en las condiciones de la modernidad del siglo venidero? Somos indígenas, negros, europeos, pero sobre todo, mestizos. Somos griegos e iberos, romanos y judíos, árabes, cristianos y gitanos. Es decir: España y el Nuevo Mundo son centros de incorporación y no de exclusión. Cuando excluimos nos traicionamos y empobrecemos. Cuando incluimos nos enriquecemos y nos encontramos a nosotros mismos.] (1992a, 379)

Fuentes proffers hope for the future with his thesis of plurality: "May we know how to nurture the plurality of our cultures so that they are reflected in our public institutions, providing them with vigor, substance, and justice" ["Que sepamos animar la pluralidad de nuestras culturas para que se reflejen en nuestras instituciones públicas, dándoles vigor, sustancia y justicia"] (1993b, 74).

Plurality and justice form a pair that Fuentes—and many other Latin Americans—hoped would lead to wider democratization in the near future. From old limiting notions of Mexican mestizo identity, Fuentes recognized the opening of Mexico in many senses as a transition to "the admission of an identity more ample than what we knew, an identification with democracy and the conviction that civil society and its culture have to be the protagonists of the future" ["una admisión de una identidad más ámplia de la que nosotros mismos vimos, una identificación con la democracia y una convicción de que la sociedad civil y su cultura tienen que ser los protagonistas del futuro"] (1996). This transition closely parallels Salinas de Gortari's 1988 campaign promises of democratic political reform and the protection of the pluricultural constituency that would benefit from it.[34] Salinas de Gortari took two important steps toward this goal: (1) when he created the IFE (Instituto Federal Electoral)[35] and (2) when he amended the constitution to term Mexico a pluricultural nation.

In his story, Fuentes discards the simplistic view of Mexicans as half Spanish (Cortés) and half indigenous (Marina) that is so prevalent in Mexican identity discourse. Instead, he uses his theory of cyclical history—in this case focusing on migratory *mestizaje*—to create an imagined space in which to postulate the difference that a modicum of multicultural recognition of difference and tolerance toward the Other would have made in the sixteenth century. As Guerrero and his Mayan soldiers take the Iberian peninsula, they mix with an already richly integrated society:

It was growing *mestizaje,* Indian and Spanish, but also Arab and Jew, that in a few years crossed the Pyrenees and spread over all of Europe.... The complexion of the old continent instantly became darker, as that of southern, Arabian Spain already was.

[Fue un mestizaje acrecentado, indio y español, pero también árabe y judío, que en pocos años cruzó los Pirineos y desparramó por toda Europa.... La pigmentación del viejo continente se hizo en seguida más oscura, como ya lo era la de la España levantina y árabe.] (1993a, 54)

The Maya then repeal exclusionist laws and unjust expulsions, readmitting both Jews and Moors, and construct a fictive literary universe, "simultaneously new and recovered, permeable, complex, fertile, born from the contact among the cultures, frustrating the fatal purifying plan of the Catholic Kings" ["a la vez nuevo y recuperado, permeable, complejo, fecundo, [que] nació del contacto entre las culturas, frustrando el fatal designio purificador de los Reyes Católicos"] (55).

The importance of tolerance and plurality in the new empire is underscored by a symbolic dream that Aguilar says he has passed on to his compatriot Guerrero. In his dream, the image of Cuauhtémoc, the last Aztec emperor, appears crying, but "instead of tears, down one cheek ran gold and down the other silver, cutting furrows in them like a knife would, leaving behind permanent wounds" ["en vez de lágrimas, por una mejilla le rueda el oro y por la otra la plata, surcándolas como cuchilladas y dejando para siempre en ellas una herida"] (Fuentes 1993a, 59). Aguilar has been haunted by Cuauhtémoc's image ever since the playful but fatal mistranslation of Cortés's words led to Cuauhtémoc's torture and, later, his death. The fact that the dream visits Aguilar upon the death of Cuauhtémoc and then reappears to Guerrero, who is seated authoritatively on a throne in the castle [alcázar] in Seville—both scenes of fallen and emerging empires—signifies the danger of losing or denying any one part of a plural heritage produced by the intersecting paths of expanding empires. Here it is ironic that Cuauhtémoc's appearance should signify the need to affirm every element of a multiracial society. In the narrative's "reverse of the conquest," therefore, we begin to see a contradiction that will plague Fuentes's story. Despite his insistent portrayal of cyclical cultural mixing and his hailing of the intersections of race as the key to a new virtual universe, Fuentes undeniably privileges a few cultural and racial elements of that society-to-come.

Multiculturalism Betrayed and a Pluricultural Mexico Proposed

Despite the text's enthusiastic portrayal of Latin American cultural plurality, Fuentes's views of Latin American identity hinge on the Spanish language in the Americas as the main cohesive component of Hispanic culture. Aguilar explains why, when he narrates the conquest of Spain by a Mayan and Caribbean armada, he maintains Spanish as the language of this fictive empire:

> The Spanish language had already learned to speak Phoenician, Greek, Latin, Arabic, and Hebrew; it was now ready to receive the contributions of Maya and Aztec, to enrich itself with them, to enrich them, to give them flexibility, imagination, communicability, and writing, turning them into living languages, not languages of empires but languages of people and their encounters, infections, dreams, and nightmares too.

[La lengua española ya había aprendido, antes, a hablar en fenecio, griego, latín, árabe y hebreo; estaba lista para recibir, ahora, los aportes mayas y aztecas, enriquerse con ellos, enriquecerlos, darles flexibilidad, imaginación, comunicabilidad y escritura, convirtiéndolas a todas en lenguas vivas, no lenguas de imperios, sino de los hombres y sus encuentros, contagios, sueños, y pesadillas también.] (1993a, 56–57)

Despite Aguilar's energetic defense of the Spanish language's ability to incorporate, adapt, and enrich, this one glaring detail—Spanish as the language of the new empire—calls into question the cultural plurality of Guerrero's Iberian Eden in "Las dos orillas." Even with the noted darkening of pigmentation and the increase in tolerance on the Iberian peninsula after Guerrero's invasion, the text fails to demonstrate its own maintenance of plurality in the end. In this text, the narration of segment "0"—the reverse—should, logic tells us, be written in an indigenous tongue or at least make an effort to appear as a translation into Spanish or an imagined Creole language. Instead, Fuentes's overvalorization of the Spanish language, thanks to his assimilationist values, once again misses the multicultural mark. Despite the possible homogenizing effect of his use of such terms as *mestizo* and *mestizaje,* here, similarly, his assertion that mere linguistic adaptability and incorporation are sufficient to transform an imperial tongue into a language of encounter completely ignores the power differential involved in conquest.

Fuentes views Spanish as perhaps the greatest legacy of the conquest. In *Geografía de la novela,* he quotes Chilean Nobel prize-winning poet Pablo Neruda as follows: "What a wonderful language mine is; what a wonderful language we inherited from the fierce conquistadors. . . . We lost. . . . We won. . . . They took the gold, and they left the gold. . . . They took everything, and they left everything. . . . They left words" ["Qué buen idioma el mío, qué buena lengua heredamos de los conquistadores torvos. . . . Salimos perdiendo. . . . Salimos ganando. . . . Se llevaron el oro y nos dejaron el oro. . . . Se lo llevaron todo y nos dejaron todo. . . . Nos dejaron las palabras"] (quoted in Fuentes 1995, 170). Although Neruda was an outspoken critic of imperialism, the utter lack of criticism here on the parts of both Neruda and Fuentes bespeaks a real denial about the cost of the colonial past that writers in other postcolonial societies do not share. As Mignolo makes clear in *The Darker Side of the Renaissance,* there is still the "need to look at the interactions between people, institutions and cultural productions aligned by relations of power and domination, and the need to look at postcolonial theories in their connections with colonial legacies" (1995, xiv).

Indeed, in other postcolonial cultures, language is and has been an important issue that calls into question the very essence of national identity. During colonial domination, "language becomes the medium through which a hierarchical structure of power is perpetuated, and the medium through which conceptions of 'truth,' 'order,' and 'reality' become established" (Ashcroft, et al. 1989, 7). Mignolo takes the concept of language's all-encompassing nature a step further in his description of "languaging." He writes that we should move "away from the idea that language is a fact (e.g., a system of syntactic, semantic and phonetic rules) toward the idea that speaking and writing are moves that orient and manipulate social domains of interaction" (1999, 56). Thus, at the moment when the imperial tongue displaces native tongues, imperial cultural control is cemented, because it is through the empire's communicative system that reality is then constituted (Kachru 1995, 293). Antonio de Nebrija, the fifteenth-century humanist, affirmed this long ago in *Gramática de la lengua castellana,* when he wrote, "Language has always been a companion of empire" ["Siempre la lengua fue compañera del imperio"] (1492, n.p.). In addition, it is reported—albeit anecdotally—that when Queen Isabel asked Nebrija about the value of his book on Spanish grammar, he responded, "Language, your majesty, is the perfect instrument of an empire" ["La lengua, Majestad, es el instrumento perfecto del imperio"]. Yet, Fuentes's text denies that the Spanish language is an imperial tool in Guerrero's fictitious Iberian conquest, characterizing it instead as one of the "living languages, not languages of empires" ["lenguas vivas, no lenguas de imperios"] (1993a, 57) because it underwent enriching transformations on American soil.[36] Yet, in the case of "Las dos orillas," how can a culture be called plural if it is, in effect—despite real cultural and ethnic diversity—forcibly monolingual?

As much as Fuentes conceives of Mexican Spanish (or the enriched Spanish in "Las dos orillas") an inclusive tongue, the fact remains that it has been displacing native languages for five centuries. In her articles "La paradoja lingüística del indígena mexicano" and "México, país plurilingüe," Rebeca Barriga Villanueva of the Centro de Estudios Lingüísticos y Literarios at the Colegio de México addresses the difficulties of being "a plurilingual country that paradoxically searches for its national identity in a common language" ["un país plurilingüe que paradójicamente busca su identidad nacional en una lengua común"] (1995a, 115). She estimates the number of indigenous languages currently being spoken in Mexico at around one hundred, each pertaining to one of fourteen linguistic families (1995b, 103). In her study of linguistic politics from the conquest through today, she underscores the danger of combining monolingualism and nationalism, since, during the nation building of independence, "Indians did not exist because their reality challenged the existence of a unified nation" ["los indios no existían porque su realidad negaba la existencia de una nación unificada"] (1995b, 106). Mignolo, insisting as he does on the coexistence of languages, literatures, memories, and spaces, would agree with the need to admit and indeed to foster linguistic plurality (1995, 4). Although Fuentes acknowledges the enriching linguistic contributions that indigenous languages lend to Mexican Spanish, his confidence in a Western linguistic common denominator betrays his focus on a single component of the same Indo-Afro-Ibero-American reality he champions.[37]

At the same time that Fuentes valorizes Latin America's plurality in his essays, he asserts, in an attempt to vindicate their Hispanic root, that Mexican and Latin American cultures are undeniably Western. He defends his position, refusing to view Latin American culture as anything but Western because "we speak Spanish and we are intimately linked to Spanish culture and, through Spanish culture, to Mediterranean culture: Greek, Roman, Arab, Jewish. So cutting ourselves off from that richness seems like sublime stupidity to me" ["hablamos español y estamos íntimamente ligados a la cultura española y através de la cultura española, a la cultura del Mediterráneo: griega, romana, árabe, judía. De manera que cortarnos de toda esa riqueza me parece una tontería sublime"] (1996). Héctor Aguilar Camín supports Fuentes on this point, saying, "Fuentes's allegation is not a traditional defense of the Spanish legacy" ["El alegato de Fuentes no es una defensa tradicionalista del legado español"] (1993b, 60). Aguilar Camín argues that Fuentes "does not want to abandon or ignore any of the dark regions of the subject" ["no quiere renunciar ni cerrar los ojos a ninguna de las zonas oscuras de su objeto"] (60). In "Las dos orillas," Fuentes's praise of Hispanic cultural roots and the Spanish language is not polemical per se; however, his unwillingness to question the *cost*—both cultural and historical—paid in the exchange of Nahuatl or Maya for Spanish surely deserves criticism. In a text that professes to treat cultural tolerance and plurality from a variety of narrative angles, Fuentes's position on language contradicts, indeed undermines, the inclusiveness of his multicultural Iberian dream, just as does his continued use of the terms *mestizo* and *mestizaje* to mean plurality.

Yet perhaps Fuentes took this insistent stance with respect to the Spanish language and the Western nature of Hispanic culture as a means to forward another agenda. In *El espejo enterrado*, Fuentes not only proclaims the rich diversity inherent in Hispanic culture but also insists on its continuity; in this way, he can advocate continental unification. He poses the ultimate question: "Can we, in the coming centuries, unite in Latin America three factors of our existence, initiating political and economic unity from our base of cultural unity?" ["¿Podemos, en el siglo que viene, unir en América Latina los tres factores de nuestra existencia, iniciando la unidad política y económica desde la base de la unidad cultural?"] (1992a, 337). A more far-reaching unity throughout the Americas would create a Latin American bloc—similar to the movements toward conglomeration demonstrated by the European Economic Community and the North American Free Trade Agreement. Reminiscent of the Latin American dreams of Simón Bolívar in his quest(s) to free and unite the continent, Fuentes's dream of unity hints at one last addendum to the cycles of empire elaborated in the stories of *El naranjo*, one that would complete the "reverse of the conquest" by allowing Latin America to turn the historical tables and use its heterogeneity as a means of ruling in the modern day and age of continual migrations.

Although the assimilation that it posits causes "Las dos orillas" to fall just short of a complete valorization of diversity, when read in conjunction with Fuentes's other writings from the early 1990s, the story fits into and often reflects the core contradictions of the author's more general projects and agendas. The circularity of time and migrations (if not miscegenations) comes full circle in "Las dos orillas" and in the other discourses that Fuentes published around the pivotal year 1992. Temporal repetitions manifest themselves in the rise and fall of real and imagined empires: Mesoamerican, European, and Iberoamerican, those of the sixteenth and twenty-first centuries, those of historical fact and of constructed fiction. Fuentes tells us that political and social inclusion will always give rise to cultural and linguistic enrichment, spreading the impulse for democracy and ultimately, he hopes, Hispanic cultural leadership for the world. Unfortunately, thanks to an inherent contradiction in Fuentes's views on plurality and cultural unity, "Las dos orillas" fails to bear out in full the inclusiveness that the author so energetically advocates.

Thus, both texts analyzed in this chapter, *Llanto: Novelas imposibles* and "Las dos orillas," continue the collective revisiting of the origins of Mexico's mestizo national identity that we saw in the works by Solares and Carrasco—works that grapple with the traumatic beginnings of a mestizo or syncretic society born of conquest. Neither Boullosa nor Fuentes, however, seeks to revitalize or revise Mexico's mestizo identity per se. Their texts instead pose urgent questions about the composition of Mexico's mestizo identity and the value of acceptance and tolerance, the very ideals that are touted by multiculturalists. Yet despite the attempts of these leading authors to explore Mexico's plurality at the end of the twentieth century, it has been evident through the beginning of the twenty-first century that the marginalized condition of Mexico's indigenous population and the reluctance of Mexican legislators would frustrate efforts to revise the citizenship status of Mexico's indigenous peoples.

4

The Interminable Conquest
of Mexico

Such works as those by Carmen Boullosa and Carlos Fuentes had begun to infuse Mexican identity discourse with multicultural understanding of difference and recognition of the many ethnicities present in Mexico. Meanwhile, however—spurred by the myriad events that represented the opening up of Mexico—a backlash had begun among other contemporary creative revisions of sixteenth-century history. The portrayal of Mexicans as "children of tragedy" ["hijos de una tragedia"] or part of a family tree with "a broken root" ["una raíz rota"] is also palatable in the works studied here. Yet in contrast with the admission of both the Western basis of mestizo culture and the diverse Mexicos in existence that we examined in Chapter 3, the representation of Mexicans as the poor indigenous, continuously victimized in terms of not only their past but also their present, permeates the works discussed in this chapter.

Recalling the history of the conquest that they were taught in grammar school, many Mexicans echo the words "They conquered us" ["Nos conquistaron"]. This outlook signals an overwhelming identification with the conquered, indigenous perspective. Furthermore, according to Magú, a cartoonist for Mexico City's *La Jornada*, in conjunction with the emphasis on being conquered, Mexican schoolchildren have been fed the concept "We were a nation that could be anything, and . . . that possibility was frustrated [by the conquest]" ["Éramos un pueblo que pudiéramos ser qualquier cosa, y . . . frustró toda esa posibilidad (la conquista)"] (1999). Ever the vanquished, then, Mexicans continue to represent themselves— even poke fun at themselves—as the indigenous people massacred by Spaniards, as the poor exploited at the hands of gringos, and even as political victims of their own twentieth-century governing machine (the Partido Revolucionario Institucional, or PRI). Like Boullosa and Fuentes, the artists discussed in this chapter bridge the sixteenth and twentieth centuries—this time, in order to demonstrate Mexicans' status as victims of the violence inherent in many of the political, economic, and social changes that were taking place in Mexico at end of the millennium. Fear of these international changes, we will see, served only to deepen popular suspicions about the cyclical nature of history and the eternal nature of the conquest.

This chapter examines the 1992 cartoon series *El Ahuizotl* and the 1998 play *La Malinche*. Both works return to the nation's sixteenth-century origins to speak allegorically about the profound transitions that were taking place in Mexico in the 1980s and 1990s. Both demonstrate Mexicans' sense that they were undergoing yet another conquest at the end of the twentieth century and their belief that there was indeed "nothing new under the sun" ["nada nuevo bajo el sol"]. The *moneros* (cartoonists) and the playwright of these texts manage to achieve this thematic and historical continuity by conflating the sixteenth and twentieth centuries and by juxtaposing traditional Mexico (a revolutionary, protectionist, safe, largely mestizo, and strongly nationalistic country) with the "modernizing" Mexico (a neoliberal, more dependent, neoindigenous, victimized country with a weak sense of nationalism). The artists discussed in this chapter draw parallels between Spanish and North American imperialism, despite the profound differences between the two, in order to emblematize the deepest fear in Mexico during the 1990s: that the PRI's deteriorating politics, neoliberal economics, and support of the North American Free Trade Agreement (NAFTA) would drastically transform Mexico's national identity. It is interesting to note that in the six years between the publication of the two texts, NAFTA went from negotiation to operation, and the 1994 uprising in the southern state of Chiapas conferred an entirely new perspective on the economic and national identity debates of the early 1990s.

Both the cartoons of *El Ahuizotl* and the play *La Malinche* capture and reflect an important moment in Mexico's changing national identity and nationalism. Although the state under President Carlos Salinas de Gortari tirelessly attempted to foment the "new nationalism—or more accurately the anti-nationalist globalism— being built around NAFTA" (Stephen 2002, xxxiii), many constituents (including those in Mexico's growing indigenous rights movement) vociferously criticized the changes at every juncture.[1] As Salinas de Gortari pushed Mexico toward modernization and globalization, fears about what the future held abounded.

Neoliberalism, NAFTA, and the End of the Protectionist State in Mexico

Fears about losing *lo mexicano*, or *la mexicanidad*, were not new either at the end of the twentieth century or when globalization became a buzzword; instead, they are stoked periodically, whenever Mexico's northern neighbor encroaches on its real or imagined territory. In 1983 Mexico's most celebrated and well-known *monero*, Rius (Eduardo del Río),[2] published a book-length comic/cartoon entitled *La interminable conquista de México*, which demonstrates five centuries of continuous colonialism in Mexico. The publication's timing, of course, had more to do with the economic changes that emerged under Mexico's President José López Portillo (1976–1982) than it did with the pending commemoration of the Quincentennial, which was still a decade away. But the text and its message nevertheless exemplify the constant debate over whether Mexico should look inward or outward.[3] Rius's attitude was provoked by the obscenely high contributions of the administration of President López Portillo (and to a lesser extent his predecessor, Luis Echeverría [1970–1976]) to Mexico's foreign debt and deepening economic dependence on the United States. Rius posits that, "deciding for an entire nation without voice or vote, the PRI changed the course of the Mexican revolution ... with the result that we see today: a country dependent on the United States, an enormous Puerto Rico" ["decidiendo por todo un pueblo sin voz ni voto, el PRI cambió el camino de la revolución Mexicana ... con los resultados que tenemos a la vista: un país dependiente de los Estados Unidos, un enorme Puerto Rico"] (1984, 143). Such was the extent of their economic folly.

Yet Rius lays only part of the blame on Mexican politicians. In his much more detailed Marxist critique of the North Americans as the "new conquistadors," Rius condemns their aggressive capitalism and economic invasion of Mexico and sounds an alarm about the deleterious effects of such economic dependence—and its concomitant cultural colonization—on Mexican national identity. This warning, of course, has since become quite common among critics of globalization; however, in the Mexico of 1983 it appeared as just another manifestation of a strong nationalist tendency in a country that shared an uncomfortable border with a superpower. In *La interminable conquista de México*, for example, young Mexicans are shown dressed in U.S. football jerseys, drinking Pepsi in front of the television, under the admonishment: "Our economy lost, we would still be consoled by the preservation of our culture, our 'national identity.' But we don't even have that! The North American conquest is a fact" ["Perdida que hemos la economía, nos quedaría el consuelo de haber conservado nuestra cultura, nuestra 'identidad cultural.' ¡Pero ni eso! La conquista cultural norteamericana ya es un hecho"] (1984, 144).

Despite Rius's seemingly sensationalized messages about Mexican economic dependency, by 1983 Mexico had witnessed only the beginnings of economic opening and cultural imperialism. Not only did Presidents Miguel de la Madrid [1982–1988] and Carlos Salinas de Gortari [1988–1994] continue the economic trend that opened Mexico to outside markets—and, some would say, gringo exploitation—but Salinas de Gortari can also be credited with tripping the flood gates, when he won Mexico a seat at the negotiating table for NAFTA in the early 1990s. The profound changes that Salinas de Gortari's neoliberalism and Mexico's inclusion in NAFTA represented for the country are evident in the cartoons of *El Ahuizotl* and in Rascón Banda's *La Malinche*.

By the time Salinas de Gortari was elected to the Mexican presidency in 1988, as we have seen, the nation had been ruled by the PRI and its interpretation of revolutionary ideals for nearly six decades. Mexican national identity, its sense of nationalism, and indeed its politics and economics had been governed by the principles of economic protectionism, political stability in the form of a single-party system, and social assimilation into the mestizo ideal (Mattiace 2003, 32). Although Salinas de Gortari was the PRI's official candidate, his election to the presidency was a blow to tradition in many ways. A Harvard-educated economist, Salinas de Gortari held views about Mexico's potential modernization that differed markedly from those of the majority of his *PRIísta* colleagues. He was a new breed of Mexican politician—a technocrat—and a staunch proponent of neoliberal economics as a means to achieve his passionate goal of modernizing Mexico.

Neoliberalism in Latin America is a term that encompasses many capitalist policies, including free-market competition and limited state regulation on trade. The term also, however, denotes certain political and social programs whose economic consequences have been criticized as impoverishing all but the most wealthy. In Mexico such policies have long been viewed with suspicion for a number of reasons. First, Americanization (now commonly interchangeable with globalization) is commonly cited as a negative consequence of Mexico's integration into world markets and less-regulated trade with such partners as the United States. Second, politically speaking, neoliberalism implies not only drastic cutbacks to some of the Mexican government's traditional welfare and corporatist spending but also a reduction in state-owned enterprises. In sharp contrast to the rampant spending and borrowing of Presidents Echeverría and López Portillo, Salinas de Gortari (as budget and programming minister under de la Madrid [Mattiace 2003, 74]) enacted far-reaching austerity plans that earned him the nickname Salinas de *Cor*tari (a play on the Spanish verb *cortar,* or "to cut").

For his commitment to neoliberal economic principles, Salinas de Gortari was said to dole out economic reforms, or *Salinastroika,* without glasnost—complementary political and cultural reforms (Preston and Dillon 2004, 186). The nicknames and puns arose from his administration's drive to cut public-sector spending and privatize the telephone, banking, and highway construction industries during his presidency. As Philip Russell notes in *Mexico under Salinas,* on paper these policies promised economic benefits, but many of them also had devastating social effects (1994, 389). After decades of protectionist tariffs, state-owned industry, a state-controlled economy, and employment protections for government workers, economic liberalism came as a shock to many Mexicans. The minimum wage plummeted under Salinas de Gortari, and the upper middle class suffered great losses (389). In part, Salinas de Gortari's image, early in his presidency, as a challenger to "the corrupt, populist bosses and inward-looking dinosaurs in the bureaucracy who had ruled Mexico for over half a century" (Cameron and Tomlin 2000, 5) enabled him to undertake many of these profound changes. Linking his image as an innovator and his neoliberal policies with his passion for modernizing

Mexico, Salinas de Gortari encouraged Mexicans to swallow his bitter economic remedies by tapping into Mexico's desire to become an industrialized nation.[4]

Nowhere was this popular aspiration toward modernization better used than in the area of trade. Although critics of Salinas de Gortari's policies balked when NAFTA negotiations began in earnest in 1991, from the technocrats' perspective, Mexico had much to gain. NAFTA is a trilateral treaty that treats the core elements of trade: tariffs, border issues, and transparency (in terms of investments and procedures) (Cameron and Tomlin 2000, 34). Yet it is historic largely because of Mexico's participation. The treaty, which originated as the Free Trade Agreement (FTA) between the United States and Canada, was originally intended to govern trade between two advanced industrial economies (33). Salinas de Gortari managed to include Mexico—a developing country—in the negotiations, thereby allowing him to pursue many of his goals. As a result of joining NAFTA, Mexico would successfully integrate into the global market, receive debt relief, attract foreign investment, and follow a path of economic liberalization (2).

The NAFTA treaty, which contains over a thousand pages, can be seen as the central achievement and most lasting legacy of the administrations that brokered it (Cameron and Tomlin 2000, 7). For Salinas de Gortari—despite the fact that the task had proved to be a monumental effort, taking five of his six years in the presidential palace (Los Pinos)—successfully negotiating the treaty was certainly a feather in his cap (Preston and Dillon 2004, 186). But to many Mexicans, NAFTA led to the disintegration of Mexico's revolutionary safety nets. No longer would there be tariffs to protect Mexican industry or agriculture. Mexican jobs would be lost. The country's restaurants, retail shelves, and television channels would be packed with Americanized products. To borrow the sexualized imagery so popularized by Octavio Paz in *El laberinto de la soledad,* NAFTA symbolically opened, violated, and raped [*abrió, chingó y rajó*] the Mexican nation.

Neoliberalism and the NAFTA negotiations were not just a shock to the Mexican economic system in the 1980s and 1990s; they also presented profound challenges to Mexico's traditionally held mestizophile national identity.[5] For the better part of the twentieth century, as we have seen, the state alleged that Mexico was constructing a "third way," both racially and economically. Racially, the state's intellectuals held, Mexicans were a "bronze race" ["raza de bronce"] (Gamio 1982) or a "cosmic race" ["raza cósmica"] (Vasconcelos 1976) that combined Spanish and indigenous heritages, thus creating a new mestizo race. Economically, the Mexican Revolution had long protected national interests from rampant capitalism, allowing two economic models to coexist. In the 1990s, then, both the liberalization of the Mexican economy and the direct negotiations with the United States, Mexico's perennial enemy, eroded the very pillars of its twentieth-century nationalism. Not only were the paternalistic principles of the Revolution called into question; the Other against which Mexico had long defined itself was now being touted as an ally (Morris 2001, 246–47).

El Ahuizotl of La Jornada: Part of a Tradition of Political Cartoons in Mexico

When the *moneros* of one of Mexico's most widely circulating daily newspapers, *La Jornada,* began their own sardonic tribute to the Quincentennial (*Quinto Centenario*) in 1992, the exploration of modern Mexican national identity was not among their stated goals. Primarily, they planned to revisit Mexico's sixteenth-century history with humor and, where applicable, make connections with current topics.

Yet in the process of "extrapolating" historical and actual moments by connecting, comparing, and contrasting historical and actual empires, the *moneros* of *La Jornada* created a particularly acute rendering and record of the issues of the day. Such subjects as politics, pollution, NAFTA, globalization, and attitudes toward Mexico's indigenous people saturate the cartoons in each issue of the newspaper's supplement, *El Ahuizotl.* By drawing a parallel between the sixteenth and twentieth centuries and by casting the Aztecs as modern-day Mexicans, the *moneros* also make an interesting observation about the state of Mexico's national identity in the last decades of the twentieth century.

Connections between the sixteenth-century conquest and colonization of the New World and twentieth-century globalization have been mapped by Walter Mignolo in such works as *Local Histories/Global Designs: Coloniality, Subaltern Knowledges, and Border Thinking.*[6] Mignolo calls the religious, economic, and epistemological missions of Western expansion "global designs," noting four constants over the past five hundred years: Christianity, a civilizing mission, development, and global markets (2000, 279). In the sixteenth century, European colonial expansion was the primary agent, and Christianizing the world was its main objective. In addition, European expansion brought a new form of mercantilism based on slavery (279) and carried out a civilizing mission that included Latin as the language of knowledge, with particular definitions of reason, philosophy, and scientific achievement, which would constitute the values and standards of civilization (297).

In the latter half of the twentieth century, however, the United States replaced Europe as the agent, with a new "non-territorial colonialism" (Mignolo 2000, 281) based primarily on economic changes that lead to transnational capitalism, (global) market power (287), and global coloniality (13). More important than Manifest Destiny in the civilizing mission of the United States is neoliberalism, which, according to Mignolo, is "a new civilizing project" (24) and not just a new economic organization (279). English, of course, is currently the "universal language of scholarship" (293), and modernity (no longer called civilization) is measured by levels of human rights, quality of life, and urbanization—not to mention adherence to nontraditional systems of knowledge, such as universal science (296–97). While transnational corporations and economic alliances gained power, the power of national states has eroded (295). This new wave of expansion, Mignolo argues, has unified much of the world under a single economic system. It has generalized communication and modern technology and disseminated basic common values, just as Europe did in the sixteenth century.[7]

Political cartoons, as a "a document of their times,"[8] capture—in a concrete and immediate way—a moment, a problem, or a concern. Their efficient visual images and their limited space for text make them a particularly terse and condensed form of political commentary. They also tend toward pedagogy, as they attempt to instruct us about the goings-on in our world.[9] For these reasons, political cartoons can recreate a moment in time and can revive its particular issues far better than can some historical narratives and far more effectively than can, for example, poll data.[10]

Political cartoons, therefore, constitute the perfect medium through which to analyze Mexico's changing social, economic, and political attitudes from the 1990s. In Mexican culture, humor and jokes are far more than entertainment. They are public opinion; they are revenge; they are *sobremesa* (after-dinner conversation). For some, they are a way of life, and, most certainly, they are art. As the writer Sara Sefchovich comments, political cartoons are indeed a necessity in Mexico because "Mexicans are not used to insulting out loud (three centuries of colonial rule and the paramilitary forces' power have accustomed them to hold their tongues), and when they do speak up, it is through jokes. Jokes and comics allow us to laugh at what is really hurting and worrying us" ["el mexicano no acostumbra decir en voz alta sus agravios (tres siglos de Colonia y el poder de las guardias blancas lo acostumbraron a callar) y cuando ya lo hace, es por medio de chistes. El chiste y la caricatura nos permiten reírnos de lo que en realidad nos está doliendo y preocupando"] (Magú and Sefchovich 2000, 40–41).[11]

Although arguably there is nothing funny about the conquest of Mexico, in 1992, the Quincentennial year, the *moneros* at the Mexican newspaper *La Jornada* succeeded in producing a humorous regular series of works that depicted the history of both the "discovery" of the Americas and the conquest of Mexico. As evidenced by the works examined in Chapter 2, recent Mexican representations of the sixteenth-century conquest evoke this distant past in order to better understand the seemingly incomprehensible historical events of five centuries ago and, more important still, to comment earnestly or scathingly (sometimes both) on Mexico's current-day national identity. The cartoons of *El Ahuizotl* forward very serious messages about twentieth-century Mexico precisely because their scathing commentary comes veiled in a comical, often bawdy, package.

Two techniques central to this particular comic series are parody and satire. As we will see, the 1992 cartoon series *El Ahuizotl* as a whole uses parody to exaggerate and distort history, making us chuckle at the absurdity of many events as it plays with the notion of historical truth. Each individual cartoon, for its part, employs cutting satirical mimicry that, depending on our reactions to the mockery of both conquered and conquerors, causes us either to roll our eyes or to roll in the aisles. Published (more or less) every third Wednesday during the Quincentennial

Figure 4.1. Masthead of *El Ahuizote*, 1874.

year, *El Ahuizotl* showcases the work of various *moneros* from *La Jornada*—among them, Ahumada, Magú, El Fisgón, Rocha, and Helguera.

The name of the series, *El Ahuizotl*, is significant for a variety of reasons. First, with the uniquely Nahuatl suffix "tl," *ahuizotl* is a (indigenized) play on the word *ahuizote*, meaning a "nuisance" or "pain in the neck." The title also serves as a tribute to various incarnations of important satirical political caricature in Mexico that "continued the erosion of the annihilated structure of a regime repudiated by the people" ["contribuyeron a erosionar la estructura aniquilosada de un régimen repudiado por el pueblo"] (Ahumada et al. 1991, x). The original *El Ahuizote*, published by Vicente Riva Palacio between 1874 and 1876, was followed by Daniel Cabrera and Ricardo Flores Magon's *El Hijo del Ahuizote* (in *Excélsior*), *El Padre del Ahuizote*, and *El Nieto del Ahuizote*. Cabrera and Flores Magon's publications emerged during Porfirio Díaz's regime, and "within their pages they attacked the dictatorship's henchmen, and they opposed a new electoral farce where surely the old general would again reign triumphant" ["atacaban en sus páginas a los esbirros de la dictadura, y se oponían a una nueva farsa de elecciones en las que seguramente resultaría triunfador una vez más el viejo general"] (Arreola Cortés 2004). More than a century later, between 1988 and 1991, the *moneros* of *La Jornada* published *El Tataranieto del Ahuizote*, in whose pages they simultaneously celebrate and lambaste the Mexican Revolution and protest the highly suspect election of Salinas de Gortari and his betrayal of revolutionary values. The 1992 *El Ahuizotl*, then, is an intellectual continuation of this strong and vociferous tradition of visual political satire and protest. The fact that its focus on pre-Columbian and sixteenth-century events also makes it appear to be a chronological precursor to its cousins, however, reinforces the sense that a return to Mexico's roots must involve a return to the indigenous past. By way of mentioning the indigenous origins of Mexican

Figure 4.2. Masthead of *El Tataranieto del Ahuizote*, 1988–1991.

Figure 4.3. Masthead of *El Ahuizotl*, 1992.

The mastheads shown in Figures 4.2 and 4.3 demonstrate the long-standing tradition of graphic political satire and protest of the cartoonists, or *moneros*, of *La Jornada* newspaper in Mexico City in the 1980s and 1990s. Courtesy of the artist, Magú.

culture, Magú has said, "Surely we have origins that we must understand in order to know ourselves, and to know how we are and how we should be, and to explain a lot of what has happened around us" ["nosotros sin duda tenemos orígenes que debemos conocer para conocernos, y para saber cómo somos y cómo debemos ser, y para explicarnos mucho todo lo que ha pasado al rededor de nosotros"] (1999).

It is interesting to note that the different incarnations of the series share not only a title but also the masthead graphic. Designed by José María Villasana in 1874, the original masthead of *El Ahuizote* (Fig. 4.1) shows an impish figure skewering the letters of its title with a trident (Ahumada et al. 1991). The enigmatic caption reads, "Ferocious weekly, although of good instincts. Bread bread and wine wine; blind man's rod and a creed's blow and stiff-straight skin" ["Semanario feroz aunque de buenos instintos. Pan pan y vino, vino: palo de ciego y garrotazo de credo y cuero y tentetieso"] (1991). Although in *El Tataranieto del Ahuizote* (Fig. 4.2), the caption remains the same, the imp has gone punk, sporting a spiked Mohawk, a safety-pin earring, and the anarchist emblem emblazoned on his chest (1991).

For *El Ahuizotl*'s 1992 Quincentennial return to the sixteenth century, the masthead was appropriately altered (Fig. 4.3). The indigenous features of an Aztec warrior, who now uses a spear instead of a trident, grin from behind a feathered headdress [*penacho*] (Ahumada et al. 1992, 1:1).[12] His earring, chest decoration, and beaded armbands mark him as indigenous, and the caption is a close, but altered, version of the original masthead caption. It reads, "Triweekly with bad instincts, though in Hispanicized Nahuatl"["Trisemanatl de malos instintos, aunque en náhuatl españolizadotl"]. In its 1992 incarnation, this *ahuizote*, or nuisance, no longer underscored the generation gap between the elderly and their (punkedout) great-great-grandchildren; it underscored the cultural abyss between indigenous Mexico and modernizing Mexico under Salinas de Gortari's political and economic policies. The "buenos instintos" of past *ahuizotes* have been jettisoned, signaling that nothing in *El Ahuizotl* will be sacred. The very language that the masthead uses to introduce itself to readers also underscores the hybridization or cultural *mestizaje* that the region experienced as a result of the events of the *encontronazo* (as the *moneros* prefer to call it) and conquest.

Conflating Past and Present: The Conquest of Chilangotitlán in *El Ahuizotl*

El Ahuizotl fuses distant history, current-day social satire, and lasting national symbols in its visual representations of the conquest. According to Magú, one of the contributing *moneros*, the conflation of past and present "is the simplest resource available for making humor, extrapolating moments in history" ["es el recurso más sencillo que se tiene para poder hacer humor, extrapolando los momentos de la historia"] (1999). Yet this fusion/confusion of past and present also serves an important purpose: It allows the cartoonists to criticize almost every aspect of modern Mexican life—down to the most sacred and taboo subjects—from a safe distance. This distancing was especially necessary given the wide circulation of *La Jornada* throughout Mexico and the long-standing limits on acceptable representations of presidents and national heroes.[13] *El Ahuizotl* takes on such controversial novelties as neoliberal economic policies and such institutional monoliths as the political monopoly of the PRI.

The 1992 series is artfully crafted to fit into *La Jornada*, as each of the sixteen issues of *El Ahuizotl* parodies a journalistic, if at times tabloid, presentation of the major historical moments of the "discovery," conquest, and colonization of the New World—especially Mexico—which the cartoonists refer to as the *encontro-*

nazo. For example, we find entire issues dedicated to the Aztec pilgrimage from Aztlán to Tenochtitlán, the arrival and advance of Spanish troops on Mexican soil, the massacres at Cholula and the Templo Mayor, the various versions of Moctezuma's death, the spread of smallpox, *Noche Triste,* and the siege and fall of the Aztec capital. The format of the front page mimics the tabloid genre, with its bold-type headlines, dramatic visuals, and titillating banners of stories to be divulged within. We feel we can expect what every tabloid promises: a sensationalized version of the truth.

On the front page of the first issue (Fig. 4.4), the headline over the graphic of an eagle eating a serpent reads, "They founded Chilangotitlán / in the middle of a lake / an eagle devouring a snake was the sign" ["Fundaron Chilangotitlán / en medio de un lago / el águila desauynándose una culebra fue la señal"] (Ahumada et al. 1992, 1:1). The visual simplicity and photographic feel of this image is similar to that of the intriguing tabloid images. Here the eagle rests not atop a *nopal* cactus, as it should, but atop a television antenna. Instantly, we recognize the fusion of the symbol of the founding of the Aztec metropolis Tenochtitlán with both the modern Mexican national symbol and the urban sprawl of current-day Mexico City. What was once a symbol of abundance, enticing the Aztecs to settle in Lake Texcoco, has been turned on its head to represent the barren landscape of today's megalopolis.[14] The television antenna, interestingly, also evokes the very purpose of *El Ahuizotl*: popular dissemination of information. Below, under the index-like category "Other Prophecies" ["Otras profecías"], is the phrase "Quetzalcóatl, Coloncóatl, and Cortescóatl, feathered snakes that will come one day from the Old World to teach them Spanish" ["Quetzalcóatl, Coloncóatl y Cortescóatl, víboras emplumadas que vendrán un día desde el viejo mundo a enseñarles español"]. Just like the tabloid-front teasers, this line draws us in by promising to reveal, and subsequently report on, predictions of the future. We are intrigued by the obvious agenda of the word play that substitutes "feathered vipers" ["víboras emplumadas"] for "feathered serpents" ["serpientes emplumadas"]: Whereas both "víboras emplumadas" and "serpientes emplumadas" denote reptiles and connote malicious persons, only "serpiente emplumada" symbolizes the (allegedly) long-awaited Aztec god Quetzalcóatl. In this verbal distancing, we see a derisive kind of satire: The Spaniards are not mistaken for gods; they are merely insulted as treacherous.

So it is that from the very first page of the inaugural issue we understand a few key characteristics of the series: First, as we notice the symbols for the founding of Tenochtitlán, we see that the series is heavily based on historic "fact." Second, it is clear that the perspective is decidedly indigenist (or Mexicanist) and quite heavily *anti-español.* This stance is evidenced in not only the Nahuatlization of Colón and Cortés into Coloncóatl and Cortescóatl but also the perversions of the *quinientos años* symbol. In this visual parody of the Quincentennial's official logo, the Spanish Crown has been redrawn to reveal a hand flashing the sign for a cuckold (the index finger and pinkie extended to represent a bull's horns). In addition, instead

Figure 4.4. The front page of the 1992 *El Ahuizotl* comic series parodies the founding of Tenochtitlán by depicting Chilangotitlán as an urban wasteland. *Chilango* is a derogatory term used to refer to residents of Mexico City. Courtesy of the artist, Ahumada.

of *años,* the commemoration symbol uses *coños,* a common but extremely vulgar swear word in Spain. Third, the fusion of the past with the present is of paramount importance; Chilangotitlán is a hybrid space incorporating both past and present—the *águila* atop an antenna. Although the solemn messages give the reader pause, the playful deconstruction of the past and its modern-day pertinence keep the reader engaged for the sheer fun of it.

The first issue also puts forth the purpose of the series. Although the goals are quite lofty, the language is cynical, incorporating obvious mockery of the Spaniards and of the call to celebrate—or commemorate—the Quincentennial. *El Ahuizotl,* it says, will "narrate the extraordinary events of the Conquest of Mexico" ["narrar los extraordinarios eventos de la Conquista de México"] (Ahumada et al. 1992, 1:2). It will participate in the 1992 attempts to "reconcile two worlds" ["reconciliar dos mundos,"] and, interestingly enough, "to contribute to the stamping out of five centuries of hate" ["contribuir al sofocamiento de (los) odios de cinco siglos"]. By October 12, the date of its last issue, the series notes,

> it is expected that the resentment felt by the conquered people has been extinguished and that they have the ability to give thanks for the great culture and civilization disinterestedly brought by the white men who left our ancestors with their mouths agape and their entrails hanging out.

> [se espera que se haya extinguido el rencor de los pueblos conquistados y estén así en aptitud de dar gracias por la tanta cultura y la tan mucha civilización que desinteresadamente nos trajeron los hombres blancos y que dejaron a nuestros antepasados con la boca abierta y las entrañas de fuera.] (Ahumada et al. 1992, 1:2)

It should be noted that this ironic self-description as reconciliatory and thankful is, of course, never fulfilled. *El Ahuizotl* is most frequently a vituperative (yet comical) condemnation of the Spaniards' violence, cultural insensitivity, imperialistic haughtiness, and poor personal hygiene.

The *moneros* of *El Ahuizotl* not only mock the traditionally Hispanophile attitude of grateful acceptance of Western culture; they also lambaste the Quincentennial's insistence on neutral language and cultural exchange over messy historical detail. As we saw in Chapter 1, the Celebration of the Discovery of America [Celebración del Descubrimiento de América] was hastily renamed the Commemoration of the Encounter of Two Worlds [Conmemoración del Encuentro de Dos Mundos]. With that retreat into euphemism, the *moneros* of *La Jornada* sarcastically lauded the "cultural transfusion" ["transfusión cultural"] brought about by the events of the sixteenth century. The military and spiritual conquest of the Americas could be described as "for the generous and altruistic purpose of teaching the first Spanish classes" ["el generoso y altruista propósito de impartir las primeras clases de español"] (Ahumada et al. 1992, 2:9) and even later was referred to as implemented so that "after torturing them, the aborigines could tell them in perfect Castilian where the hell the gold was" ["después de torturarlos, sus aborígenes pudieran decirle en perfecto castellano donde chingáos estaba el oro"] (3:2). As a result, Malinche would open her very own Instituto de Lenguas, attracting clients with such slogans as "Sign up today for the language of the future" ["Inscríbete hoy mismo al idioma del futuro"] (3:4), referencing the current-day multitude of opportunities for Mexicans, and indeed all Latin Americans, to learn European languages as a means of upward mobility. Despite this depiction of Malinche as a modern-day businesswoman, however, she did not escape ridicule as a sexualized object. On the same page, Hernán Cortés is seen wild with licentious anticipation as Malinche is described to him as "very good with the [her] tongue" ["muy buena con la lengua"] (3:4). Here, even as the *moneros* criticize their postcolonial circumstances as Spanish speakers,[15] they take great pleasure in the traditional double entendres [*albures*] so common in Mexican Spanish. This multifaceted irony, enriched by its pertinence to today's global desire for English-language skills, permeates the pages of *El Ahuizotl* and helps cement the conflation of the sixteenth and twentieth centuries in Mexican history.

As a reminder of the massacres and the battles of conquest, however, the *moneros* also describe in graphic visual terms the processes leading up to the "inevitable, and even necessary, cultural transfusion" ["inevitable y hasta necesaria transfusión cultural"] (Ahumada et al. 1992, 12:4). Preparations for the battle for and siege of Tenochtitlán begin (Fig. 4.5): An Aztec elder paints a large bull's-eye on the chest of a warrior, Spanish troops prepare for battle by watching the movie *Rambo,* and Cortés rolls into Chilangotitlán on a bulldozer outfitted with wrecking ball (12:4–5). Imminent tragedy is visually implied, and, in the aftermath of the massacre, widespread indigenous losses are attributed to Cortés's "goal of consummating as quickly as possible the epic Hispanicization and whitening of the *café con leche* race" ["propósito de consumar lo más pronto posible la epopeya de la españolización y la blanqueada de la raza café con leche"] (14:7). Clearly, because Mexican national identity and national unity have long been based on mestizophile ideals, the *moneros* seize the opportunity to deconstruct the facile notion that *mestizaje* was anything but violent, destructive, and culturally disastrous.

Thus, the plight of Mexico's indigenous people plays a prominent role in much of the humor in *El Ahuizotl,* serving as a concrete source of commentary on modern Mexican national identity. Indeed, as noted earlier, the *moneros* of *El Ahuizotl* represent Mexicans as indigenous—more specifically, Aztec—people who were massacred by the Spaniards. Moreover, the issue dedicated to the Spaniards' advance from Veracruz to Tenochtitlán draws a parallel between colonization and Americanization in the interminable conquest of Mexico, by comparing the conquest to the cola wars. We are told, "Cortés explained confidentially to the fat chief

Figure 4.5. In preparation for battle, an Aztec elder paints a bull's-eye on one of his warriors. As a result of this battle, the Spaniards seize Tenochtitlán, and the Aztec empire falls under Spanish control. Courtesy of the artist, Ahumada.

[of Cempoala] that the world was changing to Pepsi and it was time to send the rubble representing their gods to the cellars of the Museum of Anthropology" ["Entrado en confianzas, Cortés explicó al cacique gordo que el mundo estaba cambiando a Pepsi y que era el momento de mandar a las bodegas del Museo de Antropología e Historia todas las piedras esas que representaban a sus dioses"] (Ahumada et al. 1992, 4:8). The destruction of indigenous culture, resulting in the recommendation that the remaining shards of native cultures be housed in the nations' museums, is also parodied, as the Spaniards offer religious knickknacks to the indigenous people. Much in the same way that items are hawked to tourists outside the national cathedral on the *zócalo*, souvenirs are peddled to members of the indigenous community after they tithe to the Catholic church (Fig. 4.6): They are told that they can buy "crucifixes, saints' pictures, or this pretty puzzle of Huichilopochtli" ["crucifijos, estampitas o este bonito rompecabezas de Huitzilopochtli"] (4:9). The contrast between the sixteenth and twentieth centuries, of course, is that in the 1500s, as a result of Christian evangelization, the indigenous gods were razed, and now they are being sold as junk souvenirs. Indeed, in describing the Spaniards' retreat from Tenochtitlán on *Noche Triste*, the *moneros* allege

Figure 4.6. Evangelization and conversion to Christianity come at a cost. An Aztec, looking sadly at his shattered god, is asked for an offering as he is sold crucifixes and a "a pretty Huitzilopochtli puzzle" ["bonito rompecabezas de Huitzilopochtli"]. Courtesy of the artist, Magú.

that "during the flight, the gold left behind was for the Museum of Anthropology" ["en la huida, lo que dejan de oro es para el Museo de Antropología"] (10:3). This caustic suggestion that the only remains of indigenous culture are found in museums underscores the *moneros'* disdain for the indigenist policies of the government, which have been criticized as "recogniz[ing] indianness, but not Indians" (Alexander Ewen quoted in Vigil and Lopez 2004, 54).

Although the stated intentions of the series (noted earlier) indicate a corrective form of satire, none of the cited goals includes comments on or critiques of life and national identity in current-day Mexico. Despite this omission, much of this series is dedicated to the social problems and political ills of modern-day Mexico. As a result, its critical political commentary serves as the unstated impetus behind the satire and the very means through which the series contributes to the collective soul-searching that took place in 1992 and to the Mexican revision of national identity. The analysis of the cartoons of *El Ahuizotl* that follows focuses on the most severely biting criticisms of Mexico's political and economic path at the end of the twentieth century—most notably the modernization and globalization discourses of President Salinas de Gortari. The cartoons represent an ironic take on the common indigenist and nationalistic projects of the day. The conflation of the sixteenth-century conquest with twentieth-century economic policies, although it presents a sad truth, ultimately makes us laugh at the notion of conquest as globalization and evangelization as modernization.

Pointing to traces of the colonial past in current-day Mexico most often leads to negative conclusions, such as the interminable conquest and victimization of Mexicans. In *El Ahuizotl,* however, we are presented with an outright valorization of the indigenous past through the suggestion that some indigenous traditions predate their modern counterparts or are, in fact, superior to their modern gringo equivalent. Perhaps the simplest way that these comics bridge the gap between the sixteenth and twentieth centuries is through the juxtaposition of institutions, which implies that most "modern" wonders are rooted in the Aztec past. As is typical of recent indigenist movements, the cartoons attribute great cultural contributions to the pre-Columbian or pre-Cortesian Aztecs. In the first installment of the cartoon series, the canoes used by the Aztecs to cross Lake Texcoco are presented as precursors to modern-day *peseros* [buses] (Fig. 4.7): Just like the green microbuses used in Mexico City today, the canoes sport signs that read, "Unleaded only" ["Magna sin"] and "Caution: Frequent stops" ["Cuidado: Paradas contínuas"] (Ahumada et al. 1992, 2:2). Crowded public transportation gets the job done on both the ancient canals of Tenochtitlán and the vehicular arteries of modern Mexico City. We also see one of the Aztec *tamemes* [messengers]—who were famed for running fresh fish up the coast from Tabasco to the emperor in Tenochtitlán (a 300-mile journey with more than a one-mile gain in altitude)—using DHL to send his tribute (Fig. 4.8), explaining that it "absolutely, positively has be there overnight" (Ahumada et al. 1992, 2:7). This juxtaposition conveys the

Figure 4.7. Parodying the crowded green microbuses in current-day Mexico City, an Aztec canoe is labeled "Caution: Frequent stops" ["Cuidado: Paradas continuas"]. Courtesy of the artist, Magú.

message that the most modern conveniences were not unknown in Mexico before the Spaniards brought their "civilization" to the New World.

To maintain the conflation of past and present, the *moneros* even point their caustic humor at both the consumerism and violence in current-day Mexico. They liken the arrival of the first horses to the New World to the auto-envy of a capitalist society (Fig. 4.9): Upon seeing a mounted Spaniard, one Aztec exclaims, "Get

Figure 4.8. To highlight Aztec advances, a messenger, or *tameme,* uses the courier DHL to send fresh fish to the capital. In the Aztec empire, *tamemes* ran fish from the coast up to the emperor in Tenochtitlán, a 300-mile journey with a gain of more than 7,000 feet in elevation. Courtesy of the artist, Rocha.

OUUUUUUUUUT!! He's got the latest model Cavalier with turbo injection!" ["¡AÁMONOS! ¡Trae su caballier último modelo a turbo injection!"] (Ahumada et al. 1992, 4:3). The scene captures the wonder of novel invention and the undeniable quest for upgrade inherent in both the sixteenth and twentieth centuries. Perhaps one of the most tellingly comical examples of the bridging of these two

Figure 4.9. Here, the indigenous people are taken aback by their first sight of horses, brought to the New World by the Spanish conquistators. Their comment—"Get OUUUUUUT!! He's got the latest model Cavalier with turbo injection!" ["¡AÁMONOS! ¡Trae su caballier último modelo a turbo injection!"]—refers to the modern-day phenomenon of horsepower envy. Courtesy of the artist, Magú.

eras occurs when a Tlaxcalan soldier—whose tribe was long blamed and ridiculed as the traitorous indigenous group that helped the Spaniards defeat the Aztecs—reports to Cortés for duty. Emblazoned on his shield is a sign that refers to the popular late-twentieth-century view of Mexico City urbanites (*chilangos*) as rude, crude, and disruptive to idyllic provincial life (Fig. 4.10). It reads, "It's your patriotic duty: Kill a *chilango*" ["Haz madre patria: Mata un chilango"] (5:7). Ironically, of course, the saying sums up the intertribal conflict believed to have caused the fall of Tenochtitlán (currently home to the *chilangos*), which led to victory for the Spaniards. The humor of *El Ahuizotl* therefore runs the gamut between, and incorporates the derision of, both the ancient and modern worlds.

Within the drama of the conquest, the *moneros* also ridicule the PRI's stranglehold on twentieth-century Mexican politics. The cartoons that depict this state of affairs draw direct connections between the divinely sanctioned *tlatoanis* [emperors] and the perfect succession of *PRIísta* presidential candidates. When Cortés asks Moctezuma whether he might *possibly* cede the throne to the opposition, the Partido de Acción Nacional, or PAN (Fig. 4.11), we understand that he is referring not just to an end to the royal lineage of the Aztecs but also to the alternation of power in a supposedly democratic twentieth century (Ahumada et al. 1992, 9:2). Moctezuma's recalcitrant stance says it all. Then there is a cartoon that indicates the following possible campaign slogans for a politician as conqueror (Fig. 4.12): "Cortés as Captain: modernization / All three sectors (public, private, service) for Cortés / Cortés, the unity candidate" ["Cortés de Capitán: modernización / Los tres sectores con Cortés / Cortés: candidato de unidad"] (4:4). Again, the conquest is equated with modern-day globalization, and the policy of *palostroika*—or beating economic reform out of us with a stick [*palo*]. Perhaps the sweetest of the cartoons is also one of the funniest: A crestfallen Cuauhtémoc laments his fate (Fig. 4.13): "What a fucking term to be tapped [literally, 'to be touched by the man's—or lord's—finger']!" ["¡Pinche sexenio en el que me tocó el dedo del -señor!"] (11:4). Looking more like a football mascot than an emperor, Cuauhtémoc earns our sympathy. Not only do we understand that it was just plain bad timing that he ascended the Aztec throne when he did; we also appreciate the reference to the modern political practice of the *dedazo*, in which a *PRIísta* president could choose his successor with the assurance that he would win.

The anachronistic placement of certain current-day problems in a sixteenth-century context also provokes laughter: We expect the incongruous, yet we are presented with a seemingly logical resolution to some of the problems of the conquest. For example, what if there had been a "Does not circulate today" ["Hoy no circula"] system in 1521? In this modern-day system—an effort to reduce emissions and air pollution—Mexico City limits vehicular traffic by prohibiting cars from circulating one day of the week (regulated by the last digit of the license plate). Would the Spaniards have used this system to hinder indigenous resistance, or would the Aztecs have used it to hinder the Spanish invasion? Two cartoons

Figure 4.10. The Tlaxcalans, long deemed traitors for having allied themselves with the Spanish conquistadors, are shown here with shields that read, "It's your patriotic duty: Kill a *chilango*" ["Haz madre patria: Mata un chilango"]. Courtesy of the artist, Rocha.

demonstrate how Moctezuma could have used the system to keep the Spaniards at bay. In the first (Fig. 4.14), Cortés is informed that Spaniards—represented by the synecdoche (a part that stands for the whole) of a conqueror's helmet—are denied entry to Tenochtitlán because they do not circulate "every day" ["todos los días"] (Ahumada et al. 1992, 7:2). In the second (Fig. 4.15), the Spaniards aboard a *bergantín* [an impromptu boat used to seize control of Tenochtitlán] are perplexed when they are told that they need a red sticker to circulate that day (a reference to the red stickers given to cars whose license plates end in the number 3 or 4,

Figure 4.11. Cortés suggests that Moctezuma appoint an intern emperor from the opposing party (the Spaniards). In Mexico in 1992, this cartoon spoke both to the concept of Moctezuma "ceding" his empire and to hopes for alternation of power after decades of *PRIísta* rule. Courtesy of the artist, Magú.

Figure 4.12. If Cortés were a modern politician, his campaign slogans might put a positive spin on the conquest: "Cortés as Captain: modernization" ["Cortés de Capitán: modernización"] or "Cortés: the unity candidate" ["Cortés: candidato de unidad"]. Courtesy of the artist, Luis Fernando.

The Interminable Conquest of Mexico   145

Figure 4.13. Cuauhtémoc, the last Aztec emperor, laments his fate and pokes fun at the modern Mexican political tradition of the *dedazo* [literally, "big finger"], in which the outgoing president chooses his successor: "What a fucking term to be tapped!" ["¡Pinche sexenio que me tocó el dedo del señor!"]. Courtesy of the artist, Magú.

indicating that they may not circulate in Mexico City on Wednesdays). Then, conversely, a Spaniard is seen erecting a "Today no one circulates" ["Hoy no circula nadie"] banner (Fig. 4.16) to symbolize the paralysis of the Aztec capital under siege (14:2). What is today considered an inconvenience to many might have, at another time, altered the course of history.

In another creative use of Mexico City's twentieth-century environmental problem of air pollution, El Fisgón adapts the famous peregrination codex [*tira de peregrinaje*], which shows the Aztecs' mythical journey from Chicomóstoc in Aztlán to Tenochtitlán, where they were to build their empire. The title "Códice

Figure 4.14. The anachronism of the twentieth-century pollution-fighting program known as "Does not circulate today" ["Hoy no circula"] provokes laughter as the Spaniards in sixteenth-century Mexico are told that they do not circulate *every day* in Chilangotitlán. Courtesy of the artist, Rocha.

Figure 4.15. As the Spaniards seize Tenochtitlán, they advise, "Today no one circulates" ["Hoy no circula nadie"]. Courtesy of the artist, Helguera.

Figure 4.16. In another reference to Mexico's "Does not circulate today" ["Hoy no circula"] program, the Spaniards are perplexed when they are told that they cannot circulate without a red sticker on their boat. Courtesy of the artist, Magú.

Desde" is a play on the Dresden Codex, in which *Dresden* is altered to *Desde* (meaning "from")—a strong indication that the codex is meant to be an originary myth. The farcical codex in *El Ahuizotl* narrates the journey of the Imeca tribe from Ozonoxtlán made at the behest of their god Fuchipoxtli. Playing with the acronym IMECA (Índice Metropolitano de la Calidad del Aire [Metropolitan Air Quality Index])—an index used to quantify particulate and gaseous air con-tamination—the *moneros* are able to hearken back to the name Mexica (for the Aztec tribe), while they insert the word *fuchi* [yucky] into the name of the god Huichilopochtli. When the Imecas arrive in the Valley of Mexico, the punch line can be delivered: "That was how 500 Imecas [a red-alert level of pollution] de-feated 20 million inhabitants of Mexico-Tenochtitlán [the estimated population of Mexico City]" ["Fue así como 500 Imecas derrotaron a 20 millones de habitan-tes de México-Tenochtitlán"] (Ahumada et al. 1992, 1:6). Again, the sixteenth-century mystery of how five hundred Spanish soldiers could subdue an empire of Aztecs is "explained" via extrapolation. Five hundred IMECAS can paralyze a city of 20 million by plunging it into "doble hoy no circula," where unhealthful levels of pollutants mean that cars cannot circulate two days that week.

In another example of extrapolating history, we are asked to consider whether the Spaniards were met with the same corny marketing that confronts today's tourists in coastal Mexico (Fig. 4.17): One of Cortés's first interpreters, Jerónimo de Aguilar welcomes the Spaniards with trinkets and a sign that reads, "Inter-preter, translations, I move my belly, seviche [*sic*]" ["Intérprete, traducciones, se mueve la panza, seviche [*sic*]"] (Ahumada et al. 1992, 3:2). In addition, the am-bivalence with which many Mexicans greet shopping tourists today is reflected in the plainly insulting message on the cloth that they accept as a gift (Fig. 4.18): "The hieroglyphics say I hope they go straight to hell" ["Los jeroglíficos dicen que ojalá se vayan mucho a la chingada"] (4:3).

The previous two cartoons offer a fitting segue into the next topic at hand: the parallel drawn between the Spaniards and the North Americans. By equating Spaniards and gringos, the series further lampoons many of the social, economic, and political ills of Mexico in the 1990s. Consider the following images that clarify the relationship between the two. The cartoons equate (1) the Spanish military in-vasion with the North American cultural invasion and (2) the Spanish religious crusade with the North American economic crusade for "free trade." Once again, Mignolo's four constants—Christianity, a civilizing mission, development, and global markets—are shown to coexist in the cartoons of *El Ahuizotl* (in varying de-grees of importance) throughout five hundred years of Western expansion. Within this paradigm, then, Christopher Columbus recruits marines for the colonization of the New World (Fig. 4.19), much as Uncle Sam does for the imperialistic goals of the United States (Ahumada et al.1992, 5:11), and the first news of the Euro-peans' presence reaches Moctezuma along with the rough draft for the Tratado de Libre Comercio de Norteamerica (TLC), or NAFTA (Fig. 4.20). A messenger, re-

Figure 4.17. *El Ahuizotl* extrapolates history by depicting the Spaniards as tourists in Yucatan who are met by a trinket hawker (Jerónimo de Aguilar) and his corny advertisement "Interpreter, translations, I move my belly, seviche [*sic*]" ["Intérprete, traducciones, se mueve la panza, seviche [*sic*]"]. Courtesy of the artist, Luis Fernando.

Figure 4.18. The theme of a tourist invasion continues as Spaniards admire local crafts on the beaches. An indigenous man tells his friends, "The hieroglyphics say they should go straight to hell" ["Los jeroglíficos dicen que ojalá se vayan mucho a la chingada"]. Courtesy of the artist, Luis Fernando.

Figure 4.19. *El Ahuizotl* cartoons equate Spaniards and gringos as a means of suggesting an ongoing interminable conquest of Mexico. Here Christopher Columbus recruits marines for the colonization of the New World using Uncle Sam's slogan "I WANT YOU!" Courtesy of the artist, Rocha.

porting on the first sightings of the Spaniards along the coast, says, "They have the body of a deer, [they have] hair all over their faces, their feet stink, and they sent you the first draft of NAFTA" ["Tienen cuerpo de venado, (tienen) pelos en toda la cara, les apestan las patas y te mandaron el primer borrador del TLC"] (3:5). Here we are amused by the parallel between a treaty that wrenches open previously protected markets and a colonial economic monopoly that figuratively rapes a country (*wrench/rape* obviously evoking a great Mexican *albur* [double entendre] of *chingar*).

Figure 4.20. In this early account of the Spanish arrival, Moctezuma learns that the Spaniards have sent him the first draft of NAFTA. The 1992 proposal that Mexico participate in NAFTA aroused fears of globalization and Americanization. Courtesy of the artist, Ahumada.

In a cartoon by the *monero* Rocha, the Spaniards are awestruck by their first glimpse of Chilangotitlán (Fig. 4.21): "Fuck, this is wonderful!" ["¡Joer, ezto es wonderful!"] (Ahumada et al. 1992, 7:1). They are impressed not by the indigenous achievements in architecture or transportation represented in the pyramids, canals, and *calzadas* but by the evidence of industrialization and commercial integration of markets on flashy billboards. A cartoon by Magú, in turn, continues the vulgarity (Fig. 4.22): Cuauhtémoc is urged, "Listen, Guatemuz [Cuauhtémoc] . . . let's deal with the *gachupas* [a word play combining the derogatory *gachupin* (Spaniard) and the verb *chupar* (to suck), also typical of the *albures* in Mexico] by letting them put in their McDonald's [another equation of Spanish and North American economic imperialism], and then we'll kick them out" ["Oye Guatemuz . . . negociemos con los gachupas dejando que metan sus MacDonalds y luego nos los chentamos"] (14:5). Last, we see Cortés revealing financial gain as the true incentive to colonize Mexico (Fig. 4.23), as he "evangelizes" Moctezuma with a new god: the dollar (7:4). The humor lies not only in the truth contained deep within (that evangelization was secondary to the military conquest for the Spaniards) but also in the

Figure 4.21. In the 1500s, the Spaniards' first glimpse of Tenochtitlán inspired awe. Here, when they see signs of industrialization and multinationals (Coca Coatl) in Chilangotitlán, they gasp, "Fuck, this is wonderful!" ["¡Joer, ezto es wonderful!"]. Courtesy of the artist, Rocha.

Figure 4.22. This cartoon facetiously posits the sixteenth-century conquest as globalization, when Cuauhtémoc (Guatemuz) considers letting the Spaniards open a McDonald's in Mexico. Courtesy of the artist, Magú.

Figure 4.23. Cortés reveals the true incentive to colonize Mexico (financial gain, not evangelization) as he convinces Moctezuma to worship his god: the dollar. Courtesy of the artist, Rocha.

satirical derision of the materialism that the West—and now the North—have both brought to Mexican soil.

El Ahuizotl also includes textual passages that provide historical context for the visuals on each page, and it is here that the criticism of Western values and modernization/globalization is often most acute. First, in reference to Salinas de Gortari the technocrat, Quetzalcoátl is described as returning to Mexico with a Harvard degree and a plan to modernize the land, starting with a *churros con choco-late* stand atop the ruins of Chilangotitlán (Ahumada et al. 1992, 1:7). Next, the entire enterprise of conquest and colonization of the New World is deemed—to borrow a subtly Orwellian phrase from George Bush, the father—the "New World Order," wherein the *barbones* [bearded ones] would bring foreign investment, economic stability, loans, and a free-trade agreement (14:2). The indigenous groups that welcomed the Spaniards—such as those from Tabasco (3:4) and Tlaxcala (12:2)—are described in *El Ahuizotl* as embracing "the Spaniards' civilizing and modernizing project" ["el proyecto civilizatorio y modernizador de los españoles"] (11:3) or as supporting "the side of light, knowledge, free (street) trade and the glob*u*lization of collectively owned land" ["el lado de la luz, la sabiduría, el libre comercio ambulante, y la glob*u*lización del ejido"] (14:4, my emphasis). Those who resisted, however—such as Xicoténcatl and Cuauhtémoc—were mockingly seen as continuing "xenophobic policies . . . the provincial rejection of globalizing fu-

Figure 4.24. Reinforcing the parallel between the Spanish colonization and gringo globalization, a U.S. gunboat sails toward Tenochtitlán to take it by force. Courtesy of the artist, Ahumada.

sion of the cultures, and . . . outright refusal of the free-trade treaties" ["la política de xenofobia . . . rechazo provinciano a la fusión globalizadora de las culturas y . . . negativa frontal a los tratados de libre comercio"] (11:4), which were enacted by a previous conspiring emperor.

The parallels drawn between the Spanish colonization and the gringo globalization of Mexico easily extend into the realm of the military as well. In the first of these cartoons (Fig. 4.24), the impromptu boats [*bergantines*] that the Spaniards built in 1521 in order to take Tenochtitlán by water are drawn clearly as U.S. gunboats (Ahumada et al. 1992, 12:3) and are described as "therefore constituting the first motherfucking naval force, direct antecedent to the feared [U.S.] Marines" ["constituyendo así la primera fuerza naval rompemadres, antecedente inmediato de los temidos marines"] (12:3). In the second (Fig. 4.25) and third (Fig. 4.26),

Figure 4.25. Courtesy of the artist, Helguera.

the battles on Mexican soil are referred to as "High Plain Storm" ["Tormenta del Altiplano"] (5:8) and "Operation Lagoon Storm" ["Operación Tormenta en la Laguna"] (12:2), reminiscent of Operation Desert Storm of 1991—and perhaps betraying the Mexican fear that its oil fields too were dangerously of interest to and (if NAFTA offered up the national petroleum company [PEMEX] to foreign ownership) dangerously close to being within the grasp of the United States.

The cartoons of *El Ahuizotl* therefore not only play with the similarities between sixteenth- and twentieth-century history; they also evoke—very forcefully—the deepest and most urgent fears of Mexican society in the 1990s. At that time, President Salinas de Gortari had promised that it was "morning in Mexico" and that he would make Mexico into a First World nation, and this both energized and terrified many of his compatriots. These fears are evident in the title of a book of cartoons published by El Fisgón in 1996: *How to Survive Neoliberalism and Still Be Mexican* [*Cómo sobrevivir al neoliberalismo sin dejar de ser mexicano*] (Fig.4.27). In addition, the *moneros* of *El Ahuizotl* see the sixteenth-century "dis-

Figure 4.26. Courtesy of the artist, Luis Fernando.

In the cartoons depicted in Figures 4.25 and 4.26, battles on Mexican soil are named "High Plain Storm" ["Tormenta en el Altiplano"] and "Operation Lagoon Storm" ["Operación Tormenta en la Laguna"], calling to mind the 1991 Gulf War battle known as Operation Desert Storm.

covery" in terms of its current-day consequences when they refer to it as something that "modernized our destiny forever, because today, five hundred years later, we wear Calvin Klein jeans and underwear instead of loincloths and, of course, we don't wear feathers" ["modernizó para siempre nuestro destino, pues hoy, quinientos años después, traemos jeans y calzoncillos Calvin Klein en lugar de taparrabo y, desde luego, no usamos plumas"] (2:2). Behind the mocking tones that are used to describe the difficult process of transculturation that took place in both the sixteenth and twentieth centuries, lies the very real fear that Mexicans were loosing their national identity, their *mexicanidad*. In this sense, the *moneros'* conflation of past and present in *El Ahuizotl* really does facilitate a better understanding of the events of the conquest and colonization of Mexico—if only from a vanquished, indigenous standpoint. Sadly, however, equating today's Mexican population with conquered indigenous populations offers no solution; it only reaffirms the tired old saying "Poor Mexico, so far from God and so close to the United States" ["Pobre México, tan lejos de Dios y tan cerca a los Estados Unidos"].

Figure 4.27. Many Mexicans feared the effects that globalization might have on national identity. El Fisgón titled his 1996 book of cartoons *How to Survive Neoliberalism and Still Be Mexican* [*Cómo sobrevivir al neoliberalismo sin dejar de ser mexicano*].

Controversy at the Theater: *La Malinche,*
by Víctor Hugo Rascón Banda

As we have seen, the history of the conquest of Mexico and the ways it is currently represented undoubtedly serve as lightning rods of public sentiment in Mexico today. In 1998 the theatrical production of *La Malinche* in Mexico City and Guanajuato incensed and disgusted audiences. Mexico's distant past and its recent history appeared irreverently satirized and eroticized on stage. Theatergoers stormed out in midscene, shouting insults at the director. Critics described it as (1) "a vile illustration of an outsider's malice, pornographic comic, vulgar obscenity, repulsive performance, highly grotesque" ["vil ilustración de la maldad ajena, cómic pornográfico, obscenidad ramplona, espectáculo hedionda, hipergrotesco"] (Fernando de Ita quoted in Rascón Banda 2000a, 273), (2) "a unique and diverse performance that proposes a different way to face one of our most controversial myths. Desacralization of symbols" ["espectáculo único y diverso, que propone una manera diferente de encarar uno de los mitos de mayor controversia. Desacralización de los símbolos"] (Esther Seligson quoted in Rascón Banda 2000a, 273), and (3) a "monument to bad taste [that] is exhausted in its obsessive repetition, but [that] even with its weaknesses provokes an opportune revision of our prejudices, a Manichaean work, immediate, terrifying, and alive" ["monumento al mal gusto (que) se agota en su obsesiva repetición, pero (que) aún con sus debilidades provoca una oportuna revisión de nuestros prejuicios, obra maniquea, inmediata, horripilante y viva"] (Luz Emilia Aguilar quoted in Rascón Banda 2000a, 275).

Víctor Hugo Rascón Banda's[16] play, *La Malinche,* and its production emblematize the crucial debates on globalization, neoliberal economics, and national identity that raged so virulently at the turn of the millennium in Mexico. Like the cartoons of *El Ahuizotl, La Malinche* reveals twentieth-century Mexico as burdened by a tripartite configuration of dominance: the Western world (Spain) as its cultural center, the United States as its imperial center, and *PRIísta* politics as its cultural hegemony. Especially because it reflects both post-NAFTA and post-Zapatista attitudes, the play (first performed in 1998) provides a case study of the most current ways in which Mexicans use the conquest to comment on their modernizing society. Its analysis therefore provides an appropriate conclusion to our examination of Mexican national identity in the 1980s and 1990s.

First, it is important to contextualize *La Malinche* within the larger body of recent Mexican fiction that we have examined. Like many other contemporary Mexican novels, plays, and movies that rewrite the sixteenth-century conquest, *La Malinche* uses this distant point in history as a means of offering commentary on current-day Mexican national identity because the conquest is seen as the birth of the Mexican nation or, at the very least, the birth of the Mexican mestizo pueblo. Such works as *Nen, la inútil,* by Ignacio Solares; *Llanto, novelas imposibles,* by Carmen Boullosa; the stories in *El Naranjo,* by Carlos Fuentes; and the 1998 movie

La otra conquista, by Salvador Carrasco all speak clearly to issues of modern Mexican identity in their rewriting of the conquest as well.

Rather than critique or attempt to modify the Mexican community's notion of itself as did some of the aforementioned works, however, *La Malinche* sounds the alarm—much as did the cartoon series *El Ahuizotl*—that Mexico's very identity is in danger of being lost to globalization and modernization. In just two decades, Mexico had gone from a PRI-dominated, economically protectionist nation to a more democratic, economically globalizing state. More important, the homogenizing, mestizophile national identity discourse that pervaded Mexico in the twentieth century had given way to an official admission of Mexico's ethnic and linguistic diversity—or "pluriculture." The phenomenon of *La Malinche* and the public's reaction to it reveal the many tensions that exist between the Mexico of yesteryear and the Mexico of the future. The play served to openly criticize Mexico's ruling party and, in its view, the government's reprehensible handling of the Zapatista uprising and its uncritical acceptance of neoliberalism. Nationalists and Mexican artists alike objected to the hiring of the radical Austrian director Johann Kresnik, who elicited and staged the Rascón Banda play. Many protested the decision of the Instituto Nacional de Bellas Artes (INBA) to award the director's job and the play's astronomical budget to a foreigner, only to have him (mis)represent—and some say defile—all that is sacred in Mexico: the nation's heroes, its history, and its government.[17]

For those who are unfamiliar with the story behind the text, the history of the creation of *La Malinche* warrants clarification. In 1997 Rascón Banda was invited by Mario Espinosa, the president of INBA, to write a theatrical piece to be staged and directed by Kresnik. Rascón Banda is a playwright who is known for political theater that is highly critical of modern-day Mexican society (Rascón Banda 2006b). Kresnik is a director who is considered the founder of "choreographic theater," which combines acting and dance and "searches the depths of the piece for the best form of expression" ["busca lo profundo de la pieza para encontrar la mejor forma de expresión"] (Rascón Banda 2000a, 155). According to Rascón Banda, Kresnik's objective is "incitement and scandal, the enthusiasm and polemic of an extremely violent, aggressive, and shocking staging" ["la provocación y el escándolo, el entusiasmo y la polémica con (un) montaje violento, en extremo agresivo e impactante"] (2000a 163). Rascón Banda and Kresnik quickly agreed on the guiding principle of the play: Their revision of the figure of Malinche would serve as a pretext for criticism of NAFTA, neoliberalism, and the official response to the uprising in Chiapas.[18] Rascón Banda was charged with the job of providing Kresnik with texts: multiple texts, varied texts, myths, dialogues, monologues, anecdotes, and more. Rascón Banda consulted sixteenth-century historiography; Nahuatl accounts of the conquest; the writings of Subcomandante Marcos; and articles in *Milenio, Proceso, La Jornada,* and *La reforma* that addressed current affairs in Mexico. Kresnik would convert the text into theater.

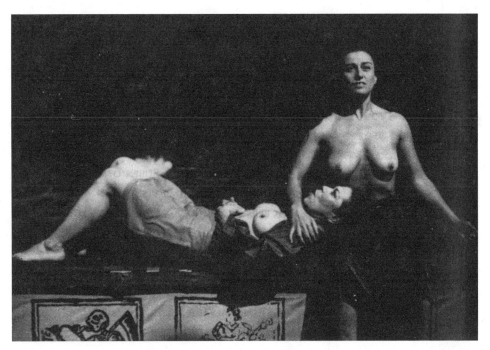

Figure 4.28. In Víctor Hugo Rascón Banda's 1998 play, *La Malinche,* an updated Malinche is seen in consultation with her psychiatrist. The two deconstruct such popular perceptions of her as that of Octavio Paz's *The Labyrinth of Solitude* [*El laberinto de la soledad*]. Photograph by Christa Cowrie. Courtesy of the playwright, Víctor Hugo Rascón Banda.

What happened next is twofold: Rascón Banda and Kresnik compiled thirty-seven texts (or chapters), each of which constitutes a scene and all of which manifest a Malinche who is brought up to date and whose diplomacy, strategy, and understanding of the processes of transculturation are depicted as far ahead of her time. The action takes place in the Congressional Chambers [Cámara de Diputados] and in flashbacks that appear to be evoked during Malinche's consultation with her therapist (Fig. 4.28). Yes, Malinche has a shrink!

The texts are surprisingly true to the history of the conquest. They represent the Spaniards' advance on Mexican soil, the massacre at Cholula, the meeting between Cortés and Moctezuma, the torture and death of Cuauhtémoc, *Noche Triste,* the siege and fall of Tenochtitlán, and the multiple consequences of these events. We note a continual and sustained infusion of both popular culture and events from the twentieth century. For example, immediately after the massacre at Cholula, the cast breaks character and sings "El corrido de Acteal," lamenting the continuing assassination of indigenous people in the 1990s. Specifically, the text links Cortés's massacre of religious leaders and civilians to the cold-blooded killing of forty-five Tzotzil people (many women and children), who were gunned down in December 1997 as they prayed in a church in Acteal. Instead of linking the violence to North Americans, the reference to Acteal—a massacre that was carried out by paramilitary troops linked to a local PRI leader (Camp 2003, 157)—places the blame squarely on the shoulders of Mexico's ruling party. A successful parallel is thus drawn (as was done in *El Ahuizotl*) between sixteenth-century history and twentieth-century actuality.

Theatrically, however, Rascón Banda believes that much of the play's message was lost, or "annulled" (2000b). Despite the common interest between Rascón Banda and Kresnik in creating political theater full of social commentary, Kresnik's aesthetic—which the playwright deemed "violent, scatological, obscene, although very poetic" ["violenta, escatológica, obscena, aunque muy poética"] (2000b)—confused audiences to the point of distraction. Whereas Rascón Banda envisioned three Malinche characters, each representing a different stage of her life, Kresnik cast *all* the women—and even some men—as Malinche. In the central scenes, in which Malinche's vindication and her role as a bridge between two worlds is explained, this vindication seems to be lost on audiences because Kresnik "staged it as two men emptied buckets of feces over her and urinated on her and masturbated on her. People saw the masturbation and the urine and the violence and did not hear the ideas she was defending" ["la puso mientras los hombres le vacían cubetas de excremento y se orinan sobre ella y se masturban sobre ella. La gente veía las masturbaciones y la orina y veía la violencia y no oía lo que ella defendía"] (2000b). Despite Rascón Banda's belief that Kresnik's staging confused the audiences, he maintains that the play captures much of Mexican popular culture. Music from the streets; a rural funeral from Tepoztlán; and many of the most common references to soccer, television, and politics make the staging of *La Malinche* Mexican to the core.

The Past in the Present:
Swapping Spaniards for Gringos

When it comes to treating the crucial debates on globalization, neoliberalism, and democratization in Mexico, as noted, Rascón Banda and Kresnik quickly came to agree on a central metaphor. Rascón Banda explains the metaphor as follows: "The Spanish conquest will be the North American conquest. The Indians will be those from Chiapas. Cholula will be Acteal. We will see the consequences of the North American Free Trade Agreement and the disagreements of San Andrés" ["La conquista española será la conquista estadounidense. Los indios serán los de Chiapas. Cholula será Acteal. Veremos las consecuencias del Tratado de Libre Comercio y los desacuerdos de San Andrés"] (Rascón Banda 2000a, 159). Spanish conquistadors thus appear as drunken gringo tourists in swim goggles. This conflation of eras again represents Mexicans' sense of the interminable conquest of

Mexico; it is an attempt on the part of the playwright to say, "Look at how there is a transformation of one identity into another. Just as it happened 500 years ago, it will happen again" ["Vean cómo hay una transformación de la identidad en otra, igual como pasó hace 500 años y como volverá a pasar"] (2000b). Whereas the sixteenth-century conquest was brought about with arms, today borders are infiltrated by free trade: "That is what the text suggests" ["Eso es lo que propone el texto"] says Rascón Banda, "another transformation, another conquest. Perhaps it isn't bloody, perhaps it isn't a bomb, perhaps it is not like that, but it is a spiritual conquest that is occurring. It will be a result of the movie industry, contact, or commerce, but it will happen" ["otra transformación, otra conquista. Quizá no es cruenta, quizá no es una bomba, quizá no es con eso, pero es una conquista espiritual que se está dando. Será por el cine, será por el contacto, o por el comercio, pero será"] (2000b).

One of the first scenes that clearly signals this continuum of conquest and the unavoidable consequences in terms of national identity is entitled "The Seven Plagues" ["Las siete plagas"]. In this scene, two Malinches (one adult, one elderly) enumerate the scourges brought by the Spaniards in the sixteenth century: small-pox, measles, typhoid fever. They then seamlessly continue:

Old Malinche:	But now there are new plagues that are killing us.
Adult Malinche:	Halloween kills Día de Muertos.
Old Malinche:	Mall kills *tianguis* [Aztec market].
Adult Malinche:	Harvard kills UNAM [Mexico's largest public university].
Old Malinche:	NAFTA kills commerce.
Adult Malinche:	Lumberjacks kill forests.
Old Malinche:	Ozone kills *chilango*.
[Malinche Vieja:	Pero ahora hay nuevas plagas que están matándonos.
Malinche Adulta:	Halloween mata Día de Muertos.
Malinche Vieja:	Mall mata tianguis.
Malinche Adulta:	Harvard mata UNAM.
Malinche Vieja:	TLC mata comercio.
Malinche Adulta:	Taladores matan bosques.
Malinche Vieja:	Ozono mata chilango.] (Rascón Banda 2000a, 98)

Here we see the stinging criticism of a globalizing plan that supplants authentic cultural rituals, that commodifies and commercializes exchange, and that replaces a locally educated governing elite with technocrats who then force foreign theories on a nation's economic and political systems.[19]

In the scene "Interrupted Party" ["Fiesta interrumpida"], the two conquests converge anew. At a party that could well be the Spaniards celebrating their victory over the Aztecs—for Tenochtitlán has fallen and Cuauhtémoc and Moctezuma have been killed—we see "high-class Mexicans and foreigners" ["mexicanos y extranjeros de etiqueta"] (Rascón Banda 2000a, 117) celebrating, instead, the passage of NAFTA, when the indigenous community arrives armed. The reference here, of course, is to the January 1, 1994, confluence of the enactment of NAFTA and the commencement of the Zapatista uprising. The actor who has portrayed Cortés is now dressed in a white dinner jacket, is referred to as *Licenciado,* and is spouting *PRIísta* policies at Malinche, who must then try to persuade the indigenous people to leave. The character tells Malinche, "Kill them now. . . . Make sure no one sees them" ["Mátenlos en caliente. . . . Que nadie los vea"] (118). Later he instructs, "Have these people enter through the back door" ["Haz pasar a esta gente por la puerta trasera"] (118). Then he asks, "What do they want? To ruin the party? Scare my guests/the foreigners? This is a historic day. Today we are entering the First World" ["¿Qué se han propuesto? ¿Echar a perder la fiesta? ¿Espantar a mis invitados/extranjeros? Este es un día histórico. Hoy estamos ingresando en el primer mundo"] (118). Here the apprehension and dramatic tension of the significance of becoming part of the First World are painfully obvious. Because of the risk that they might "scare off" the gringos and Canadians, the Lacandon, Tzotzil, and Chamula people are denied entry. They are accused of being a nuisance, inappropriately dressed, an eyesore, and a bunch of party poopers. Still, the two groups agree to sit down at the negotiating table in San Andrés. But in the scene entitled "San Andrés Disaccords" ["Desacuerdos de San Andrés"], the indigenous people are nowhere to be found and it is up to Malinche and *Licenciado* to attempt to come to a compromise on the language of the demands that will become the reality—and enforceable law:

Malinche:	[. . .] They are asking "*to agree collectively* to the use and enjoyment of the natural resources of their territories."
Licenciado:	All right, but I would do away with the *collectively agree* and would add "respecting the limitations established by the constitution." Is it too much to ask?
Malinche:	It's just that it changes the meaning.
[Malinche:	(. . .) Están pidiendo "*acceder de manera colectiva* al uso y disfrute de los recursos naturales de sus territorios."
Licenciado:	Está bien, pero yo quitaría lo de *manera colectiva* y agregaría "respetando las limitaciones establecidas por la constitución." ¿Es mucho pedir?
Malinche:	Es que cambia el sentido.] (127)

Here the language closely mirrors the government legalese that many felt was used to thwart any progress made toward securing indigenous rights in the 1996 San Andrés Accords. As noted in Chapter 1, despite the agreement of the 1996 accords on such basic issues as indigenous autonomy, collective land rights, and control of natural resources, the 2001 indigenous rights law passed by the Mexican House and Senate represented a radical departure from these tenets. In both the halls of Mexico's political power and the play *La Malinche,* the indigenous people have again been turned away from the negotiating tables. After this act of silencing them, what more could they loose? Ironically in the play, in the rapidly globalizing world, their very identity is consumed—once again—by a dominant conquering culture.

Soon after, the updated Malinche, too, appears as an agent of global free trade, when we see her in a scene entitled "New Body, New Skin" ["Nuevo cuerpo, nueva piel"], which is staged as an infomercial. She is the poor consumer who has tried every product to alleviate her problems. At first, we think that the products NEW BODY and CLARITY SKIN are the typical miracle weight loss and skin-firming salves hawked on television. But then Malinche is asked, "Do you have problems at home or in the office because of the dark color of your skin?" ["¿Tienes problemas en la casa o en la oficina por el color oscuro de tu piel?"] (Rascón Banda 2000a, 132). Malinche is seductively advised, "With CLARITY SKIN you can leave that all in the past" ["Con CLARITY SKIN todo puede quedar en el pasado"] (132). We now realize that the play is suggesting that the future of global consumerism and marketing constitutes a form of racial and cultural whitewashing and that it therefore represents a real threat to *mexicanidad* and Mexico's multicultural attempts at maintaining diversity among its indigenous and mestizo populations.

The exchange that ends the scene has the two vendors imploring Malinche to embrace the new, First World, white persona that she could and should embody:

Woman 1:	New skin, new body, new life.
Woman 2:	Be thin!
Malinche:	It's a miracle!
Woman 4:	Be white!
Malinche:	I can't believe it.
Woman 3:	Be happy!
Malinche:	I am you!
Woman 3:	Dare!
Malinche:	Heavens!
Man 2:	Call us!
Malinche:	Oh my God!

[Mujer 1:	Nueva piel, nuevo cuerpo, nueva vida.
Mujer 2:	¡Sé delgada!
Malinche:	¡Es un milagro!
Mujer 4:	¡Sé blanca!
Malinche:	No puedo creerlo.
Mujer 3:	¡Sé feliz!
Malinche:	¡Ésa soy tú!
Mujer 3:	¡Atrévete!
Malinche:	¡Santo cielo!
Hombre 2:	¡Llámanos!
Malinche:	¡Oh my God!] (Rascón Banda 2000a, 133)

At this point, Malinche cries, as a man grabs her breast—indicating just how desirable and objectified she has become. Then she continues:

Woman 2:	Limited time offer!
Malinche:	Thanks to NEW BODY I am totally . . . happy.

[Mujer 2:	¡Oferta limitada!
Malinche:	Gracias a NEW BODY. Soy totalmente . . . feliz.] (133)

And mimicking what those who are familiar with Mexican television and advertising have come to expect at the end of a plug for a particularly pernicious or unhealthful product, the dialogue continues:

Man 1:	Pending permits from the Department of Health and Consumer Rights.
All:	Eat fruits and vegetables!

[Hombre 1:	Permisos de la Secretaría de Salud y del Consumidor en trámite.
Todos:	¡Come frutas y verduras!] (133)

Yet the cosmetic erasure of Mexicans' color and authenticity that is proposed by the fictitious products is merely skin deep, as they say. In the final scene, the therapist and Malinche verbally affirm her enduring presence in and pertinence to Mexico, as they visually participate in a sort of wrestling match. An old indigenous woman extinguishes the candles on stage and lies down, as corn rains down from the heavens and the curtain closes.

In some ways, the play and its production represent a successful collaboration and a fulfillment of the goals of Rascón Banda and Kresnik. First, through its revision of the figure of Malinche, the play succeeds in demonstrating that opening Mexico's economy to free trade and global markets leads to the loss of Mexico's varied and unique social, cultural, and racial characteristics—the very material of a multicultural national identity. Once again, the conquest provides Mexican artists with the backdrop they need to explore the complex realities of modern Mexico. In a scene in which Cuauhtémoc and Marcos lament the fall of Tenochtitlán, the following lines (the last of which quotes *La visión de los vencidos*) are pertinent not only to sixteenth-century Mexico but to post-NAFTA Mexico as well:

| Marcos: | Weep, my friends. |
| Cuauhtémoc: | Be it understood that for these reasons we are losing the Mexican nation. |

| [Marcos: | Llorad, amigos míos. |
| Cuauhtémoc: | Tengan entendido que por estas razones estamos perdiendo la nación mexicana.] (Rascón Banda 2000a, 77)[20] |

Yet in the play *La Malinche,* we note a contradiction in the attitude toward cultures in contact, transculturation, or the wrenching and violent transformations of the sixteenth and twentieth centuries. How can a mestizo nation celebrate its racial and cultural crosscurrent as enrichment while it fears that new influences are diluting? This same contradiction exists, metaphorically, in the fear that Kresnik's production annulled Rascón Banda's text although, at the same time, it captured Mexican popular culture. Mexican nationalism and national identity, therefore, straddle an uncomfortable line when it comes to attitudes toward external influence.

Second, this play was a successful collaboration because of whom it touched and how. It is true that Kresnik's aesthetic and Rascón Banda's text confused and insulted many. But, according to Rascón Banda, the collaborators' efforts were roundly embraced by young people: "Young people went crazy over the play. They stood up, they filled the theater, they yelled, and it was scandalous because it communicated very well to young people, because young people have no prejudices, because young people belong to another century and they do not carry the weight and cultural baggage that adults have" ["Los jóvenes se enloquecían con la obra. Se ponían de pie, llenaban el teatro, gritaban, y era un escándolo aquello porque se comunicaba muy bien con los jóvenes, porque los jóvenes no tienen prejuicios, porque los jóvenes son de otro siglo y no tienen ese peso y ese bagaje cultural que tienen los adultos"] (2000b). But, it is worth pointing out, young people loved this play precisely because it is (1) about them and about the Mexico in which they live and (2) a product of globalization. Kresnik's aesthetic is, after all, much like the violent, vulgar, eroticized, and sexualized international cyber culture that so engages the world's youth. Yet their ebullient reception of *La Malinche*'s irreverent and uncomfortable production can be read in two ways: To traditionalists, it confirms fears of a vacuous, post-NAFTA McCulture accepted by today's Americanized young Mexicans. But to others, the enthusiasm of Mexico's young people speaks to an emerging globalized border culture in which local politics can advocate indigenous rights and, at the same time, fall back on the tired disingenuous *indigenismo* contained in the statement "Todos somos indios."

5

Concluding Remarks

The texts analyzed here demonstrate the suitability of the period from the late 1980s through the 1990s for the revisitation, revision, and realignment of Mexican national identity with turn-of-the-millennium Mexican national sentiment. As we have seen, this large-scale revisitation of national origins was necessitated by the deepening crisis in Mexican national identity, provoked by acute political and economic failings. Because of the faltering state of the nation's main political party, Mexican intellectuals sensed the need to reexamine the emblem around which the Partido Revolucionario Institucional (PRI) had constructed national unity for decades: the mestizo. Officially hailed as a harmonious synthesis of two races, two cultures, two peoples, *mestizaje* as an ideal was being undermined by many factors at the end of the twentieth century, not the least of which were the Quincentennial debates, increasing awareness of multiculturalism, and the growing indigenous rights movement in Mexico.

When the Quincentennial year brought mestizo origins into sharp focus, such artists as Ignacio Solares, Salvador Carrasco, and Carmen Boullosa demonstrated the impossibility of the concept of harmonious mestizo beginnings. Ending with the indigenous protagonists crushed and silenced, their works highlight not only the real imbalance of powers at play in the sixteenth century but also the real absence of diversity—or even duality (cultural synthesis)—in mainstream mestizo culture. Despite the desire of all three authors to demonstrate—as they had been taught since primary school—the rich indigenous and Spanish contributions to Mexico's racial and spiritual essence, their texts leave us sensing not only indigenous absence but also the true state of Otherness to which the indigenous people had been relegated.

Our examination of the results of works that revisit mestizo origins showed how texts by Carmen Boullosa and Carlos Fuentes, in their attempts to ascribe plurality to Mexican culture, call into question the very concept of mestizo culture as synthesis. These authors concur with Roger Bartra, who writes that democratization at the end of the twentieth century meant the end of a culture of duality (1991, 18). Although Boullosa's text concludes by advocating multicultural understanding, the despairing note is undeniable in her positing of the first Mexican as a Spaniard rather than as an *indígena* or a mestizo. This ending is yet another indication of Mexico's heavy alignment not only with Hispanic culture and language at the expense of the indigenous but also with the falsehood of indigenous presence. Using the misnomer *mestizaje*, "Las dos orillas," by Fuentes, makes even greater strides toward true valuation of cultural and racial diversity, but it too ultimately betrays a real bias for Western Hispanic culture. What the failed attempts of these texts clearly demonstrate is that although the Mexican people were beginning to acknowledge the nation's pluriculture in the late 1980s and early 1990s, the government and the nation as a whole had failed to generate policies that would give that acknowledgment meaning in real concrete terms (Morris 2001, 245).

It is interesting to note that in this collective revision of Mexican national identity, as Chapter 4 demonstrates, one defining element of the *fin del siglo* proved capable of profoundly influencing Mexican national identity discourse: the issue of modernization. The cartoons of *El Ahuizotl* and Víctor Hugo Rascón Banda's play *La Malinche* demonstrate how the specter of modernization could effect a very real backlash in nationalist sentiment. No longer the culturally dual mestizos, when threatened with modernization (perceived as concomitant with globalization and Americanization), Mexicans defensively represented themselves as the vanquished indigenous people of the sixteenth century. Fear of losing their Mexican way of life fueled their new identification with the indigenous people of the sixteenth century precisely because of the perception that their culture, society, and language had been razed.

Yet how could Mexican national identity face the prospect of "losing" its indigenous root? The admission that mestizos are not really a cultural synthesis, that they are instead largely Western (Hispanic), is an admission of the assimilationist impulse within mestizophile philosophy to view indigenous people as Others. How could mestizo Mexico then trace its glorious past through indigenous cultures? How could Mexicans be and feel that they are countrymen and -women of the indigenous groups—who are Other both culturally and linguistically—that currently inhabit Mexican territory?

On January 1, 1994, this question of indigenous person as Other or as self would be irremediably altered. The momentous events in Chiapas, and the Mexican and global reaction to them, undoubtedly and profoundly altered much about Mexican national identity. As Stephen D. Morris demonstrates in his article "Reforming the Nation: Mexican Nationalism in Context," the Zapatista movement challenges Mexico's myth of national unity and "forces the dominant *mestizo* culture to come to grips with the now glaring contradiction between the concept of the *indio* contained within its own (*mestizo*) image of itself and the situation, and the demands of the current indigenous population" (1999, 375). For this reason, the analyses of creative works published during the Carlos Salinas de Gortari *sexenio* that are contained in this book are instructive and important: They provide an in-depth probe into not only the state of Mexico's mestizo national identity in the years leading up to Chiapas but also the various constructions of self and Other within national identity discourses at the time.

At stake, of course, in the squaring off of self and Other is the very concept of Mexican national unity. If for decades the nation had been told that its unity, its strength, and its greatness revolved around the figure of the mestizo and flowed from the harmony and synthesis embodied in the process of *mestizaje,* around what would Mexicans now rally? What would hold the nation together? Fortunately, Mexicans in 1994 possessed a high level of identification with their nationality. In a survey carried out by the Universidad Nacional Autónoma de México, 37 percent of those polled identified more with Mexico than with their state, 18 percent identified as much with Mexico as with their state, and 19 percent identified only with Mexico (*Los mexicanos de los noventa* 1996, 86).

Another boon to national unity in the late 1990s, of course, was the evident opening of Mexico to real alternation of power and democracy. Swept by the excitement of the elections in 2000 and the possibility for change, the Mexican electorate turned out in record numbers and Mexican citizens living abroad (mostly in the United States) flooded the border states to cast their votes, largely for the candidate of the Partido de Acción Nacional (PAN), Vicente Fox.

All of this, of course, still leaves us with the question of Mexican national unity in the years to come. Perhaps, as the election in 2000 demonstrated, a civic-mindedness will bind Mexicans to their fellow countrymen and -women. Perhaps an inclusive ideology such as multiculturalism will embrace all and will even afford rights as bestowed by a government convinced of its nation's pluriculture. In *La guerra y las palabras: Una historia intelectual de 1994,* the young Mexican writer Jorge Volpi—citing the popularity of Subcomandante Marcos and the lack of attributability of that popularity to a rebirth of either Marxism or utopian socialism—argues that the unifying force may be a combination of both civic-mindedness and an inclusive ideology. According to Volpi, Marcos and the Ejército Zapatista de Liberación Nacional (EZLN) prefigured a new left—one based on consolidating democracy and civil society while also fighting for indigenous rights and against the inequalities of neoliberalism (2004, 395). This new left, he continues, is "more citizenry than partisanship and more socially than politically active— which we usually identify with antiglobalization movements" ["más ciudadana que partidista y más activa social que políticamente que ahora identificamos con los movimientos antiglobalización"] (395–96). Whether or not the left provides Mexico with unity in the future, one obvious area of fallout from both the postrevolutionary PRI crumbling and Fox's presidency involves the very issue of national history. If Mexican society no longer balances on the pillars of *PRIísta* mestizophile discourse, then no longer must the nation and its institutions trace their lineage back to the encounter of two worlds or to the great indigenous past.

As if cued by the cyclical Aztec notion of time, Fox's appointees at the Secretaría de Educación Pública (SEP) announced their plans for the next printing of *Libros de texto gratuitos* in June 2004. Nearly every president who reissues the texts faces public outcry (especially with respect to the history texts). Under the Reforma Integral de la Educación Secundaria in 2004, history, it was revealed, would be one of the materials dramatically cut from the curriculum for Mexican schoolchildren. Beginning in 2005, in order to "avoid repetitions" ["evitar repeticiones"] and "ensure greater depth" ["asegurar mayor profundidad"], Mexican high school students would study one year of history (rather than three). As a result, both their national and their world history texts would begin with the fifteenth century.[1]

The public outcry, as expected, was immediate and vociferous. "How could Fox cut prehistory—especially pre-Hispanic Mexican history?" the Mexican people asked. Gone would be the Mesoamerican cultures (Fig. 5.1): the Maya, the Teotihuacanos, the Zapotecs, the Mixtecs, and the Toltecs (Ahumada 2004). The historian Alfredo López Austin opined that the cuts "would be lamentable in Mexico, because students would be left unarmed when faced with today's national reality as a cultural mosaic. This would impede understanding of the very nature of Mexico" ["en el caso de México sería lamentable, porque el estudiante quedaría desarmado frente a la realidad actual del país como un mosaico cultural. Esto impediría entender la propia naturaleza de México"] (quoted in Mac Masters et al. 2004, 2). The historian Miguel León-Portilla wrote an entire article for *La Jornada* in which he extolled the bases of Mexican identity: "We Mexicans have constructed our identity on a rich, dual cultural legacy. . . . To be unaware of this legacy is to be disconnected from the millenary roots that give life to the country's being" ["Los mexicanos hemos construido nuestra identidad a partir de un doble y muy rico legado cultural. . . . Desconocer este legado es desentendernos de las raíces milenarias que dan sustento al ser del país"] (2004, 1). In addition, he echoed fears about the loss of Mexican identity: "Today as never before, there are rampant processes of cultural globalization coming from the most powerful country on earth. Are they trying to strip us of our roots?" ["Hoy, como nunca antes, existen procesos de rampante globalización cultural provenientes del país más poderoso del planeta, ¿se pretende acaso extirpar la conciencia de nuestras raíces?"] (2). The ethnographer José del Val Blanco even alleged, "If they erase history from our secondary school texts, they erase adolescents' identification with Mexican essence. The social and national implications are a betrayal of the country; erasing Mexico's history from secondary education is a betrayal of the country" ["Si nos borran la historia de los libros de texto de secundaria, se borra en los adolescentes la identificación con la matriz mexicana. Las implicaciones sociales y nacionales son de traición a la patria; borrar la historia de México en la educación secundaria es tración a la patria"] (quoted in Ponce 2004, 1).

Figure 5.1. In response to President Vicente Fox's announced plans to reduce the history curriculum for schoolchildren in 2004—especially the pre-Hispanic Mexican history curriculum—Ahumada drew this cartoon of a Mayan figure being tossed out of a public school. Courtesy of the artist, Ahumada.

It appears that more than a decade later the discourse that surrounds history and national identity has changed—but not all that much. Although Mexican society and its identity are still viewed as dual (indigenous and Spanish), now there appears the image of a cultural mosaic. Identity stems from knowledge of our roots, and now more than ever—as Mexico is faced with cultural globalization—it is essential to instill that identity in Mexico's youth. Perhaps most menacing, as we have seen, is Fox's apparent ability to reduce the curriculum of a subject that has long been sacred in the Mexican public education system.

As usual, the criticisms of the curriculum cuts also turned against the president himself. The history teachers at the Colegio de Jefes de Enseñanza in Mexico City charged Fox with demonstrating a "neoliberal, conservative, utilitarian, and reactionary bias" ["carga ideológica neoliberal, conservadora, utilitarista y retrógrada."] ("Plan de SEP" 2004, 1). The writer Federico Campbell, for his part, was quoted as saying of Fox and his functionaries in the SEP, "They are people who believe that the present comes out of nowhere and is not a product of historical and social workings. Therefore, it appears to me to be one more act of foolishness on the part of Vicente Fox's educational politics and culture" ["Son personas que creen que el presente es una invención de la nada, y no un producto del quehacer histórico social. Entonces, me parece una tontería más de la política educativa y cultural de Vicente Fox"] (quoted in Mac Masters et al. 2004, 4). The *moneros* of *La Jornada* also took up the attacks—personal at times—against Secretary of Public Education Reyes Tamez Guerra. In one cartoon, Rocha depicts the secretary commenting on the controversy as he reads about it in the daily paper (Fig. 5.2): "Why do you want to hear an Indian story? Better yet, I'll tell you a cowboy tale" ["¿Para qué quieren que les cuente la historia de los indios? Mejor les cuento una de vaqueros"] (Rocha 2004b). Here it is not bad enough that the secretary is seen as a yes-man for the president; to top it off, Fox is accused of cutting the ancient history curriculum specifically to make room for the inclusion of his own campaign, victory, and presidency in the pages of *Mi libro de historia* (a charge that was leveled against Salinas de Gortari in the 1990s as well). In a cartoon entitled "Plucking

LA HISTORIA SECUNDARIA ◑ Rocha

Figure 5.2. Many Mexicans believed that the Fox administration intended to minimize historical accounts about pre-Hispanic (indigenous) events in order to maximize historical accounts about Fox (known as the cowboy for the boots he wears). In this illustration, an administrator tells a class, "Why do you want to hear an Indian story? Better yet, I'll tell you a cowboy tale." Courtesy of the artist, Rocha.

History" ["Desplumando la historia"] (Rocha 2004a), Tamez Guerra's attempts to reduce the size of the indigenous headdress he is wearing leave him with two feathers that crown him with donkey ears (Fig. 5.3). The message is clear: He who cuts indigenous history makes an ass of himself.

Admittedly, the uprising in Chiapas and nearly two decades of neoliberal policies in Mexico have dramatically altered Mexico's national identity and have exposed many new nuances. Yet the core issues discussed in the novels, the movie, the play, and the cartoons analyzed here remain salient. First, Mexico's origins—whether political, racial, spiritual, or cultural—continue to be a dramatic source of storytelling. And the stories they evoke will, in turn, always speak to the question of who today's Mexicans are. Moreover, history—whether mythified or not—is ever-present in Mexico and continues to be employed by the state to aid in inculcating in its youth both national identity and specific civic values. And finally, race—indigenous, European, or mestizo—will continue to challenge this nation whose mestizophile identity discourse long skewed many Mexicans' notion of their nation.

What is, and will be in the future, in flux in Mexican national identity are the very issues that so vexed the creative works discussed in this book. To begin with, Mexico's diversity, or pluriculture, is undeniable yet inadequately defined in the minds of many. Despite clear promises in Salinas de Gortari's constitutional

DESPLUMANDO LA HISTORIA □ Rocha

Figure 5.3. When the administrator from the Secretaría de Educación Pública (SEP) cuts indigenous history (the feathers), he is left with a donkey's ears, thus making an ass of himself. Courtesy of the artist, Rocha.

reform to protect and promote, governmental inconsistency in its dealings with indigenous groups has added to the nation's befuddlement over what to do about its national diversity. In addition, the very attitudes of multiculturalism espoused by Fuentes, and to a lesser extent by Boullosa, may develop slowly on a national level—if they reach that goal at all—and may nevertheless fail to lead to consensus. And finally, as we saw in Chapter 4, modernization and the effects of opening Mexico to the exterior—so long a source of national hand-wringing—will be, perhaps, the new lightning rod for issues of national identity, affecting the future of the very state of *mexicanidad*.

Notes

Chapter 1
Issues of Nation, Identity, and History in Mexico

1. Officially, Mexico declared its mestizo status an asset and produced a national identity based on mestizophile thought. Mestizophile thought, as defined by Agustín Basave Benítez (1993, 13) is "the idea that *mestizaje*—that is the mixing of two races and/or cultures—as a phenomenon is a desirable event" ["la idea de que el fenómeno del mestizaje—es decir, la mezcla de razas y/o culturas—es un hecho deseable"]. He goes on to note that the mestizophile writings of Andrés Molina Enríquez—Mexico's greatest champion of *mestizaje*—state that the Mexican mestizos, "those who have a mixed, Hispanic-indigenous lineage, are Mexicans par excellence, the authentic depositaries of *la mexicanidad*" ["quienes poseen un linaje mixto hispano-indígena, son los mexicanos por antonomasia, los auténticos depositarios de la mexicanidad"] (13).

2. Numerous other Latin American governments—including those of Colombia, Ecuador, Nicaragua, Panama, and Venezuela—also faced their nations' ethnic diversity in the 1990s. See Shannan Mattiace's description of "constitutionally codified, ethnically defined autonomy regimes" (1993, 40–46 and conclusion) and Donna Lee Van Cott's study of "multicultural constitutionalism" (2000, 257–80).

3. The term *multiculturalism*, coined in Canada in the 1960s, describes "both the ideals of a democracy that values cultural diversity and the policies necessary to realize these goals" (Van Cott 2000, 281). In his book *We Are All Multiculturalists Now*, Nathan Glazer states that the term first surfaced in the 1970s and 1980s in publications from Australia and Canada and that it is just the latest in a long series of terms that describe how a multiethnic society should respond to its diversity (1997, 8). Indeed, terms such as *cultural pluralism* have been around since 1915 (Aguilar Rivera 2004, 95).

4. The term *politics of recognition* is from Taylor 1992.

5. Natividad Gutiérrez admits that the shift toward recognition of plurality "is an

incomplete project still undergoing conceptual clarification and requiring further legislation" (1999, 110).

6. In her study of the indigenous rights movement in Chiapas and Oaxaca, Lynn Stephen writes more specifically that these terms are defined in Mexico as "respect for the internal practices and decision-making modes of indigenous pueblos . . . the participation of indigenous communities in levels of economic, political, cultural and legal decision-making associated with the government" as well as the ability of "local and regional forms of ethnic and cultural identities to function both within the larger indigenous movement and within the nation" (2002, 328–29). As such, in Mexico indigenous demands reflect Jacob Levy's third, sixth, seventh, and eighth categories of policies that respect diversity.

7. Primary among the rebels' complaints was Salinas de Gortari's 1992 end to agrarian reform and modification of Article 27 of the 1917 constitution. For detailed discussions of this aspect of the Zapatista uprising, see Stephen 2002 (62–72) and Mattiace 2003 (79–81).

8. In her comparative study of the politics of diversity and constitutional reform in Latin America, Van Cott states that—in varying degrees—the multicultural constitutional reforms share the following five elements: "(1) rhetorical recognition of the multicultural nature of their societies and the existence of indigenous peoples as distinct, substate social collectivities, (2) recognition of indigenous peoples' customary law as official, public law, (3) collective property rights protected from sale, dismemberment or confiscation, (4) official status or recognition of indigenous languages, and (5) a guarantee of bilingual education" (2000, 265). The self-determination issue, she writes, "is an obstacle to the adoption of a UN or OAS declaration of indigenous rights acceptable to the most radical and internationalized indigenous organizations. This is unfortunate since most indigenous organizations in Latin America seek not the full independence that a minority insist must be codified as a legal alternative, but rather, a sphere of autonomy within the state and a greater role in decision-making that affects them" (265).

9. For a detailed discussion of the semantic and legal differences in the terms *peoples* and *communities*, see Levi 2002 (34).

10. In August 2005, the Zapatista leader, known as Subcomandante Marcos, reappeared metaphorically and physically on Mexico's political scene. Just as the leading parties chose their presidential candidates for the 2006 election, Marcos appeared in public for the first time in four years to criticize the candidates and to challenge the candidate for the leftist Partido Revolucionario Democrático [Democratic Revolutionary Party]), Andrés Manuel López Obrador, to debate. As the nation geared up for the 2006 presidential election, it appeared that the EZLN and Marcos intended to reenter national political dialogue. In the end, however, they had no impact on the election results.

11. A perhaps unforeseen consequence of this identity crisis has been noted by Ingelhart and colleagues: "We find a declining sense of nationalism, which bodes well for the future evolution of international cooperation, and for a potential North American free-trade zone in particular" (1996, 85). As Chapter 4 demonstrates, in Mexico in the 1990s, this prospect was highly contentious.

12. These six works were selected specifically because they combine historical fiction with *identity discourse* (a term that is defined in the corresponding discussion). The pieces analyzed here are unique among the large body of works from the same time period that rewrite the events of the discovery and conquest, because they relate to Mexican national identity and mestizophile ideology. For an excellent review of historical novels published in Mexico and throughout Latin America that deal with the discovery and conquest, see the Introduction to Lopez 2002.

13. Rascón Banda's play *La Malinche,* analyzed in Chapter 4, was written in 1997, produced in 1998, and published in 2000. However, its irresistible combination of historical revision of the conquest, scathing political criticism, and eroticized national identity discourse set in a post-NAFTA, post-Chiapas Mexico make it a fitting text with which to culminate the book's discussion.

14. The following quotation by Max Parra, which is worth citing at length, illuminates the specific intricacy of Mexico's twentieth-century nationalism—the defining discourse of the nation: "What we understand as nationalism is the strategy employed by the State that arose from the Revolution in order to acquire legitimization and exercise power with the consent of the masses, a strategy that foments national unity for the purpose of inhibiting social practices antagonistic to the established order. This State discourse is, consequently, interested in creating a collective identity that transcends class differences, elaborating an official historical memory that adapts to the intentions of the State, placing emphasis on the conquests of the Revolution, on harmonic social development, on national progress." ["Por nacionalismo entendemos la estrategia del Estado surgido de la Revolución para adquirir legitimación y ejercer el poder con el consentimiento de las masas, estrategia que fomenta una unidad nacional con el propósito de inhibir prácticas sociales antagónicas al poder establecido. Este discurso del estado interesa, por consiguiente, en forjar una identidad colectiva que trascienda las diferencias de clase, elabora una memoria histórica oficial que se amolde a los designios del Estado, pone énfasis en las conquistas de la Revolución, en el desarrollo social armónico, en el progreso nacional"] (1996, 28). Here Parra touches on the ever-present role that the Mexican state, in the form of the Partido Revolucionario Institucional, or PRI, played in fomenting nationalism throughout the twentieth century. The PRI's interpretation of Mexico's past simultaneously served to legitimize its own power and to create a version of national unity that, in turn, offset any questioning of its rule.

15. Although Mexico's deep and often aggressive nationalist tradition can be attributed to many factors, far and above the others is its proximity to the United States and the many consequential geographical, political, and economic clashes. Indeed, in his *Los orígenes del nacionalismo mexicano,* David Brading defines *nationalism* as a reaction to foreign threat (1981, 11). Furthermore, Mexico has suffered numerous threats, attacks, invasions, and occupations from *other* nations. After citing both the shadow cast by the United States and the PRI's need to consolidate power, Alan Riding adds Mexico's renowned machismo and inferiority complex to the equation (1989, 18–20). Although it can be argued that these characterizations are somewhat facile, Riding contends that the sense of vulnerability they foster feeds Mexican

nationalism. Henry Schmidt offers a similar thesis in his claim that Mexico's need to define itself has been "stimulated by the desire to enter the larger world, to emerge from its isolated, colonial status and convey an image of equality with other nations" (1978, 161).

16. Brazilian intellectuals also continually ponder their nation's identity. Most noted for his contributions to the field is Gilberto Freyre. In Argentina, Ezequiel Martínez Estrada figures, and both Peruvian and Puerto Rican intellectuals also debate the concepts of nation and identity.

17. In the following quotation, the Mexican historian, author, and political analyst Héctor Aguilar Camín demonstrates how difficult the definition and separation of these two concepts can be: "Identity is nothing more than a mixture of history, myth, official inventions, and collective inventions. Our national or cultural identity is something that comes from the past, from our memory and our traditions, but it is also something that is in gestation, that comes from beyond and is the result of the outcomes of our present" ["La identidad no es sino una mezcla de historia, mitos, invenciones oficiales e invenciones colectivos. Nuestra identidad nacional o cultural es algo que viene del pasado, de nuestra memoria y nuestras tradiciones, pero también es algo que está en gestación, que viene de adelante y es el resultado de los desenlaces de nuestro presente"] (1993a, 59). This vague definition presents national identity as interchangeable with nationalism in general, or national consciousness, which is the populace's awareness of its national characteristics and nationalist discourses. To a certain extent, this is true, but it is nonetheless a poignant reminder that the complexity and interrelation of these terms aids little in their definition or analysis.

18. A few of the key works on Mexican national identity published in the twentieth century include *Forjando patria* (1916) by Manuel Gamio, *La raza cósmica* (1925) by José Vasconcelos, *El perfil del hombre y la cultura en Mexico* (1934) by Samuel Ramos, *El laberinto de la soledad* (1950) by Octavio Paz, and *La jaula de la melancolía* (1987) by Roger Bartra. These works are treated in greater detail in the pages that follow.

19. Henry Schmidt, who documents the beginnings of the *lo mexicano* movement in prerevolutionary Mexico, notes that it reaches its apogee between the years 1920 and 1959 when "the term *lo mexicano* became a 'sacred phrase' and assumed popular as well as academic meanings as the question of what is Mexico and the Mexican was asked. *Lo mexicano* refers to the Mexican ethos as well as to its study and became a driving principle for the growth of knowledge relating to Mexico. With its allied terms *mexicanidad, mexicanismo,* and *el mexicano,* it cut across disciplines and engaged historians as well as philosophers and psychologists" (1978, x). Whereas Creoles and liberals in the nineteenth century had defined nationhood only along historiographic and political lines, postrevolutionary thinkers sought out the unique characteristics of Mexican being and touted them through culturally nationalist works.

20. In a June 1994 poll taken by the Universidad Nacional Autónoma de México (UNAM), when asked whether they identify more with their nation or their state of birth, 37 percent of respondents said that they identify more with Mexico. The

authors conclude, "The fact that people perceive themselves as having a common nationality does not mean they do not perceive differences among themselves. National diversity (linguistic and ethnic) within the state questions the normative order that proposes uniformity among citizens in the name of nation and state congruency" ["El que las personas se perciban como poseedores de una nacionalidad común, no quiere decir que no adviertan diferencias entre sí. La diversidad nacional (lingüística y étnica) dentro del estado cuestiona el orden normativo que plantea la uniformidad entre los ciudadanos en nombre de la congruencia entre Estado y nación"] (*Los mexicanos de los noventa* 1996, 86). Mexico's great ethnic diversity is evident in Rebeca Barriga Villanueva's study of plurilingualism in present-day Mexico, in which she demonstrates the existence of no less than 122 indigenous languages (1995a, 125–31).

21. Vasconcelos (1976) embarked on a national postrevolutionary project to integrate and educate the Mexican population that revolved around the concept of racial and cultural *mestizaje* as a harmonious, third "cosmic race" ["raza cósmica"]. Molina Enríquez, seen as the father of *mestizofilia*, also regarded the mixing of races and cultures as desirable for Mexico and believed mestizos to be "Mexicans par excellence, the authentic depositaries of *la mexicanidad*" ["los mexicanos por antonomasia, los auténticos depositarios de la mexicanidad"] (quoted in Basave Benítez 1993, 13). Molina Enríquez based his views of Mexican citizenry as essentially mestizo on Gamio's ideas originally published in 1916 in *Forjando patria*. In this text, Gamio concludes that the fusion of races would produce a coherent, strong, well-defined nation (1982, 183). For more in-depth analysis of Mexico's budding mestizophile national identity, see Doremus 2001.

22. In his article "Ambigüedad de la identidad, fluctuación de la nación, avatares de lo mexicano, a través de los siglos," Jacques Lafaye demonstrates the blurring of concepts such as nation, pueblo, state, *patria*, and race in the past century and a half in Mexico (1996, 62–66). Analyzing the writings of Gamio and Vasconcelos, he writes that "the concept of 'race' had the greatest importance in the Mexican nation" ["el concepto de 'raza' tuvo la mayor importancia de la nación mexicana"] (66).

23. Although the text does not mention the exclusion of the Niños Héroes, for a demonstration of the representation of the Salinas de Gortari regime's pro–United States stance in Mexico's elementary school texts, see Gilbert 1997 (283–89). Morris 2005 (85–127) examines the issue in texts from the 1960s to the 1990s.

24. Alfredo López Austin, a well-known Mexican historian has written that "the coat of arms reduces, unifies, and simplifies *la mexicanidad*, evoking a story that is in itself an allegory" ["el escudo reduce, unifica, simplifica la mexicanidad evocando un pasaje que ya de suyo es alegoría"] (1995, 16).

25. Perhaps the best study of nationalistic culture is by Néstor García Canclini. In *Culturas híbridas,* he states, "It is logical that, among Latin American countries, Mexico is, due to the nationalist orientation of its postrevolutionary policy, the country that has been most concerned with expanding its visual culture, preserving its patrimony, and integrating it into a system of museums and archeological and historical centers" ["Es lógico que, entre los países latinoamericanos, sea México,

por la orientación nacionalista de su política postrevolucionaria, el que más se ha ocupado de expandir la cultura visual, preservar su patrimonio e integrarlo en un sistema de museos, centros arqueológicos e históricos"] (1990, 161).

26. For an excellent study of Vasconcelos—his thought and works—see Luis A. Marentes's *José Vasconcelos and the Writing of the Mexican Revolution* (2000). The book is particularly illuminating in terms of the evolution of Vasconcelian thought and how modern-day views of Vasconcelos contradict many of his later writings. In the chapter on his Ministry of Public Education, Marentes carefully documents Vasconcelos's political and ideological conflicts with the muralists as well.

27. Ever since Mexico gained independence in 1821, Mexican intellectuals have played an active role in the development of texts for elementary school instruction. In the 1890s, however, the teaching of history throughout Mexico became official—that is, its function became to legitimize the state and further the ideals of integration and citizenship (Vázquez 1995, 54).

28. Josefina Zoraida Vázquez, who has studied Mexican education in the past century and a half, believes that "education has been an instrument the government has used to mold the collective consciousness of a country and awaken the loyalty of its inhabitants toward a nation-state" ["la educación ha sido, pues, un instrumento que el gobierno ha utilizado para modelar la conciencia colectiva de un país y despertar la lealtad de sus habitantes hacia el estado-nación"] (1995, 8). For a discussion of how national heroes can be manipulated to embody national values, thus making school texts veritable ideological tools of the state, see her detailed analysis of history textbooks (Vázquez 1970). For a discussion of similar political educational policies around the world, see Farnen 1994 (60–71), which reviews a large body of scholarship on the subject.

29. Two scholars who have studied the *Libros de texto gratuitos* and their ramifications as identity discourses since the books became mandatory are Lorenza Villa Lever and Lilian Álvarez de Testa. Their works (Villa Lever 1988; Álvarez de Testa 1992) analyze social representations manifested in the treatment of the history, indigenous cultures, and heroes of Mexico.

30. Mexico City is commonly referred to as a palimpsest because of its multiple architectural and archaeological layers. Especially at the Templo Mayor, we see the practice of palimpsest building, wherein a hybrid site is constructed by erecting temples one atop another—often by reusing the very materials of the razed temple. For example, because it was common for each newly crowned Aztec emperor to build larger, more grandiose temples atop the existing temples, excavations of the Templo Mayor by Eduardo Matos Moctezuma and his colleagues reveal no less than seven stages of construction (1988a, 59–83). The square, once framed by symbols of Aztec religion (the Templo Mayor) and government (Moctezuma's palace), is now delimited by the traditional powers of the Spanish Crown: the church (the cathedral) and viceroyalty (the National Palace, built atop Moctezuma's palace).

31. For additional critiques of the texts' representation of Mexican ethnicity, see Aguilar Rivera (2004, 71), which argues that the books overvalue Mexico's uniqueness as a mestizo society, and Gutiérrez 1999 (77), which demonstrates how the books favor the Hispanist legacy and minimize indigenous heritage.

32. This image will be interesting to keep in mind during the later discussion of Salinas de Gortari's presidential campaign discourses. To assuage popular fears of change and the "gringoization" that government policies of modernization could effect, Salinas de Gortari stresses diversity within consensus and the Mexican way of life. In essence, he is saying that a Mexican—though Westernized—is still a Mexican.

33. In June 2004, under President Vicente Fox, the Secretaría de Educación Pública caused controversy again when it released the details of a planned reform of the secondary school curriculum (the reform was announced in May 2003; the details were not immediately known). Most hotly debated was the elimination of Mexico's pre-Hispanic history, which would be taught only in elementary schools. Although Mexico does not issue mandatory textbooks for secondary school as it does for elementary school (Aguilar Rivera 2004, 237 n. 111), scholars hotly debated the ramifications of this change in terms of Mexico's national identity (León-Portilla 2004; Salinas Cesareo 2004). The reform took effect in September 2005 (Beltrán Enviada 2005).

34. For a detailed study of the reaction to the 1992 texts and analysis of the ideological changes in content, see Gilbert 1997 and Aguilar Rivera (2004, 65–72).

35. Salinas de Gortari's economic neoliberalism can be defined, in a nutshell, as favoring the free-market, free-trade ideology espoused by both Ronald Reagan and Margaret Thatcher in the 1980s. It involves rapid privatization of state assets to raise capital, often to pay off huge debts, and an opening of the economy to foreign interests. Chapter 4 discusses this topic in more depth.

36. Again, Gilbert 1997 provides detailed analysis of this point.

37. The following quotation clearly demonstrates the depth of the general political crisis in which Salinas de Gortari found himself: "For an important sector of the citizenry, the Salinista government is questionable and illegitimate, because it is the product of a fraudulent election and in frank deterioration for its use of political methods that do not correspond to the call for plurality that is becoming more and more urgent" ["Para un sector importante de ciudadanos, el gobierno salinista es cuestionado, ilegítimo por ser producto de una elección fraudulenta y en franco deterioro al utilizar métodos políticos que no corresponden al reclamo de pluralidad que cada vez se hace más urgente"] (Aguirre 1992a, 19).

38. In his acclaimed *Politics in Mexico: The Democratic Transformation*, Roderic Ai Camp writes that "the unpredictable economic, political and social conditions of Mexican life in the 1980s and 1990s" (2003, 58) explain many Mexican attitudes toward various institutions—especially the low regard they hold for state institutions such as the presidency and government (55). Although this affirms the present analysis of 1982–1992 as a decade of crises, Camp goes on to say that "serious political and economic events throughout 1994 and the first half of 1995 . . . [brought] perceptions of the presidency and governmental institutions to new lows" (71). Although I agree with this analysis and concede that events such as the Zapatista uprising cemented Mexico's transition toward multiculturalism, the events of 1994 and 1995 occurred too late to play a seminal role in the early debates and initial opening of Mexican society.

39. The *dedazo* (literally, "big finger") refers to the process by which, for decades during the twentieth century, Mexican presidents "tapped," or chose, their successors.

40. Elena Poniatowska's *La Noche de Tlatelolco* (published in English as *Massacre in Mexico*) is a remarkable compilation of testimonial accounts of that night. In his introduction to the English edition, Octavio Paz states simply, "A political, social, and moral crisis ensued [after that night] that has not yet been resolved" (quoted in Poniatowska 1975, vii).

41. Because of the PRI's overwhelming authoritarianism, Mexican elections were famous for being "historically almost all form and no content" ["históricamente casi pura forma y nada de contenido"] (Meyer and Aguilar Camín 1994, 280). In 1988 Cuauhtémoc Cárdenas—an engineer; a former governor of the state of Michoacán; and the son of a former president, Lázaro Cárdenas—changed all this, when he did the unthinkable: He broke with the PRI, formed a coalition called the Frente Democrático Nacional (FDN [National Democratic Front]), and ran for president himself.

42. During his campaign, Salinas de Gortari promised both economic and political liberalization (democratization). Yet despite the progress he made in economic liberalization, Salinas de Gortari markedly centralized his political decision-making control (Camp 2003, 255).

43. Ironically, diversity (especially ethnic diversity) and modernization are often viewed as mutually exclusive in Mexico. The 1994 UNAM poll, which asked about Mexico's indigenous population vis-à-vis national development, found that "the idea that the indigenous people should no longer be indigenous in order to transform themselves into Mexicans and modern citizens still pervades. In this sense, modernization and Mexicanization have been seen, by the people and by the government, as polar opposites of traditional life. This is due, in part, to the concepts that propose the construction of a nation as a homogeneous whole" ["aún predomina la idea de que los indígenas deberán dejar de serlo para convertirse en mexicanos y ciudadanos modernos. En este sentido, la modernización y la mexicanización han sido contempladas, tanto por las personas como por el gobierno, como polos opuestos a la vida tradicional. Ello se debe, en parte, a las concepciones que postulan la construcción de la nación como un todo homogéneo"] (*Los mexicanos de los noventa* 1996, 86).

44. Interestingly, the term *mestizo* was not easily dropped when the semantic shift to such terms as *multiple* and *plural* occurred in Mexico's national identity discourse. Consider the following quotation by Matos Moctezuma, which insists on using *mestizo* to refer to a more broadly defined ethnicity: "History speaks to us about the multiple face of Mexicans. . . . [From our history], a new *mestizo* face must be derived so that, little by little, it takes on multiple forms wherein we see the undeniable presence of the indigenous face, subjugated and subdued, and of the Western, Christian, peninsular face. This is where the plural face of today's Mexico originates" ["La historia nos habla del rostro múltiple del mexicano. . . . (De nuestra historia), habrá de derivarse un nuevo rostro mestizo que, poco a poco, cobra formas múltiples en donde vemos la presencia innegable del rostro indígena, sometido y sojuzgado, y del rostro peninsular cristianizado y occidental. De ahí proviene el rostro plural

que es el México de hoy"] (1988b, 25). Indiscriminate use of the terms *mestizo* and *mestizaje* reveals a contradictory stance on plurality and multiculturalism, as Chapter 3 demonstrates. Whereas the term *multicultural* can be used adjectivally to mean "including several cultures," *multiculturalism* is used herein to refer to both a state of cultural pluralism and attitudes of tolerance toward it.

45. In his *Culturas híbridas: Estrategias para entrar y salir de la modernidad,* García Canclini (1990) takes an interdisciplinary approach to the remarkable cultural diversity—or what he calls the multitemporal heterogeneity—of modern Latin American nations.

46. For a detailed study of the term *salinastroika,* the policies associated with it, and the conditions that brought it about, see Centeno 1994 (chap. 1). It is important to note that, in *The Making of NAFTA: How the Deal Was Done,* Maxwell A. Cameron and Brian Tomlin allege that salinastroika (economic opening) was not accompanied by glasnost (political opening) as promised by Salinas de Gortari and as witnessed in Russia under Mikhail Gorbachev (2000, 6).

47. The novelist and poet Carmen Boullosa recalls how she, like so many Mexicans, truly wanted to believe this message: "Salinas and the Salinista project, which is also an intellectual project and one in which many writers became involved and actively participated, wanted to take us beyond being a revolutionary country, to being a modern country . . . and to say, 'Well, this is a first world country; we are a modern country.' And I would like us to be a modern, democratic country. Of course, I would like that. But we are not, and Salinas said we were" ["Salinas y el proyecto salinista, que es un proyecto intelectual también y en que muchos escritores se involucraban y participaban de manera activa—quiso llevarnos más allá de un país revolucionario, llevarnos a un país moderno ¿no? . . . y decir, 'Bueno, éste es un país del primer mundo, somos un país moderno.' Y a mí, me encantaría que fuéramos un país moderno, democrático. Claro que me encantaría. Pero no lo somos y Salinas decía que lo éramos"] (1996).

48. For a detailed account of the Salinas de Gortari presidency, see Russell 1994.

49. David Brading, a modern scholar, theatrically rephrases Sierra's "beautiful words" ("palabras bellas"): "If the Mexican homeland was born with the shout at Dolores, the Mexican nation was born with the first kiss between Malinche and Hernán Cortés" ["Si la patria mexicana nació con el grito de Dolores, la nación mexicana nació con el primer beso entre la Malinche y Hernán Cortés"] (1994, 41).

50. The historian Enrique Florescano writes that "this construction of national memory insisted on erasing the Hispanic past of the viceroyalty and blaming it for the huge national problems that faced republican governments" ["esta construcción de la memoria nacional se empeñó en borrar el pasado hispánico del virreinato, y en culparlo de los grandes problemas nacionales que encaraban los gobiernos republicanos"] (1989, 30). In other writings, Florescano demonstrates how, until recently, this nationalism had effectively denied the historical era its due analysis in Mexican historiography.

51. León-Portilla also pointed out that as early as 1957 he had used the phrase "encounter of two worlds" ["encuentro de dos mundos"] in his introductory comments to *La visión de los vencidos,* a compilation of indigenous narratives of the

conquest. The text reads, "The calm examination of the encounter between those two worlds, the indigenous and the Spanish, from whose dramatic union Mexico and Mexicans descend, will help to better appraise the profound source of our conflicts, our grandeurs and our miseries and, in a word, evaluate our own 'face and heart,' expression of our physiognomic culture and ethnicity" ["El examen sereno del encuentro de esos dos mundos, el indígena y el hispánico de cuya dramática unión México y los mexicanos descendemos, ayudará a valorar mejor la raíz más honda de nuestros conflictos, grandezas y miserias, y en una palabra del propio 'rostro y corazón,' expresión de nuestra fisonomía cultural y étnica"] (1989, xxxi).

52. "Mexico is advancing toward a new historical era that bids farewell to the dearest traditions and the most intolerable vices of the historical heritage we know as the Mexican Revolution. [México avanza hacia una nueva época histórica que dice adios a las tradiciones más caras y a los vicios más intolerables de la herencia histórica que conocemos como Revolución Mexicana] (Meyer and Aguilar Camín 1994, 8).

Chapter 2
The Trauma of Mexico's Mestizo Origins

1. Although the words *mestizo* and *mestizaje* carry with them burdensome sexual baggage, a topic explored in more detail in Chapter 3, here the terms are used when the artists themselves use them to refer to cultural processes.

2. Malintzin, or Malinche, represents one of the most irreconcilable conundrums in Mexico's national identity discourse. Despite her noble indigenous roots, she has been reviled as a traitor and a concubine. Yet recent academic feminist and Chicano works seek to vindicate Malintzin, by showing her to have been of paramount importance to the Spaniards for her multiple linguistic and strategic-planning abilities. For more on the role that Malinche plays in Mexico's gendered sense of identity, see Bartra 1987, Cypess 1991, Paz 1993, and Glantz 1994. For more on the role that Malinche plays in Mexico's national identity, see Bartra 1987, Cypess 1991, and Glantz 1994.

3. A very strong term in Mexico, *chingar* is commonly used to mean "to fuck" or "to screw" and *hijo de la chingada* to mean "son of a bitch" and "motherfucker."

4. Interestingly, Cortés and Malinche have not always been viewed so negatively. In discussing the birth of the Mexican nation, Justo Sierra, a powerful nineteenth-century intellectual, wrote that "Hernán Cortés was, as the Conquest's main personality, the founder of nationalism; Hidalgo, as independence's personality, is the father of the homeland" ["Hernán Cortés fue, como la personalidad capital de conquista, el fundador de la nacionalidad, Hidalgo como la personalidad de la independencia, es el padre de la Patria"] (quoted in Vázquez 1970, 106). As mentioned in Chapter 1, note 49, David Brading and Justo Sierra contend that "the Mexican nation was born with the first kiss between Malinche and Hernán Cortés" ["la nación mexicana nació con el primer beso entre la Malinche y Hernán Cortés"] (Brading 1994, 41). Significantly, for Sierra and Brading, Mexico's nationality is exemplified in its mestizo beginnings, but Mexico's nation begins as it throws off the yoke of colonialism.

5. During the Mexican Revolution, Francisco (Pancho) Villa's army, formally known as the División del Norte, was also referred to as Dorados. In 1914, while battling the armies of Venustiano Carranza, Villa and his troops held (in part or all) the northern states of Chihuahua and Durango.

6. Muñoz was the author of such well-known novels of the Revolution as *Memorias de Pancho Villa* (1923) and *¡Vámonos con Pancho Villa!* (1931).

7. In his article "Where Was the Brazilian Malinche? Myths of National Origin in Brazil and Mexico," Thomas Skidmore, the prominent historian who specializes in Brazil, also cites the nineteenth- and twentieth-century histories of the two nations in order to demonstrate that Mexico's postindependence experience; stronger anti-Spanish sentiment; larger, more present indigenous population; and 1910 Revolution contributed to the different directions taken by Octavio Paz and Gilberto Freyre, respective theoreticians of national character. He concludes, "There was undoubtedly rape in Brazil and tenderness in Mexico, but it is not the facts of the matter which theoreticians of national character most often use. Rather it is their practice to construct myths of national origin in order to explain (and often justify) the societies which have emerged" (1996, 130).

8. Compare this quotation to one by Henry Schmidt referring to the positivist decade of 1900–1910: "The sociocultural type [of the mestizo had] a strong Indian element and a less significant Creole or European one" (1978, 55). Here we see the unfixed nature of the national concept of mestizo identity in Mexico. At times it is deemed predominantly indigenous, at times predominantly Western or Hispanic, despite official discourses that declare a fifty-fifty balanced ratio as the basis of societal unity and harmony.

9. Solares—who was born in Ciudad Juárez in 1945 and now lives in Mexico City—is a noted playwright, reporter, and novelist. His narrative works include *Anónimo, Casas de encantamiento, Madero, el otro,* and *La noche de Ángeles* (which won the Diana-Novedades prize in 1989). His play *El gran elector* received the award for the best work presented in 1992. In 1996 Solares was awarded not only the Fuentes Mares prize for *Nen, la inútil* but also a Guggenheim fellowship. His most recent novels include *El espía del aire* (2001) and *No hay tal lugar* (2003).

10. After being shipwrecked on the Yucatan peninsula with a number of other European sailors in 1511, Guerrero was enslaved for a time before he married into a Mayan tribe and sired children—years before Cortés arrived to Mexico. As a result, Guerrero has been hailed as Mexico's founding father (Brushwood 1992, 837) and the father of Mexican mestizos (J. Johnson 1988, 26). When Cortés sent for Guerrero and for Jerónimo de Águilar to act as translators in the approach to Tenochtitlán, Guerrero refused, ultimately dying alongside the Mayans as they fought off the Spaniards. Aguilar accompanied Cortés's men but was eventually replaced as a translator by Malintzin, an Aztec princess who had been enslaved by the Tabascans and was later given to the Spaniards. Cortés took her on as a translator, guide, slave, and lover.

11. The 1992 commemorative edition of *La visión de los vencidos* was the thirteenth Spanish edition. According to León-Portilla, the book is the eighth overall best

English seller for Beacon Press, which has printed nearly 150,000 copies under the title *The Broken Spears* (León-Portilla 1996) since its publication in 1992.

12. Díaz del Castillo writes of these encounters in the Yucatan in chapters 27 and 29 of his *Historia verdadera de la conquista de la Nueva España* (1992).

13. It is important to note that Solares focuses exclusively on the dual nature of the mestizo in *Nen, la inútil*. Much official discourse does the same, with only a footnote or a sentence that mentions the black presence along the Mexican coast. See, for example, Basave Benítez 1993 (17) and Álvarez de Testa 1992 (15).

14. In a 1989 article, John Brushwood observes a growing trend of the "trans-real" in Mexican literature, which he attributes to "a time when stable bases have disappeared or are disappearing" (1989, 16). The Mexican crises of the 1980s and 1990s will fuel writers' narrative material, especially identity discourses.

15. Although many scholars believe in the occurrence of these auguries (which perhaps added to Moctezuma's fear of the Spaniards), others question their authenticity. There are those who believe that the Spaniards invented or exaggerated them in order to justify and explain the success of the conquest and divert attention from the cruelty and bloodshed of the warfare they had waged. In any event, it is worth noting that the Spaniards arrived in 1519, or the year Ce-Acatl (Uno Caña [One Reed]), which would have been the end of a fifty-two-year cycle (or Aztec century) in which the Aztecs awaited renewal of the universe through the ritual of Fuego Nuevo, a fact that lends credence to the existence of the apprehension-causing auguries.

16. Homi Bhabha theorizes the existence of a "third space" between binaries, which *needs* the two oppositional poles of a binary in order to exist in their interstices and in order to create something new through the process of melding or joining. Yet Bhabha contends that neither the term *third space* nor the phenomenon resolves the tension between the two cultures (Bhabha 1994, 113). Rolena Adorno confirms this indeterminacy in her article "The Colonial Subject and the Cultural Construction of the Other." She borrows from Bhabha's theorization of "a paradox of difference and similarity" in her demonstration of a complex interrelation of subjects, discourses, and relationships that constitute the vision of the colonial Other (1990–1991, 149).

17. This denial can also be manipulated toward a positive end. For example, if, in denying, one is simultaneously celebrating a newfound uniqueness, then a sense of pride may result. For example, in another work—celebrating America's uniqueness and echoing the Creole patriotism that existed until the nineteenth century followed by the pan-Americanism evident in such writings as José Martí's "Nuestra América" (1939 [first published in 1891])—Paz writes, "The mestizo is neither Spaniard nor Indian, nor is he a European looking to establish himself: he is the product of American ground, a new product" ["El mestizo no es español ni indio; tampoco es un europeo que busca arraigarse: es un producto del suelo americano, el nuevo producto"] (1979, 46).

18. Solares added that Guerrero's life had been treated in a number of other texts, the best-known Mexican treatment being Eugenio Aguirre's *Gonzalo Guerrero: Novela histórica* (1991). Other novels about Guerrero include Aguirre Rosas 1975, Pisani 1992 (originally published in French in 1991), Meza 1994, and Villa Roiz

1995 (which is more historiographic). For a well-documented discussion of the construction of Guerrero as a cultural icon through his treatment in sixteenth-century historiography, see Adorno 1996.

19. Reflected in this passage is Sigmund Freud's pleasure principle. Solares's knowledge of psychoanalysis stems principally from a course taught by Erich Fromm that he audited (González 1995, 117), and Solares mentions Freud's writings as having the most influence on and resonance for him.

20. In my interview with Solares, he referred to Martín Luis Guzmán's *Las memorias de Pancho Villa,* which "people consult as if it were a biography. . . . What Martín Luis Guzmán invented is now more real than is anything that could have been real. So I think that imagination writes reality as well" ["la gente consulta como si fuera una biografía. . . . Lo que inventó Martín Luis Guzmán ya es más real de lo que pudo haber sido real. Entonces yo creo que también la imaginación escribe la realidad"] (1996).

21. Through his discussion of the cultural construction of the two sides of the modern Mexican woman—the Virgin of Guadalupe and Malinche—Bartra demonstrates the sadomasochistic relationship that the Mexican male develops with the Mexican woman whom he knows "has been raped by the *macho* conquistador, and [whom] he suspects . . . has enjoyed and even desired the rape" (1992, 158). Here it is evident that the pleasure is merely perceived by the macho.

22. Although a full discussion of the patriarchal undertones of this scene falls outside the scope of this chapter, it is worth mentioning that, as we have seen, the male perceives the female as inviting his aggression. The narrative point of view, as well, allows for the unfathomable justification for and revision of a rape scene. A fascinating literary parallel to this romanticization of rape into love exists in Fuentes's 1962 *La muerte de Artemio Cruz.* See Sommer 1993 (27–29) for discussion of this "pretty lie." Sommer also notes that in nineteenth-century romantic narratives, love and productivity were closely linked to the nineteenth-century goals of bourgeois Europe; productivity and *passion,* however, could be played out only in a "realizable utopia" such as America.

23. In this section, I use the terms *mestizo* and *syncretic* to mean "mixed," either culturally or spiritually. It is important to note that *syncretism* is commonly defined as a reconciliation or fusion of beliefs (*American Heritage College Dictionary* 1993, 1376), whereas *mestizaje* simply connotes the mixing of two races. Therefore, *mestizaje* can be traumatic or romantic, but the definition of syncretism includes a value judgment that excises conflict.

24. Carrasco's film was first released in March 1999 at the Muestra de Cine Mexicano in Guadalajara. In April 1999, it was shown throughout Mexico by Twentieth Century Fox, marking the first time a Mexican film was distributed in Mexico by a U.S. company. The film was released in April 2000 in selected theaters in southern California. According to Carrasco (2004), it is the highest-grossing Mexican dramatic film ever released in that country and one of the most costly to produce ($4 million).

25. Born in Mexico City in 1967, Salvador Carrasco (director/screenwriter/editor) attended the Universidad Nacional Autónoma de México's Centro Universitario

de Estudios Cinematográficos (CUEC-UNAM) and graduated from New York University's Tisch School of the Arts in 1991. He and producer Alvaro Domingo formed Carrasco and Domingo Films in 1992; *La otra conquista* was their first feature film. Today Carrasco lives in Los Angeles with his wife and three children.

26. Carrasco's statement conflates the concepts of *mestizaje* and syncretism, leveling them in the field of cultural mixing. Despite the downside of this terminological confusion, the two terms continue to be used interchangeably. Carrasco's statement also highlights the pliant nature of Mexico's mestizo identity. Stress on the violent conquest of native Mexicans by invading Spaniards can be used to foment nationalistic sentiment and distrust of foreigners, as occurred in the decades following the Revolution. Or the depiction of *mestizaje* and its spiritual component, syncretism, as harmonious and balanced processes can allow Mexico to claim (falsely) to have integrated its indigenous population—a topic that is treated in greater detail ahead.

27. In his *Local Histories/Global Designs: Coloniality, Subaltern Knowledges, and Border Thinking,* Walter Mignolo reframes the debate between assimilation (global designs) and multiculturalism (local histories) in terms of knowledge (epistemology) and ways of knowing (hermeneutics). Writing about Ortiz's concept, he says he "do[es] not find anything wrong with the notion of transculturation" (2000, 14) and credits the concept with moving the discourse on race into the realm of the discourse on culture (167). Yet he avoids the term, he says, because it continues to be "attached to a biological/cultural mixture of people" and thus "maintains the shadows of *mestizaje*" (14).

28. Fray Diego appears to be a composite of various historical figures. According to the film's website, he is loosely based on Fray Juan de Zumárraga, a protector of the indigenous people and bishop of Mexico in 1531. In the film's chronology, however, Fray Diego arrives in the New World in 1526, two years before Zumárraga. In a previous version of the script (June 14, 1995, cited with permission by the director), Fray Diego is described as one of the original twelve Franciscan apostles.

29. The act of strangling Tecuichpo in the film calls to mind the scandal in which Cortés allegedly strangled his first wife, Catalina Xuárez Marcaida, soon after she arrived in Mexico and joined him in Coyoacán in 1522 (Martínez 1992, 404–6). He was then free to marry Juana de Zuñiga, daughter of Don Carlos Ramírez de Arellano, the Segundo Conde de Aguilar (Martínez 1992, 527), which allowed him to insert himself into the circle of Spanish nobility. As Hugh Thomas comments in the genealogy entitled "La entrada de Cortés en la nobleza," "This genealogy suggests that although Cortés was the son of a poor hidalgo, he was rich in family relations" ["Esta genealogía sugiere que, si bien Cortés era hijo de un hidalgo pobre, era rico en relaciones familiares"] (1994, 686).

30. Carrasco refers to a quotation by Paz, which appears in the introduction to Jacques Lafaye's groundbreaking work *Quetzalcóatl y Guadalupe: La formación de la conciencia nacional en México, 1531–1815*: "Tonantzin/Guadalupe was our imagination's answer to the sense of orphanhood that Indians were left with after the conquest" ["Tonantzin/Guadalupe fue la respuesta de la imaginación a la situación de orfandad en que dejó a los indios la conquista."] (Paz 1995, 22). Carrasco's omission of the

word *imagination* might have been unintentional, but it serves to highlight the blurring of lines between cultural constructions and the reality that they constitute for believers. Although Paz posits the Virgin of Guadalupe as, first and foremost, a savior to the indigenous, the work of many foreign scholars establishes the Virgin of Guadalupe and her apparition legends as primarily Creole constructions in the early days of evangelization (the late 1500s and early 1600s).

31. Interestingly, this opening scene in the Templo Mayor replaced a June 14, 1995, version. Previously, the first scene showed the Virgin of Guadalupe as she appears on Juan Diego's tunic and then zoomed in for a closeup of her pregnant belly. In this version, Carrasco seemed to frame his work as a birth: the birth of Guadalupe as icon and the birth of the Mexican people as her children. This gestation, the movie implies, took more than a decade, from 1520 to 1531. In this version of the script, the film was entitled *La visión absuelta* [The Absolved Vision] (see Carrasco 1995).

32. Carrasco's film is based on numerous historical and historiographic texts. The director cites as useful to his work such sixteenth-century texts as the Aubin and Ramírez Codices and the writings of Bernardino de Sahagún, Ixtlilxóchitl, Bernal Díaz del Castillo, and Hernán Cortés. Carrasco also makes use of not only such works on the conquest as those by Miguel León-Portilla, José Luis Martínez, Georges Baudot, Hugh Thomas, and William Prescott but also Jacques Lafaye's text on Guadalupe. With respect to writings on Mexican national identity, he lists works by Octavio Paz, Samuel Ramos, and José Vasconcelos.

33. Carraso has written that Topiltzin's death at the end of the film is a "Christlike self-sacrifice, which makes him transcend his enemies and become a symbolic figure" (Carrasco 2002, 176). However, as we will see, these nuances of Christian redemption are ultimately lost on the audience.

34. In *Nen, la inútil,* Solares also uses these dream-like or surreal narrative techniques when he recounts the massacre in the Templo Mayor and the rape and crushing to death of Nen. Felipe recounts to a friend the role he played in the massacre, saying he felt he was intoxicated or bewitched in some way, and Nen experiences the rape as a déjà vu from her lifelong nightmares, and thus the culmination of her destiny.

35. Carrasco's interpretation of Topiltzin's actions, however, *is* reflected in the 1995 version of the script. Topiltzin delivers such lines as these: "All of the world's evil is contained within the icon of the Great Lady with white skin. It is necessary to take possession of her, but that is not enough . . . Why should it be I—who decided this—who must hide her in my chest, absorb her pitiful soul, and lose my powers?" ["Todo el mal del mundo está contenido dentro del icono de la Gran Señora de piel blanca. Es necesario apoderarse de ella, pero eso no basta . . . ¿Por qué he de ser yo—quién lo decidió—el que la oculte en mi pecho para absorber su penosa alma y que pierda sus poderes?"] (1995, 109) and "I shall overcome or be defeated forever, although it's all the same to me. 'Saint Topiltzin of Victory or Saint Tomás of the Honorable Death.' . . . I will die with her and for her. No one before me had dared to tear out evil in a single gesture, from the root. But is there space for both? No, only death" ["Venceré o seré derrotado para siempre, aunque para mí eso sea indiferente. 'San Topiltzin de la Victoria o Santo Tomás el-de-la-Honrosa-Muerte.' . . . Moriré con ella y por ella. Nadie antes de mí se había atrevido a arrancar el mal

de un solo impulso, desde la raíz. ¿Pero, hay lugar para ambos? No, sólo la muerte"] (110). According to Carrasco, as a director, he realized he could express this message cinematographically through Topiltzin's actions in twenty minutes of dialogue-free scenes. Cinematographically, I agree that he chose the most effective device. Unfortunately for the film's message, these monologues were not part of the final product.

Chapter 3
Moving toward Multiculturalism

1. Carmen Boullosa, born in Mexico City in 1954, began her literary career as a poet (*La salvaja, La Delirios,* and *La bebida*) and playwright (*Cocinar hombres, Aura y las once mil vírgenes,* and *Mi versión de los hechos*). She has published novels (*Mejor desaparece* [1987], *Antes* [1989], *Papeles irresponsables* [1989], *Son vacas, somos puercos* [1991], *El médico de los piratas* [1992], *Llanto: Novelas imposibles* [1992], *La milagrosa* [1993], *Duerme* [1994], *Cielos de la tierra* [1997], *Treinta años* [1999], *De un salto descabalga la reina* [2003], and *La otra mano de Lepanto* [2005]). She has received funding from the Guggenheim Foundation, the Centro Mexicano de Escritores, and the DADD Künstlerprogramm in Berlin, as well as numerous awards. She spent a semester as a distinguished guest at San Diego State University, and in 1989 she won the Premio Xavier Villarrutia. Her works have been translated into German, French, and English.

2. Boullosa herself, in comparing to *Son vacas, somos puercos* two of her novels published before 1991 (*Mejor desaparece* and *Antes*), comments that the earlier works are "somewhat more internal novels; their construction is mostly introspective.... They belong to the domestic sphere" ["novelas un poco más internas, la construcción es en gran parte introspectiva.... Pertenecen al mundo de la casa"] (quoted in "Carmen Boullosa: Escritora por oficio" 1991a, 7). Her early fiction, which concerns such interior spaces as the home and the mind of the child, is therefore characteristically subjective, intimate, and personal. As a result, the leap to historical fiction meant for Boullosa a radical adjustment of perspective, discourse, and material.

3. Although Boullosa employs this spelling of the Aztec emperor's name, deemed by Tzvetan Todorov a "more precise" ["más exacto"] spelling (1989, 61), I use the more common "Moctezuma" throughout.

4. Interestingly, in her interview with Kristine Ibsen, Boullosa confesses that she wrote this novel three times, each in a different genre: "I wrote it three times until it ended up in this way: the first was like an adventure novel, a bit banal; I thought it was wrong and that I had not approached it correctly; the second one did not work out, and the third was that, a non-novel, a nonliterary novel, a peculiar narrative, unnarrated" ["La escribí tres veces hasta que me quedó como terminó siendo: la primera era como una novela de aventuras, un poco banal, pensé que estaba mal, que no la había abordado yo bien; la segunda no me salió, y la tercera fue eso, una no-novela, una novela no-literaria, una narrativa peculiar, desnarrada"] (1995, 55–56). This creative indecision appears in *Llanto* as a number of the narrators discuss these very genres and techniques while they, too, brainstorm for the novel. In the end,

Boullosa terms the finished product a "novela de ideas" (53, 57). This term is useful because it reflects the novel's many narrative projects.

5. Boullosa reveals these details in "Personajes y obra," a talk that took place at the Palacio de Bellas Artes in Mexico City on February 19, 1997. Elena Poniatowska also pointed out the connections in her 1993 review of the novel (28).

6. These quotations are taken from a clipping provided by Carmen Boullosa.

7. Boullosa relies on such historiographic sources as ancient codices, whose glyphs are open to interpretation. According to Todorov, "The codex drawings only keep the principle points of history that, in that form, are unintelligible; the accompanying ritual discourse makes them understandable" ["los dibujos de los códices sólo conservan los principales puntos de la historia que, en esa forma, son ininteligibles; los vuelve comprensible el discurso ritual que los acompaña"] (1989, 88).

8. Despite the tragedy inherent in this misunderstanding, Poniatowska admits that the affection she feels for Moctezuma stems from the fact that "he thought that if he sent Hernán Cortés more and more gifts, he would go away satisfied. What an incorrect tactic, poor thing, one that would occur only to an innocent man" ["él creía que si le enviaba más y más regalos a Hernán Cortés, éste acabaría por largarse satisfecho. ¡Qué táctica equivocada, pobrecito mío, sólo a un inocente se le ocurriría!"] (1993, 27). This again demonstrates the tendency to infantilize the emperor, viewing him as confused and child-like. By explaining the cultural basis for some of his actions, Boullosa tries to modify this common perception to some extent.

9. Todorov's theories on the Other were cited frequently (and largely without question) in Mexican literature and in articles about the Quincentennial and the resultant reevaluation of the discovery and conquest of the Americas. In a 1992 article, José Alberto Abud uses Todorov's theory throughout his discussion of the misunderstandings that occurred five centuries ago. He concludes, as many did, that the Quincentennial was nothing to celebrate but that it should merely be commemorated (12–18).

10. Significantly, the date is August 13, 1989, the anniversary of the fall of Tenochtitlán to the Spaniards. Four hundred sixty-eight years have passed, marking nine full cycles of fifty-two years (equivalent to an Aztec "century").

11. In her talk that took place at the Palacio de Bellas Artes in Mexico City, Boullosa was asked to speak on the subject "El autor como personaje de su obra." She contends that she is not a character; instead, she says, "I am like a wind that appears in the novel, a soft wind that disperses the need to write the reappearance of Moctezuma II in Mexico City. Here the author as character in her work is a wind that travels to advise other writers that Moctezuma has arrived and urges them to write about him" ["Soy como un viento que aparece en la novela, un vientecito suave que dispersa la necesidad de escribir la reaparición de Moctezuma II en la Ciudad de México. El autor como personaje de su obra es aquí el viento que viaja para avisar a los pies de otros escritores que ya llegó Moctezuma, que lo escriban"] (1997, 5–6).

12. See J. H. Elliott's introduction to Anthony Padgen's translation of *Hernán Cortés: Letters from Mexico* for a detailed account of the underlying circumstances that surround the writing of Cortés's *Cartas de relación*. Stephanie Merrim's "The First

Fifty Years of Hispanic New World Historiography: The Caribbean, Mexico and Central America," in the *The Cambridge History of Latin American Literature,* also includes a discussion of these circumstances, framed in an analysis of Cortés's verbal craft (1996, 71–78).

13. Todorov sums up the intensity of the clash between circular and linear concepts of time, saying, "Instead of this time that is cyclical, repetitive, fixed on an unalterable sequence, where everything is already foretold, where a singular action is no more than the realization of omens that have always been present, instead of this time dominated by the system, a unidirectional time comes to impose itself, the time of the apotheosis of fulfillment, in the same way that Christians come" ["En lugar de este tiempo cíclico, repetitivo, fijado en una secuencia inalterable, donde todo ya está predicho, donde el hecho singular no es más que la realización de presagios ya presentes desde siempre, en lugar de este tiempo dominado por el sistema, viene a imponerse el tiempo unidireccional, el tiempo de la apoteosis del cumplimiento, tal como vienen entonces los cristianos"] (1989, 95).

14. Fuentes is by far Mexico's best known and most internationally published novelist. His narrative includes such titles as *La región más transparente* (1958), *La muerte de Artemio Cruz* (1962), *Cambio de piel* (1967), *Zona sagrada* (1967), *Terra Nostra* (1975), *La cabeza de la hidra* (1978), *Gringo viejo* (1985), *Cristóbal nonato* (1987), *La campaña* (1990), *El naranjo, o los círculos del tiempo* (1993), *La frontera de cristal* (1995), *Los años con Laura Díaz* (1999), *Instinto de Inez* (2001), and *Inquieta compañía* (2004). He has also published literary criticism and essays: *Tiempo mexicano* (1970), *Valiente mundo nuevo* (1990), *El espejo enterrado* (1992), *Geografía de la novela* (1993), *Nuevo tiempo mexicano* (1994), *En esto creo* (2002), and *Contra Bush* (2004). In 1994 he was awarded the Premio Príncipe de Asturias.

15. See Raymond Williams's discussion of the narrative cycle and the works that it encompasses, in *The Writings of Carlos Fuentes* (1996, 110–38).

16. Leopoldo Zea, another respected Mexican intellectual and philosopher who greatly influenced Fuentes's own theories on such issues as time and identity, also comments on the idea of a culturally amalgamated Latin America: "Let's remember that the Spaniard who arrives to America is accustomed to *mestizaje.* . . . He learned to live with other cultures and other races. That is why, despite his arrogance, his haughtiness, and his greed, he did not struggle with the *mestizaje* that gave origin to the world we form part of" ["Recordemos que el español que llega a América está acostumbrado a la mestización. . . . Aprendió a convivir con otra cultura y con otra raza. Por eso, a pesar de su arrogancia, de su altanería y de su codicia no le costó trabajo el mestizaje que dio origen al mundo del cual formamos parte"] (quoted in Ochoa Sandy 1992, 48). Zea, like Fuentes, lacks a critical eye in evaluating the processes of colonization. Zea first equates Latin American *mestizaje* with the cohabitation of Spaniards and Moors under Muslim rule and then no more than alludes to the violent rape of Amerindians in the conquest of the Americas.

17. Raúl Bueno differentiates the terms as follows: "Cultural *mestizaje,* like its homologue racial *mestizaje,* tends to create a new specimen within an agglutinate lineage, dissolving differences. Its characteristic is the solubility of ingredients, meaning, its capacity to establish an existential continuum, without apparent fissures,

attributable, as has been seen, to the notion of homogeneity. . . . Heterogeneity, on the other hand, tends toward the individualization of specimens in contact, within an altering lineage based on the affirmation of these differences. Its characteristic is the insolubility of the elements at play, meaning, its capacity to confirm cultural discontinuity, that is, to mark the fissures established by pluriculturalism" ["El mestizaje cultural, como su homólogo, el mestizaje racial, tiende a la creación de un nuevo espécimen dentro de la línea aglutinante, disolvente de las diferencias. Su característica es la solubilidad de los ingredientes, es decir, su capacidad de establecer un *continuum* existencial, sin fisuras aparentes, adscribible, como se ha visto, a la noción de la homogeneidad. . . . La heterogeneidad, en cambio, tiende a la individuación de los especímenes en contacto, dentro de la línea alterizante basada en la afirmación de las diferencias. Su característica es la insolubilidad de los elementos en juego, es decir, su capacidad de confirmar la discontinuidad cultural, esto es, de marcar las fisuras que establecen la pluricultura"] (1996, 28). For more on *mestizaje* as the erasure of difference, see Spitta 1995 (186) and F. Schmidt 1996 (43).

18. For more on this subject, see Anne Doremus's article "Indigenism, *Mestizaje* and National Identity in Mexico during the 1940s and the 1950s" (2001) and Roberto Fernández Retamar's comments on Antonio Cornejo Polar's work in *Asedios a la heterogeneidad cultural* (1996, esp. 48).

19. I should mention here the unlikelihood that Díaz del Castillo's account is entirely accurate. Penned approximately fifty years after his participation in the conquest, the *Historia verdadera de la conquista de la Nueva España* was an attempt to write the brave but unsung heroic soldiers into history. Díaz del Castillo took umbrage with historians who not only did not witness the events they retold but also focused exclusively on the principal men: Hernán Cortés, Pedro de Alvarado, and Francisco de Montejo. This fact and the immensely distorting role that time plays in memory contribute to the fictional nature of this testimonial historiography.

20. In a longer version of this article, in Glantz's *La Malinche, sus padres y sus hijos,* she also provides a detailed account of Cortés's various translators and their experiences (1994, 75–95).

21. For more on the role of translation in "Las dos orillas," see Jay 1997 and Mac Adam 1993.

22. It is important to understand that, according to Aguilar's own version of events in "Las dos orillas," the other interpreter, Malintzin, learned Spanish around the time of their stay in Cholula and replaced him as interpreter months before their meetings with Cuauhtémoc. The impossibility of his participation in these events highlights both the message of this scene (words construct reality) and Fuentes's project of "rescuing" this historically marginal figure.

23. For a clear and authoritative discussion of the historical circumstances that surround Cortés's conquest, see Elliott 1986 (xi–xxxvii).

24. In relating language (tongue/*lengua*) to such sexual issues as cultural rape, it is interesting to point out that the image of a forked tongue, which Aguilar mentions here, symbolizes emasculation, as it reflects feminist refutations of Jacques Lacan. Whereas Lacan contends that male identity is constructed around the phallus, and

therefore female identity is constructed around lack, such feminists as Luce Irigaray reply that the female genitalia are, in fact, plural, a sex that is not one. In this sense, the cutting of Aguilar's tongue "feminizes" him.

25. Cultures with written languages have always viewed orality with suspicion, as Walter Mignolo points out in *The Darker Side of the Renaissance: Literacy, Territoriality and Colonization,* his seminal work on power and language: "People without letters were thought of as people without history, and oral narratives were looked at as incoherent and inconsistent" (1995, 3).

26. In her article "La estatua de Gonzalo Guerrero en Akumal," Rolena Adorno studies mentions of Guerrero and Aguilar in sixteenth-century texts. She points out that, although, in some, Guerrero and Aguilar are given voices, they are later renditions of the conquest and therefore probably mere elaboration on the part of the authors. Interestingly, however, neither Marina's voice nor her words are ever recorded in Spanish chronicles (Glantz 1994, 86).

27. The figure of Corazón de los Cielos appears in a novel that deals with Guerrero's total assimilation into life on the Yucatán. Originally published in French and written by Francis Pisani, *Huracán, Corazón-del-Cielo* ends with the hurricane as an undeniable symbol of unification. Emblematic of the *mestizaje* that Guerrero's life embodies, "the hurricane unites the earth and sky, the five cardinal points, the rain and wind, heaven and hell, yesterday, today, and tomorrow" ["huracán une el cielo y la tierra, los cinco puntos cardinales, la lluvia y el viento, el paraíso y el infierno, ayer, hoy y mañana]" (1992, 345).

28. The Mesoamerican "century" consists of fifty-two-year cycles. To mark the end of one cycle and the beginning of another, the ceremony of *Fuego Nuevo* dramatically illustrates the awaited renewal of the universe. All fires in the kingdom were extinguished on that night and, if the gods willed the universe to continue, a new ritual fire would ignite and be carried to all the villages. Homero Aridjis (born in Michoacán in 1940), a Mexican poet and novelist, bases *¿En quién piensas cuando haces el amor?* (his 1996 book) on this concept. Having calculated that the next *Fuego Nuevo* is due in 2027, he sets a story of intrigue and sixteenth-century cultural *mestizaje* in a futuristic Mexico City (1996).

29. It is significant that Fuentes's description of this plaza and its construction mirrors the creation of Mexico City's actual central plaza [*zócalo*]. In "Las dos orillas," the colonial practice of palimpsest buildings takes place again, this time, ironically, in Spain, reaffirming the cyclical nature of history in the story.

30. In his article "Translation, Invention, Resistance: Rewriting the Conquest in Carlos Fuentes's 'The Two Shores,'" Paul Jay argues that translation plays a subversive role here: one of resistance. Although I agree with this in terms of the scenes concerning Aguilar and Malinche that I have analyzed, I take issue with his characterization of the "reverse of the conquest" where he writes that it "reverses the players, but it leaves the mechanisms of conquest in place and so dramatizes the Mayans' appropriation and transformation of the methods of the Spanish. In this way the conquest of New Spain is seamlessly translated into the conquest of Spain" (1997, 419–20).

31. Malintzin was an Aztec princess who was sold into slavery upon the death of her father. Eventually she was acquired by the Tabascans. They gave her to the Spaniards, who took her along as they marched back into her natal territory.

32. In her discussion of the late sixteenth-century *Historia de Tlaxcala,* by the mestizo Diego Muñoz Camargo, Adorno reveals what may be the inspiration for this aspect of "Las dos orillas." As in this text, "it is Aguilar [not Guerrero] who becomes indigenous and is married—not to a Mayan woman but to Malintzin herself" ["es Aguilar (no Guerrero) quien se convierte en indio y se casa—no con una mujer maya sino con la propia Malintzin"] (1996, 918).

33. It is important to note that contributing to his resentment and paranoia is the fact that the character Aguilar believes that Marina has chosen Cortés of her own accord. Most colonial texts make it clear that Cortés, in fact, took her for his own.

34. As we saw in Chapter 1, in such public speeches as "Cultura e identidad nacional," Salinas de Gortari and the intellectuals who supported him praised Mexico's "pluricultural" nature and promised that democratization and modernization would in no way compromise Mexico's unique confluence of multiple cultures, traditions, and ways of life.

35. The importance of this institution (begun under Salinas de Gortari) cannot be overstated in terms of opening the Mexican electoral system to more democratic practices at the end of the twentieth century.

36. In 1997 Fuentes delivered the keynote address during the Celebration of the Day of the Spanish Language at Brown University, where he also received his doctorate in humane letters. In his speech, entitled "Spanish: A Language of Encounters," Fuentes described how the quintessential language of empire (Spanish) has become one of encounter.

37. In her article on this story, Carmen Rivera discusses Fuentes's use of *mestizaje,* yet she sees no reason to critique it. She writes instead that he creates an America based on "the richness of equally mixed components" ["la riqueza de unos componentes igualmente mezclados"] (1995, 57).

Chapter 4
The Interminable Conquest of Mexico

1. For more on how the PRI's loss of political consensus translated into differing "nation views" in Mexico, see the preface to Lynn Stephen's *Zapata Lives! Histories and Cultural Politics in Southern Mexico* (2002).

2. Rius (born Eduardo del Río in 1934) celebrated fifty years as a cartoonist in 2004. His lengthy body of works includes such titles as *Cuba para principiantes, Lástima de Cuba, Marx para principiantes, Mao para principiantes, Rius para principiantes,* and *Manual del perfecto ateo.* His books, or *historietas,* combine history, political commentary, and his irreverent questioning of social and political institutions. Many have been translated into English, German, and Italian. His participation in such comic series as *Los Agachados, Los Supermachos* and *El Chahuistle* has been inspirational to generations of *moneros* in Mexico.

3. For a fascinating and detailed account of the debate over cosmopolitanism versus

state-supported cultural nationalism among Mexican intellectuals in the 1950s and 1960s, see Cohn 2002 (89–103).

4. In April 1991 the inaugural issue of *Este País*—Mexico's leading source of social and political polls—cited the 1990 *Encuesta mundial de valores* [World Values Survey]. It reported that, if it meant a higher quality of life, 59 percent of Mexicans polled were in favor of merging with the United States into a single country. The authors concluded, "This dramatic data suggests that Mexican nationalism is dwindling and that one of the most important undermining factors has been the economic crisis" ["Esta dramática cifra sugiere que el nacionalismo mexicano está mermado y que uno de sus corrosivos más importantes ha sido la crisis económica"] ("Integración económica y nacionalismo" 1991, n.p.).

5. For an in-depth analysis of this phenomenon, see Morris 2001 (239–55).

6. Because Mignolo's theories are both dense and multifaceted, my synthesis of a few of his main points herein cannot do justice to the overall arguments in his work. His acute delineation of globalization as neocolonialism, however, is worth summarizing before undertaking an analysis of the cartoons of *El Ahuizotl*.

7. It is important to note that Mignolo is also highly critical of the ways in which global designs invariably displace local histories and diverse forms of knowledge. He advocates new ways of knowing, or "border thinking," to combat the subjugation of knowledge and the homogeneity of globalization.

8. Pedro Pérez del Solar demonstrates the use of this term in his article "Old Fashions for New Times: *El Desencanto* in Spanish Comics" (2003, 85–101). The article studies the comic magazine *Cairo* and the ways it visually captures the profound sense of disenchantment in the post-Franco Spain of the 1980s.

9. See the introduction to Magú and Sefchovich 2000 (38–39) for an enumeration of these and other characteristics of political cartoons.

10. In my interview with Magú, however, he commented that, although there was some consideration about whether to try to publish the supplement *El Ahuizotl* in book form, it was ultimately decided that updating or modifying much of the topical humor would be too difficult (1999). I would respectfully disagree with the need to update the humor, in view of the fact that the 1992 comics continue to speak so clearly to the issues at hand in this study.

11. In Latin America in general, cartoons (both comic strips and comic books) have warranted serious critical study since the 1970s. Two book-length studies available in English are *How to Read Donald Duck: Imperialist Ideology in the Disney Comic*, by Ariel Dorfman and Armand Mattelart (first published in Spanish in 1972), and Dorfman's follow-up, *The Empire's Old Clothes: What the Lone Ranger, Babar, and Other Innocent Heroes Do to Our Minds*. Although these Marxist analyses focused on the capitalist and culturally imperialistic messages found in First World comics (especially Disney) produced for export to the Third World, they are important because they opened up academic discourse about popular culture and its effects on consumers in Latin America. In 1989 David William Foster published *From Mafalda to Los Supermachos: Latin American Graphic Humor as Popular Culture*, and in 1992 Harold E. Hinds, Jr., and Charles M. Tatum published *Not Just for Children: The Mexican Comic Book in the Late 1960s and 1970s*. These were two of the first

critical studies of comic books produced in Latin America and available in English. Since then, Anne Rubenstein's *Bad Language, Naked Ladies and Other Threats to the Nation: A Political History of Comics Books in Mexico* has continued the trend of solid critical examination of Mexican comic books. The study of comics and cartoons continues to produce useful and interesting scholarship as part of the larger and still emerging fields of popular culture and cultural studies.

12. The headdress of the Aztec emperors is a concrete symbol of national pride in Mexico. But Moctezuma's original headdress, adorned with over five hundred green feathers of the sacred quetzal bird, was taken from Mexican soil in the sixteenth century. Since the 1920s, it has been housed in the Vienna Museum of Ethnology. Negotiations for its return to Mexico have been ongoing in recent decades. In the movie *La otra conquista,* a replica of Moctezuma's headdress appears in the scene in which Cortés takes Tecuichpo by force. The background image of the *penacho* represents not only the violation and decapitation of the Aztec empire but also the nostalgia for an indigenous people now relegated to museums.

13. In my interview with Magú, he related an anecdote from the time of *El Tataranieto del Ahuizote* (1988–1991) about a television comic who was sanctioned (by being suspended for three programs) for telling a joke about national hero Benito Juárez. Magú added, "It was a time when Mexican heroes were almost untouchable, almost like presidents in office. And poking fun at them was not easy" ["Era un tiempo en que los héroes mexicanos eran casi intocables, eran casi como presidentes en turno. Y hacer humor sobre ellos no era sencillo"] (1999).

14. As Chapter 1 demonstrated, the fact that this image has become the national emblem constitutes a controversial privileging of Aztec roots and a conceptual centralization of Mexico as a nation.

15. In the well-known postcolonial studies primer *The Empire Writes Back: Theory and Practice in Post-colonial Literatures,* Bill Ashcroft, Gareth Griffiths, and Helen Tiffin demonstrate the profound issues that surround language in postcolonial nations. Paramount among them is "questioning the appropriateness of an 'imported' language to describe the experience of place in post-colonial societies" (1989, 24). Because of the pervasiveness of Spanish in Mexico, this issue is infrequently debated among intellectuals; it is, however, treated herein, in the analysis of "Las dos orillas," by Fuentes.

16. Víctor Hugo Rascón Banda was born in Uruáchic, Chihuahua, in 1948. As a playwright, he has published *El baile de los montañeses* (1982), which won first prize at the tenth Festival Internacional Cervantino in Guanajuato; *Voces en el umbral* (1983); *Teatro del delito: Manos arriba; La fiera del Ajusco; Máscara versus Cabellera* (1985); *Tina Modotti y otras obras de teatro* (1986); *Guerrero negro y Cierren las puertas* (1988); and *Volver a Santa Rosa* (1996). His novel *Contrabando* (1993) was awarded the 1991 Premio Juan Rulfo for a first novel. In addition to writing, Rascón Banda serves as the corporate director of Banco Cremi. He has also served as president of the SOGEM (Sociedad General de Escritores de México).

17. This resentment of the foreign at the expense of *lo mexicano* can easily be deemed *malinchismo* (or the selling out of Mexico). Interestingly, as Stuart Day points out in a chapter entitled "La Malinche in the Neoliberal '90s," *malinchismo* "has become

more a question of consumer patterns than one of punishable treason" in post-NAFTA Mexico (2004, 138).

18. For detailed analysis of the play's revision of Malinche as both a mythic historical figure and a nationalist symbol, see van Delden 2004 (13–17) and Day 2004 (124–29).

19. In his article "Reforming the Nation: Mexican Nationalism in Context," Stephen D. Morris explains how fears of modernization can trigger a nationalist backlash such as this (1999, 293–95).

20. These lines refer specifically to the "cantares tristes" [*icnocuícatl*], or "sad songs," transcribed in *La visión de los vencidos*. Composed after the conquest (1523), the text entitled "The *Mexica* (Aztec) Nation Has Been Lost" ["Se ha perdido el pueblo mexica"] reads, "Weep, my friends. / Be it understood that with these events / we have lost the *mexica* nation." ["Llorad, amigos míos, / Tened entendido que con estos hechos / hemos perdido la nación mexicana"] (León-Portilla 1989, 165).

Chapter 5
Concluding Remarks

1. It soon became evident that the reforms in fact targeted secondary schools only and that pre-Hispanic Mexican history would continue to be taught in primary schools (specifically in the fourth grade).

Works Cited

Abud, José Alberto. 1992. "El V Centenario: La visión del otro." *Cultura Sur* 3, no. 21 (September–October): 12–18.

Adorno, Rolena. 1990–1991. "The Colonial Subject and the Cultural Construction of the Other." *Revista de Estudios Hispánicos* (Río Piedras, P.R.) 17–18:149–65.

———. 1996. "La estatua de Gonzalo Guerrero en Akumal: Íconos culturales y la reactualización del pasado colonial." *Revista Iberoamericana* 62, nos. 176–77 (July–December): 905–23.

Aguilar Camín, Héctor. 1988. "Hacía una cultura del consenso." *Diálogo Nacional* (Revista de la consulta popular—IEPES/PRI) 18 (February 12): 22–23.

———. 1993a. "Notas sobre nacionalismo e identidad nacional: La invención de México." *Nexos* 16, no. 187 (July): 49–61.

———. 1993b. "Por una historia patria para adultos." *Nexos* 184 (April): 59–63.

———. 1993c. *Subversiones silenciosas: Ensayos de historia y política de México.* Mexico City: Aguilar.

———. 1995. "La obligación del mundo: Los cambios del fin de siglo y la transformación de México." *INTI* 42 (Fall): 37–47.

Aguilar Rivera, José Antonio. 2004. *El sonido y la furia: La persuasión multicultural en Mexico y Estados Unidos.* Mexico City: Taurus.

Aguirre, Eugenio. 1991. *Gonzalo Guerrero: Novela histórica.* Mexico City: Editorial Diana.

Aguirre M., Alberto. 1992a. "A Guevara Niebla lo están utilizando para legitimar al gobierno, dice Raúl Alvarez Garin." *Proceso* 825 (August 24): 18–19.

———. 1992b. "Zedillo almacenó libros por 12,026 millones y editó otros por 19,819 millones." *Proceso* 834 (October 26): 12–15.

Aguirre Rosas, Mario. 1975. *Gonzalo de Guerrero: Padre del mestizaje iberomexicano.* Mexico City: Editorial Jus.

Ahumada. 2004. "N.R.D.A." *La Jornada Virtu@l.* June 23. Available at www.jornada.unam.mx.

Ahumada, El Fisgón, Helguera, Magú, Rocha, and Ulises. 1991. *El Tataranieto del Ahuizote.* Mexico City: Ediciones de *La Jornada.*

Ahumada, Helguera, El Fisgón, Luis Fernando, Magú, Rocha, and Ulises. 1992. *El Ahuizotl*. In *La Jornada* (March 4 and 25; April 22; May 6 and 27; June 17; July 1, 15, and 29; August 12 and 26; September 9, 23, and 30; and October 7 and 12).

Alvarado Tezozómoc, D. Hernando. 1980. *Crónica mexicana.* (Escrita por D. Hernando Alvarado Tezozómoc hacia el año de MDXCVIII; anotada por Manuel Orozco y Berra, y precedida del Códice Ramírez, manuscrito del siglo XVI intitulado Relación del origen de los indios que habitan esta Nueva España según sus historias, y de un examen de ambas obras, al cual va anexo un estudio de cronología mexicana por el mismo Orozco y Berra.) 3rd ed. Mexico City: Editorial Porrúa.

Álvarez de Testa, Lilian. 1992. *Mexicanidad y libro de texto gratuito.* Mexico City: Universidad Nacional Autónoma de México.

American Heritage College Dictionary, The. 1993. 3rd ed. New York: Houghton Mifflin.

Arenal Fenochio, Jaime del. 1993. "La desmitificación de la historia de México." *Istmo* 204 (January–February): 4–8.

Aridjis, Homero. 1996. Personal Interview. May 24.

Arreola Cortés, Raúl. 2004. "Semblanza biográfica de Don Belisario Domínguez." March 3. Available at www.senado.gob.mx/medalla_belisario.php?ver=biografia.

Ashcroft, Bill, Gareth Griffiths, and Helen Tiffin. 1989. *The Empire Writes Back: Theory and Practice in Post-colonial Literatures.* New York: Routledge.

Barriga Villanueva, Rebeca. 1995a. "México, país plurilingüe." *INTI* 42 (Fall): 115–31.

———. 1995b. "La paradoja lingüística del indígena mexicano." *INTI* 42 (Fall): 103–12.

Barros Valero, Javier. 1988. Introduction. *Diálogo Nacional* (Revista de la consulta popular—IEPES/PRI) 18 (February 12): 21.

Bartra, Roger. 1989. "Hacia una sociedad postdemocrática." *La Jornada Semanal* December 3:21–25.

———. 1991. "La venganza de la Malinche: Hacia una identidad postnacional." *Este País* 1 (April): 17–19.

———. 1992. *The Cage of Melancholy: Identity and Metamorphosis in the Mexican Character.* Translated by Christopher J. Hall. New Brunswick, N.J.: Rutgers University Press.

———. 1993. "Espejo y diáspora." *La Gaceta* 269 (May 1993): 13–14.

———. 1996. *La jaula de la melancolía: Identidad y metamorfosis del mexicano.* Mexico City: Grijalbo.

Basave Benítez, Agustín. 1993. *México mestizo: Análisis del nacionalismo mexicano en torno a la mestizofilia de Andrés Molina Enríquez.* Mexico City: Fondo de Cultura Económica.

Becerra, Ricardo. 1993. "Libro de texto: Historia oficial e historia por consenso." *El Libro del Año* (*El Nacional*) pp. 370–76.

Beltrán Enviada, Claudia Herrera. 2005. "En septiembre, la reforma a la educación secundaria: Fox." *La Jornada Virtu@l.* May 19. Available at www.jornada.unam.mx.

Benítez, Fernando. 1992. *1992 ¿Qué celebramos, qué lamentamos?* Mexico City: Ediciones Era.

Bhabha, Homi K. 1994. *The Location of Culture.* New York: Routledge.

Bonfil, Guillermo, Rolando Cordera Campos, Enrique Florescano, Luis González y González, and Arturo Warman. 1991. "Rumbo a 1492." *Nexos* 168 (December): 43–47.

Bonfil Batalla, Guillermo.1996. *México Profundo: Reclaiming a Civilization.* Translated by Philip A. Dennis. Austin: University of Texas Press.Boullosa, Carmen. 1991a. "Carmen Boullosa: Escritora por oficio." *El Canario de Coyoacán.* December 19:7.

———. 1991b. "Retazos de la conquista." *Epitafios* 1, no. 2 (September–November): 34–38.

———. 1992. *Llanto: Novelas imposibles.* Mexico City: Ediciones Era.

———. 1995a. "El que gira la cabeza y el fuego: Historia y novela." *Revista de Literatura Hispanoamericana* 30 (January–June): 5–16.

———. 1995b. "La destrucción en la escritura." *INTI* 42 (Fall): 215–20.

———. 1996. Personal interview. July 23.

———. 1997. "Personajes y obra: El autor como personaje de su obra." Talk given at the Palacio de Bellas Artes, Mexico City, February 19.

Braden, Charles S. 1930. *Religious Aspects of the Conquest of Mexico.* Durham, N.C.: Duke University Press.

Brading, David. 1981. *Los orígenes del nacionalismo mexicano.* Translated by Soledad Loaeza Ricárdez. Mexico City: Ediciones Era.

———. 1994. "De nacionalismos y patriotismos." *Este País* 44 (November): 37–43.

Bruni, Frank, and Ginger Thompson. 2002. "Bolstering Faith of Indians, Pope Gives Mexico a Saint." *New York Times,* August 1.

Brushwood, John S. 1989. "Narrating Parapsychology: The Novels of Ignacio Solares." *Chasqui* 18, no. 2 (November): 12–17.

———. 1992. "Discoveries of America: Wonder, Promise, Refuge." *Hispania* 75 (September–December): 836–43.

Bueno, Raúl. 1996. "Sobre la heterogeneidad literaria y cultural de América Latina." In *Asedios a la heterogeneidad cultural: Libro de homenaje a Antonio Cornejo Polar.* Edited by José Antonio Mazzotti and U. Juan Zevallos Aguilar. Philadelphia: Asociación Internacional de Peruanistas.

Burkhart, Louise M. 1993. "The Cult of the Virgin of Guadalupe in Mexico." In *South and Meso-American Native Spirituality: From the Cult of the Feathered Serpent to the Theology of Liberation.* Edited by Gary H. Gossen. Vol. 4 of *World Spirituality: An Encyclopedic History of the Religious Conquest.* New York: Crossroad Publishing.

Cameron, Maxwell A., and Brian Tomlin. 2000. *The Making of NAFTA: How the Deal Was Done.* Ithaca, N.Y.: Cornell University Press.

Camp, Roderic Ai. 2003. *Politics in Mexico: The Democratic Transformation.* 4th ed. New York: Oxford University Press.

Carrasco, Salvador. 1995. *La visión absuelta.* Original screenplay. June 14. Carrasco and Domingo Films.

———, writer/director. 1998. *La otra conquista.* Twentieth Century Fox.

———. 2002. *The Invisible Sight.* In *The Zapatista Reader.* Edited by Tom Hayden. New York: Thunder's Mouth Press/Nation Books.

———. 2004. Personal interview. July 23.

Caso, Antonio. 1988. *The Aztecs: People of the Sun.* Translated by Lowell Dunham. Norman: University of Oklahoma Press.

Castañón, Adolfo. 1996. Personal interview. June 11.

Cazés, Daniel. 1992a. "La nueva historia oficial" (pt. 1). *La Jornada* August 29:9.

———. 1992b. "La nueva historia official" (pt. 2). *La Jornada* September 5:15.

Centeno, Miguel Ángel. 1994. *Democracy within Reason: Technocratic Revolution in Mexico.* University Park: Pennsylvania State University Press.

Codex Aubin. 1963. (Historia de la nación mexicana; reproducción a todo color del Códice de 1576 [Códice Aubin] Edición, introd., notas, índices, versión paleográfica y traducción directa de náhuatl por Charles E. Dibble.) Madrid: J. Porrúa Turanzas.

Cohn, Deborah N. 2002. "La construcción de la identidad cultural en México: Nacionalismo, cosmopolitismo e infraestructura intelectual 1945–1968." *Foro hispánico.* Special edition: *Cultura y política en México desde la Revolución hasta el neozapatismo.* Edited by Maarten van Delden and Kristine Vanden Berghe. 22:89–103.

"Constitución política de los Estados Unidos Mexicanos, actualizada hasta reforma de 14.08.2001." 2001. *Political Database of the Americas.* December 13. Available at www. georgetown.edu/pdba/Constitutions/Mexico/mexic02001.html.

Cypess, Sandra Messinger. 1991. *La Malinche in Mexican Literature, from History to Myth.* Austin: University of Texas Press.

Day, Stuart. 2004. *Staging Politics in Mexico: The Road to Neoliberalism.* Lewisburg, Pa.: Bucknell University Press.

"Diálogo." 1988. *Diálogo Nacional* (Revista de la consulta popular—IEPES/PRI) 18 (February 12): 6–14.

Díaz del Castillo, Bernal. 1992. *Historia verdadera de la conquista de la Nueva España.* 2nd ed. Mexico City: Editores Mexicanos Unidos.

Domínguez Michael, Christopher. 1995. "La civilización sin alma." *Vuelta* 220 (March): 40–41.

Doremus, Anne. 2001. "Indigenism, *Mestizaje,* and National Identity in Mexico during the 1940s and the 1950s." *Mexican Studies/Estudios Mexicanos* 17, no. 2 (Summer): 375–402.

Eco, Umberto, Richard Rorty, Johnathan Culler, and Christine Brooke-Rose. 1992. *Interpretation and Overinterpretation.* New York: Cambridge University Press.

Editorial. 1994. *Chicomóztoc* 4 (September): 1–2.

Elliott, J. H. 1986. "Cortés, Velázquez, and Charles V." Introduction to *Hernán Cortés: Letters from Mexico.* Translated by and edited by Anthony Padgen. New Haven, Conn.: Yale University Press.

Farnen, Russell F., ed. 1994. *Nationalism, Ethnicity, and Identity.* New Brunswick, N.J.: Transaction Publishers.

Fernández Retamar, Roberto. 1996. "Comentarios al texto de Antonio Cornejo Polar 'Mestizaje, transculturación, heterogeneidad.'" In *Asedios a la heterogeneidad cultural: Libro de homenaje a Antonio Cornejo Polar.* Edited by José Antonio Mazzotti and U. Juan Zevallos Aguilar. Philadelphia: Asociación Internacional de Peruanistas.

Fisgón, El [Rafael Barajas]. 1996. *Cómo sobrevivir al neoliberalismo sin dejar de ser mexicano.* Mexico City: Grijalbo.

Florescano, Enrique. 1989. "El viaje de Crístobal Colón y sus interpretaciones." *La Jornada Semanal* December 17:26–32.

Flores Olea, Víctor. 1995. "Identidad y cambio: Los rostros en movimiento." *INTI* 42 (Fall): 73–79.

Frost, Elsa Cecilia. 1994. "El símbolo del triunfo." In *La Malinche, sus padres y sus hijos*. Edited by Margo Glantz. Mexico City: Facultad de Filosofía y Letras, Universidad Nacional Autónoma de México.

Fuentes, Carlos. 1962. *La muerte de Artemio Cruz*. Mexico City: Fondo de Cultura Económica.

———. 1980. "Fuentes on his *Terra Nostra*." *Hispania* 63, no. 2 (May): 415.

———. 1990. *Valiente mundo nuevo: Épica, utopía y mito en la novela hispanoamericana*. Madrid: Narrativa Mondadori.

———. 1992a. *El espejo enterrado*. Mexico City: Fondo de Cultura Económica.

———. 1992b. *Tiempo mexicano*. Mexico City: Cuadernos de Joaquín Mortiz.

———. 1993a. *El naranjo, o los círulos del tiempo*. Mexico City: Alfaguara Literaturas.

———. 1993b. *Tres discursos para dos aldeas*. Mexico City: Fondo de Cultura Económica.

———. 1995. *Geografía de la novela*. Mexico City: Fondo de Cultura Económica.

———. 1996. Personal Interview. November 13.

Fuentes Mares, José. 1981. *Cortés, el hombre*. Mexico City: Grijalbo.

Gamio, Manuel. 1982. *Forjando patria*. 3rd ed. Mexico City: Editorial Porrúa.

García Canclini, Néstor. 1990. *Culturas híbridas: Estrategias para entrar y salir de la modernidad*. Mexico City: Grijalbo.

Garrido, Javier. 1992. "La historia oficial." *La Jornada* August 28:10.

Gilbert, Dennis. 1997. "Rewriting History: Salinas, Zedillo, and the 1992 Textbook Controversy." *Mexican Studies/Estudios Mexicanos* 13, no. 2 (Summer): 271–97.

Gilly, Adolfo. 1995. "Las transfiguraciones del nacionalismo mexicano," *Nexos* 207 (March): 61–64.

Glantz, Margo. 1994. "La Malinche: La lengua en la mano." In *La Malinche, sus padres y sus hijos*. Edited by Margo Glantz. Mexico City: Facultad de Filosofía y Letras, Universidad Nacional Autónoma de México.

Glazer, Nathan. 1997. *We Are All Multiculturalists Now*. Cambridge, Mass.: Harvard University Press.

Goldman, David. 1990. "A Revolution You Can Invest In." *Forbes* July 9:48–53.

González Ayala, Jorge E. 1995. "Fin del siglo." *La Reforma* December 17:El Ángel 1–2.

Gruzinski, Serge. 2001. *Images at War: Mexico from Columbus to Blade Runner (1492–2019)*. Translated by Heather MacLean. Durham, N.C.: Duke University Press.

Gutiérrez, Natividad. 1999. *Nationalist Myths and Ethnic Identities: Indigenous Intellectuals and the Mexican State*. Lincoln: University of Nebraska Press.

Herrera, Willebaldo. 1992. "En la portada de los libros, una mujer olvidada." *Proceso* 827 (September 7): 11.

Hinojosa, Juan José. 1992. "Cristóbal Colón." *Proceso* 833 (October 19): 38–39.

Historia: Quinto grado. 1994. Mexico City: Secretaría de Educación Pública.

Hunt, Harry T. 1989. *The Multiplicity of Dreams: Memory, Imagination, and Consciousness*. New Haven, Conn.: Yale University Press.

Ibsen, Kristine. 1995. "Entrevistas: Bárbara Jacobs/Carmen Boullosa." *Chasquí* 24, no. 2 (November): 46–63.

Inglehart, Ronald F., Neil Nevitte, and Miguel Basañez. 1996. *The North American Trajectory: Cultural, Economic, and Political Ties among the United States, Canada, and Mexico*. New York: Adeline de Gruyter.

Iniciarte, Esteban. 1992. "Vasco de Quiroga y Bartolomé de las Casas: Dos actitudes indigenistas." *Plural* 253 (October): 60–67.

"Integración económica y nacionalismo: Canadá, Estados Unidos y México." 1991. *Este País*. April 1. Available at http://web.lexis-nexis.com.

Janzen, Rod. 1994. "Melting Pot or Mosaic?" *Educating for Diversity* 51, no. 8 (May): 9–11.

Jay, Paul. 1997. "Translation, Invention, Resistance: Rewriting the Conquest in Carlos Fuentes's 'The Two Shores.'" *Modern Fiction Studies* 43 (2):405–31.

Johnson, Harvey L. 1980. "The Virgin of Guadalupe in Mexican Culture." In *Religion in Latin American Life and Literature.* Edited by Lyle C. Brown and William F. Cooper. Waco, Tex.: Baylor University Press.

Johnson, J. Holbrook. 1988. "Father of the Mexican Mestizos." *Américas* 40, no. 2:26–29.

Kachru, Braj B. 1995. "The Alchemy of English." *The Post-colonial Studies Reader.* Edited by Bill Ashcroft, Gareth Griffiths, and Helen Tiffin. New York: Routledge.

Kymlicka, Will. 1995. *Multicultural Citizenship: A Liberal Theory of Minority Rights.* New York: Oxford University Press.

Kymlicka, Will, and Wayne Norman, eds. 2000. *Citizenship in Diverse Societies.* New York: Oxford University Press.

Lafaye, Jacques. 1996. "Ambigüedad de la identidad, fluctuación de la nación, avatares de lo mexicano, a través de los siglos." In *Visiones cortazarianas: Historia, política y literatura hacia el fin del milenio.* Mexico City: Aguilar.

———. 1995. *Quetzalcóatl y Guadalupe: La formación de la conciencia nacional en México 1531-1813.* Translated by Ida Vitale and Fulgencio López Vidarte. Mexico City: Fondo de Cultura Económica.

Latapí, Pablo. 1992. "La nación en busca de su historia." *Proceso* 828 (August 31): 34–35.

Le Clézio, J. M. G. 1993. *The Mexican Dream: Or the Uninterrupted Thought of Amerindian Civilizations.* Translated by by Teresa Lavender Fagan. Chicago: University of Chicago Press.

León-Portilla, Miguel. 1989. *La visión de los vencidos: Relaciones indígenas de la conquista.* Introduction, selection, and notes by Miguel León-Portilla. Translated from *Nahua* texts by Angel María Garibay K. 12th ed. Mexico City: Coordinación de Humanidades, Universidad Nacional Autónoma de México.

———. 1992. *The Broken Spears: The Aztec Account of the Conquest of Mexico.* Translated by Lysander Kemp. Boston: Beacon Press.

———. 1996. Personal interview. November 28.

———. 2004. "Socavar nuestra identidad." *La Jornada Virtu@l.* June 22. Available at www.jornada.unam.mx.

Levi, Jerome M. 2002. "A New Dawn or a Cycle Restored? Regional Dynamics and Cultural Politics in Indigenous Mexico, 1978–2001." In *The Politics of Ethnicity: Indigenous Peoples in Latin American States.* Edited by David Maybury-Lewis. Cambridge, Mass.: Harvard University Press.

Libro integrado: Primer grado. 1994. Mexico City: Secretaría de Educación Pública.

Limón, Dante. 1992. "Conocer mejor la historia, para mejorar el futuro." *Época* 59 (August 10): 18–20.

Loaeza, Guadalupe. 2002. "San Juan Diego." *Reforma.com.* August 1. Available at www. reforma.com/nacional/articulo/216067.

López, Kimberle S. 2002. *Latin American Novels of the Conquest: Reinventing the New World.* Columbia: University of Missouri Press.

López Austin, Alfredo. 1995. "El águila y la serpiente." In *Mitos mexicanos.* Coordinated by Enrique Florescano. Mexico City: Aguilar, pp. 15–20.

Mac Adam, Alfred J. 1993. "Carlos Fuentes y 'Las dos orillas': Tradittore/Traduttore." In *Literatura mexicana/ Mexican Literature.* Edited by José Miguel Oviedo. Philadelphia: University of Pennsylvania Press.

Mac Masters, Merry, Arturo Jiménez, Mónica Rodríguez, Fabiola Palapa, Jorge Ricardo, Fernando Camacho, Carlos Paul, and Ángel Vargas. 2004. "Crece reclamo contra planes para *recortar* la historia." *La Jornada Virtu@l.* June 19. Available at www. jornada.unam.mx.

Magú. 1999. Personal Interview. June 22.

Magú and Sara Sefchovich. 2000. *Las PRIelecciones: Historia y caricatura del dedazo.* Mexico City: Plaza y Janés.

Marentes, Luis A. 2000. *José Vasconcelos and the Writing of the Mexican Revolution.* New York: Twayne.

Martí, José. 1939. *Nuestra América.* Buenos Aires: Editorial Losada.

Martínez, José Luis. 1992. *Hernán Cortés.* 2nd ed. Mexico City: Universidad Nacional Autónoma de México/Fondo de Cultura Económica.

Matos Moctezuma, Eduardo. 1988a. *The Great Temple of the Aztecs: Treasures of Tenochtitlán.* Translated by Doris Heyden. London: Thames and Hudson.

———. 1988b. "Tradición y modernidad." *Diálogo Nacional* (Revista de la consulta popular—IEPES/PRI) 18 (February 12): 25–26.

———. 1996. Personal interview. June 13.

Mattiace, Shannan. 2003. *To See with Two Eyes: Peasant Activism and Indian Autonomy in Chiapas, Mexico.* Albuquerque: University of New Mexico Press.

Mejía, Mauricio. 2002a. "Barroquismo católico, asunto de casta." Editorial. *Proceso.* August 1. Available at www.proceso.com.mx.

———. 2002b. "La canonización del indio Juan Diego, sin indígenas." Editorial. *Proceso.* August 1. Available at www.proceso.com.mx.

Merrim, Stephanie. 1996. "The First Fifty Years of Hispanic New World Historiography: The Caribbean, Mexico and Central America." *The Cambridge History of Latin American Literature.* Edited by Roberto González Echevarría and Enrique Pupo-Walker. New York: Cambridge University Press.

Los mexicanos de los noventa. 1996. Mexico City: Instituto de Investigaciones Sociales, Universidad Nacional Autónoma de México.

Meyer, Lorenzo. 1993. "La disputa por la historia patria." Interviewed by Tania Carreño King and Angélica Vázquez del Mercado. *Nexos* 191 (November): 41–49.

———. 1996. Personal interview. July 24.

Meyer, Lorenzo, and Héctor Aguilar Camín. 1994. *A la sombra de la Revolución Mexicana: Un ensayo de historia contemporánea de Mexico, 1910–1989.* Mexico City: Cal y Arena.

Meza, Otilia. 1994. *Un amor inmortal, Gonzalo Guerrero, símbolo del orígen del mestizaje mexicano: Novela histórica.* Mexico City: ALPE.

Mi cuaderno de trabajo de sexto año. 1964. Mexico City: Secretaría de Educación Pública.

Mignolo, Walter D. 1999. "Linguistic Maps, Literary Geographies, and Cultural Landscapes: Languages, Languaging, and (Trans)nationalism." In *The Places of History: Regionalism Revisited in Latin America.* Edited by Doris Sommer. Durham, N.C.: Duke University Press.

———. 2000. *Local Histories/Global Designs: Coloniality, Subaltern Knowledges, and Border Thinking.* Princeton, N.J.: Princeton University Press.

———. 1995. *The Darker Side of the Renaissance: Literacy, Territoriality, and Colonization.* Ann Arbor: University of Michigan Press.

Mi libro de historia de México: Sexto grado. 1992. Mexico City: Secretaría de Educación Pública.

Mi libro de segundo: Parte 2. 1982. Mexico City: Secretaría de Educación Pública.

Monsiváis, Carlos. 1988. *Entrada libre: Crónicas de la sociedad que se organiza.* Mexico City: Ediciones Era.

———. 1994. "Notas sobre la cultura mexicana en el siglo XX." In *Historia general de México.* 4th ed. Vol. 2. Mexico City: Colegio de México.

Morris, Stephen D. 1999. "Reforming the Nation: Mexican Nationalism in Context." *Journal of Latin American Studies* 31:363–97.

———. 2001. "Between Neo-liberalism and *Neo-indigenismo*: Reconstructing National Identity in Mexico." *National Identities* 3, no. 3:239–55.

———. 2005. *Gringolandia: Mexican Identity and Perceptions of the United States.* New York: Rowman and Littlefield Publishers.

Muñoz, Lorenza. 2000. "Preparing a 'Conquest.'" *Los Angeles Times,* April 19.

Nebrija, Antonio de. 1492. *Gramática de la lengua castellana.* Available at http://www.jabega.net/nebrija/index.html.

Ochoa Sandy, Gerardo. 1992. "La exigencia de Carlos Fuentes para levantar una estatua a Cortés, impugnada por Monsiváis, Everaert, Tovar y Zea." *Proceso* 802 (March 16): 46–49.

Orozco y Berra, Manuel. 1880. *Historia antigua y de la conquista de México.* Mexico City: Tip. De G A Esteva.

Ortega, José. 1992. "Conmemoración del genocidio de las Indias." *La Palabra y el Hombre* 81 (January–March): 11–19.

Ortiz, Fernando. 1947. *Contrapunteo cubano del tabaco y el azúcar (Cuban Counterpoint: Tobacco and Sugar).* New York: Knopf.

Padgen, Anthony, trans. and ed. 1986. *Hernán Cortés: Letters from Mexico.* New Haven, Conn.: Yale University Press.

Parra, Max. 1996. "El nacionalismo y el mito de 'lo mexicano' en Octavio Paz y José Revueltas." *Confluencia* 12, no. 1 (Fall): 29–37.

Pastor, Beatriz. 1992. "Silencio y escritura: La historia de la conquista." In *Crítica y descolonización: El sujeto colonial en la cultura latinoamericana.* Caracas, Venezuela: Editorial. de la Universidad Simón Bolívar.

Paz, Octavio. 1979. *El ogro filantrópico: Historia y política 1971–1978.* Mexico City: Joaquin Mortiz.

———. 1993. *El laberinto de la soledad.* Mexico City: Fondo de Cultura Económica.

————. 1995. Introduction to *Quetzalcóatl y Guadalupe: La formación de la conciencia nacional en México, 1531–1813* by Jacques Lafaye. Translated by Ida Vitale and Fulgencio López Vidarte. Mexico City: Fondo de Cultura Económica.

Pereyra, Carlos. 1968. Prologue to *Historia verdadera de la conquista de la Nueva España*, by Bernal Díaz del Castillo. 2nd ed. Madrid: Espasa-Calpe.

Pérez del Solar, Pedro. 2003. "Old Fashions for New Times: *El Desencanto* in Spanish Comics." *International Journal of Comic Art* 5, no. 2 (Fall): 85–101.

Pisani, Francis. 1992. *Huracán, Corazón-del-Cielo*. Translated by Raúl Falcó. Mexico City: Editorial Joaquín Moritz.

"Plan de SEP oculta 'carga ideológica neoliberal.'" 2004. *La Jornada Virtu@l*. July 1. Available at www.jornada.unam.mx.

Pohlenz, Ricardo. 1994. "Noveletas de Carmen Boullosa e Ignacio Solares: Dos paseos novelados en el siglo XVI mexicano." *El Semanario* (Mexico City) December 11:4–5.

Political Constitution of the Mexican United States. 1994. Mexico City: Instituto Federal Electoral (IFE).

Ponce, Roberto. 2004. "Borrar la historia, traición a la esencia nacional." *Proceso*. July 13. Available at www.proceso.com.mx.

Poniatowska, Elena. 1975. *Massacre in Mexico*. Translated by Helen R. Lane. Columbia: University of Missouri Press.

————. 1993. "Llanto por el tlatoani." *La Jornada* February 27:27–28.

Preston, James J., ed. 1982. *Mother Worship: Theme and Variations*. Chapel Hill: University of North Carolina Press.

Preston, Julia, and Samuel Dillon. 2004. *Opening Mexico: The Making of a Democracy*. New York: Farrar, Straus, and Giroux.

"El Quinto viaje: Claroscuros." 2002. Editorial. *La Jornada Virtu@l*. July 31. Available at www.jornada.unam.mx.

Ramírez, Ignacio. 1992. "Avalancha sobre los libros de historia: Deformados, erráticos, contradictorios, esquemáticos, simplistas, tendenciosos . . ." *Proceso* 827 (September 7): 6–7.

Ramos, Samuel. 1976. *El perfil del hombre y la cultura en México*. 6th ed. Mexico City: Espasa-Calpe Mexicana.

Rascón Banda, Víctor Hugo. 2000a. *La Malinche*. Mexico City: Plaza y Janés.

————. 2000b. Personal Interview. June 20.

Reid, Anna. 1995. "Interview with Carmen Boullosa." *Journal of American Cultural Studies* 4, no. 2:145–51.

Reyes, Alfonso. 1952. *La X en la frente: Algunas páginas sobre México*. Mexico City: Porrúa y Obregón.

Riding, Alan. 1989. *Distant Neighbors: A Portrait of the Mexicans*. New York: Vintage Books.

Ríos, Julián. 1996. "*El naranjo, o los círculos del tiempo* narrativo de Carlos Fuentes." *INTI* 43–44 (Spring–Fall): 231–36.

Rius [Eduardo del Rio]. 1984. *La interminable conquista de México*. Mexico City: Grijalbo.

Rivera, Carmen. 1995. "Las dos orillas de Carlos Fuentes: Una visión posmoderna de la conquista de México." *Torre de Papel* (Iowa) 5:1 (1995): 49–59.

Roa Bastos, Augusto. 1987. "El quinto centenario." *Nexos* 128 (December): 5–8.

Robles, Manuel. 1992. "Con los ceros se van también los próceres de las monedas." *Proceso* 843 (December 28): 22–25.

Rocha. 2004a. "Desplumando la historia." *La Jornada Virtu@l.* June 21. Available at www.jornada.unam.mx.

———. 2004b. "La historia secundaria." *La Jornada Virtu@l.* June 18. Available at www.jornada.unam.mx.

Roman, José Antonio, and Rosa Elvira Vargas. 2002. "Visita papal." Editorial. *La Jornada Virtu@l.* August 1. Available at www.jornada.unam.mx.

Romero Jacobo, César. 1992. "El 'pecado' del nuevo texto de historia: Es mejor." *Época* 67 (September 14): 10–15.

Russell, Philip L. 1994. *Mexico under Salinas.* Austin, Tex.: Mexico Resource Center.

Salinas de Gortari, Carlos. 1988. "Cultura e identidad nacional." *Diálogo Nacional* (Revista de la consulta popular—IEPES/PRI) 18 (February 12): 15–19.

Salinas Cesareo, Javier. 2004. "El gobierno foxista intenta socavar la identidad nacional." *La Jornada Virtu@l.* June 22. Available at www.jornada.unam.mx.

Schmidt, Friedhelm. 1996. "¿Literaturas heterogéneas o literatura de transculturación?" In *Asedios a la heterogeneidad cultural: Libro de homenaje a Antonio Cornejo Polar.* Edited by José Antonio Mazzotti and U. Juan Zevallos Aguilar. Philadelphia: Asociación Internacional de Peruanistas.

Schmidt, Henry C. 1978. *The Roots of "Lo Mexicano": Self and Society in Mexican Thought, 1900–1934.* College Station: Texas A&M University Press.

Shirk, David A. 2005. *Mexico's New Politics: The PAN and Democratic Change.* Boulder, Colo.: L. Rienner.

Skidmore, Thomas E. 1996. "Where Was the Brazilian Malinche? Myths of National Origin in Brazil and Mexico." *Horizontes Antropológicos* (Porto Alegre, Brazil) 2, no. 4 (January–June): 127–30.

Smarr, Janet Levarie. 1993. Introduction to *Historical Criticism and the Challenge of Theory.* Edited by Janet Levarie Smarr. Chicago: University of Illinois Press.

Solares, Ignacio. 1994. *Nen, la inútil.* Mexico City: Alfaguara.

———. 1996. Personal Interview. May 31.

Sommer, Doris. 1993. *Foundational Fictions: The National Romances of Latin America.* Berkeley and Los Angeles: University of California Press.

Spitta, Silvia. 1995. *Between Two Waters: Narratives of Transculturation in Latin America.* Houston, Tex.: Rice University Press.

Stavenhagen, Rodolfo. 2003. "Mexico's Unfinished Symphony: The Zapatista Movement." In *Mexico's Politics and Society in Transition.* Edited by Joseph S Tulchin and Andrew D. Selee. Boulder, Colo.: L. Rienner.

Stephen, Lynn. 2002. *Zapata Lives! Histories and Cultural Politics in Southern Mexico.* Berkeley and Los Angeles: University of California Press.

Taylor, Charles. 1992. *Multiculturalism and "The politics of recognition": An essay.* Princeton, N.J.: Princeton University Press.

Thomas, Hugh. 1994. *La conquista de México.* Translated by Víctor Alba. Mexico City: Editorial Patria.

Thomas, Kevin. 2000. "'Conquest' Reveals Clash, Fusion of Spirit." *Los Angeles Times,* April 19.

Todorov, Tzvetan. 1989. *La conquista de América: El problema del otro.* Mexico City: Siglo Veintiuno Editores.

Torres Fierro, Danubio. 1992. "Conversación con Carlos Fuentes: La fortaleza mexicana." *La Gaceta* (nueva época) 254 (February): 55–57.

Van Cott, Donna Lee. 2000. *The Friendly Liquidation of the Past: The Politics of Diversity in Latin America.* Pittsburgh: University of Pittsburgh Press.

van Delden, Maarten. 2004. "Past and Present in Víctor Hugo Rascón Banda's *La Malinche* and Marisol Martín del Campo's *Amor y Conquista.*" *South Central Review* 21, no. 3 (Fall): 8–23.

Vargas, Rosa Elvira. 1992. "'Desapareció' la historia en los nuevos textos: Taibo II." *La Jornada* August 26:6.

Vasconcelos, José. 1976. *La raza cósmica.* Mexico City: Espasa-Calpe.

Vázquez, Josefina Zoraida. 1970. *Nacionalismo y educación en México.* Mexico City: Colegio de México.

———. 1995. "La historia y su enseñanza." *Memorias de la Academia de la Historia Mexicana* 38:47–59.

Velazco, Salvador. 1999. "Entrevista con Salvador Carrasco." *La Jornada Semanal* April 18:4.

Vera, Rodrigo. 1992. "González y González los defiende: 'No hay satanizaciones ni canonizaciones; hay hombres de carne y hueso." *Proceso* 827 (September 7): 13–14, 16–17.

Vigil, James Diego, and Felipe H. Lopez. 2004. "Race and Ethnic Relations in Mexico." *Journal of Latino/Latin American Studies* 1, no. 2 (Spring): 49–73.

Villa Lever, Lorenza. 1988. *Los libros de texto gratuitos: La disputa por la educación en México.* Guadalajara, Mexico: Universidad de Guadalajara.

Villa Roiz, Carlos. 1995. *Gonzalo Guerrero: Memorial olvidada, trauma de México.* Mexico City: Plaza y Janés.

Villegas, Abelardo. 1992. "Los textos y la conciencia nacional." *Proceso* 828 (September 14): 34.

Villoro, Juan. 1996. Personal interview. November 28.

Villoro, Luis. 1950. *Los grandes momentos del indigenismo en México.* Mexico City: Colegio de México.

Volpi, Jorge. 2004. *La guerra y las palabras: Una historia intelectual de 1994.* Mexico City: Ediciones Era.

Williams, Raymond L. 1996. *The Writings of Carlos Fuentes.* Austin: University of Texas Press.

Wolf, Eric R. 1958. "The Virgin of Guadalupe: A Mexican National Symbol." *Journal of American Folklore* 71:34–39.

Zeran, Faride. 1994. "Carlos Fuentes y el poder de la literatura." *La Gaceta* (nueva época) 280 (April): 31–34.

Index

Pages that include relevant figures are printed in **bold**.